Acclaim for
THE BOOK OF BLUFFS

Lessinger is uniquely qualified to write *The Book of Bluffs,* and I wholeheartedly recommended it. I'm sure it will help every player.

> —Alan Schoonmaker, columnist, *Card Player,*
> and author of *The Psychology of Poker*

This book will do more for poker education than *Caro's Book of Poker Tells.* I wish it was written sixty years ago.

> —Amarillo Slim Preston

One of the brightest people I have ever known, Lessinger has a deep understanding of both the mathematics and the psychology of the game of poker. His writing style is concise, yet he skips none of the important details.

> —Peter Landolfo, supervisor,
> Claridge Casino, Atlantic City

I was a beginner at Texas hold 'em when Matt began coaching me. He has elevated my playing skills and knowledge to a completely different level, and I've won multiple online and live-play tournaments since he helped me. I couldn't have done it without him. His expertise can help anyone from the beginner level to the seasoned veteran.

> —Cheryl Sakamo*
> Matt's #1 p(

THE
BOOK
OF
BLUFFS

♣ ♦ ♥ ♠

How to Bluff and Win at Poker

MATT LESSINGER

WARNER BOOKS

NEW YORK   BOSTON

Copyright © 2005 by Matt Lessinger

Warner Books

Time Warner Book Group
1271 Avenue of the Americas, New York, NY 10020
Visit our Web site at www.twbookmark.com.

Printed in the United States of America

First Edition: October 2005

10 9 8 7 6 5 4 3 2 1
Library of Congress Cataloging-in-Publication Data
Lessinger, Matt.
      The book of bluffs : how to bluff and win at poker / Matt Lessinger.
      —1st ed.
        p. cm.
      ISBN 0-446-69562-9
      1. Poker   I. Title.
    GV1251.L46 2005
    795.412—dc22
2005015535

Book design and text composition by Stratford Publishing Services

Cover design by Brigid Pearson

Cover photo by Herman Estevez

For Renee and Len (G & G),
who never wanted their grandson to be a poker player
or a bachelor, but love him and support him just the same.

Acknowledgments

First and foremost, thank you, Alan Schoonmaker, for your hundreds of hours of editing and general support. Your contributions have been invaluable. This book could not have been done without you.

Thank you, Greg Dinkin and Frank Scatoni at Venture Literary, for taking a good idea and turning it into a great proposal.

Thank you, Colin Fox, Andrea Girolamo, and everyone at Warner Books, for putting up with my constant phone calls, and for collaborating to create this finished product.

Thank you, Crandall Addington, Bobby Baldwin, Nolan Dalla, Chris Moneymaker, and Ron Stanley, for your insightful interviews. It was a pleasure talking with each of you.

Thank you, Mike Caro, for taking the time to write a foreword. Your *Book of Tells* was a tremendous inspiration for me.

Thank you, John Tibbetts, Mike Fink, Larry Thomas, Wayne Hirao, and John Larosa of the Oaks Club for allowing me the time off to work on this book, and for providing me with such an enjoyable workplace. To everyone else at the Oaks Club, thank you for your continued encouragement and support.

Thank you, Jeremy, Ysaaca, the gang at 1018 Verdemar, my folks at Hagen Oaks, Jason, Pete, Tim, and everyone else who has supported me through this process with their friendship, advice, and humor.

Thank you, Mom and Dad, Linda and Lou, Kristen and Casey, Michael, Renee, Danielle, Zoe, Howie, Sheila, Kenneth, Dale, Helene, Ira, and everyone else in my family who has been there for me.

Finally, I thank you for reading this book. I hope that you enjoy it, and that it pays for itself a hundred times over.

Contents

Foreword

By Mike Caro

"The Mad Genius of Poker"

Without bluffing there can be no poker. When I teach the game to beginners, I begin by defining what makes poker poker. Oddly, cards don't even figure into the definition. Yes, by convention, we all use a deck of cards to play. But you wouldn't need one.

I describe a ranch house with a bunch of bored people sitting around, wondering what to do next. They invent a game. There are three elements. Here's how it goes . . .

Elements

Element 1. Everyone wagers $1 in advance, and all the money is put on the kitchen table. It forms an initial prize pool that only one player will eventually win. In poker, you know this as "the pot." You need something to motivate you, before you can begin to play poker and make further wagers. Otherwise, players would just wait till they held something unbeatable, and nobody would match the bet unless they had the same thing. Doing anything less would be folly—and whoever played by that obvious perfect strategy would win. That would be boring. So, you need an incentive in advance of making any further wagers. Those dollars at the ranch house comprise something we call an "ante" in poker. We can generate the same motivation to make further bets with "blinds" (another poker term you probably know well), as is the case in hold 'em. But, whatever it is, there needs to be something to start people fussing and fighting over the pot.

Element 2. We pass out paper bags and everyone goes into the pasture to find the biggest cow chip they can and hide it in their bag.

That's the equivalent in poker, as played with cards, of holding a secret hand. Without having a secret, you can't play poker.

Element 3. Everyone returns to the kitchen table and bets on the size of their secret cow chips. Now here's the scary part—you have to have courage to bet *and* courage to call. Let's say everyone else only found medium-sized cow chips in the pasture. So you bet. You bet a lot. You make a *very* big bet. If anyone equals your bet (that's "calling" in poker terms), you need to open your bag and compare sizes. Biggest cow chip wins. But if nobody calls your bet, you simply scoop up all those dollars and pocket the money. You don't even have to open your bag to prove anything. Do you see where this is getting us? Right! Everyone is terrified of your big bet and they decide not to call. You win the dollars! But with what? Actually, your bag was empty! You didn't even find a cow chip in the pasture, but you won the pot. Congratulations, you just bluffed!

That's what this book is about—Element 3. If nobody calls your bet, you win. And it doesn't matter what you have.

Now at Mike Caro University of Poker, I spend a lot of energy researching and talking about the bluff. Without the bluff—or at least the threat of the bluff—you could forget about playing poker. Bluffing is married to poker's nature.

Cover to Cover

Well, now comes Matt Lessinger with a whole book on bluffing, stuffed cover to cover with advice that is sure to build your bankroll. There's never been a book like this—taking one primal aspect of poker and providing its complete anatomy. And Matt does this with the same skill, clarity, and patience he exhibits in his popular columns.

Near the very beginning, he'll tell you that a good bluff should be misleading, but not confusing. That's a critical vision and one that will save you a lot of money, once you make it part of your everyday tactics. But Matt goes far, far beyond explaining the nature of bluffing. He tells you how to do it successfully and often incorporates player personalities into the equations. Again and again, you'll be confronted with exact situations that you'll recognize from your past poker exploits and that you'll meet again the next time you play. By the time you get to Bluff #29—"Jeez, What a River!" you'll truly appreciate—as I did—that the book you're now holding can help you bluff your way to abundant new profit you may never have realized existed.

And this journey into the strategies and science of bluffing begins on the very next page.

Mike Caro, often known as "The Mad Genius of Poker," is generally regarded as the world's foremost authority on poker strategy, psychology, and statistics. He is founder of Mike Caro University of Poker, Gaming, and Life Strategy, found online at www.poker1.com.

Introduction

It was 1:30 A.M. on the fifth day of the most grueling and prestigious poker tournament in the world. The board on the turn showed 9♠2♦ 6♠8♠. Through the magic of lipstick television cameras, everyone watching could see that the pro held Q♠9♥, top pair and a queen-high flush draw. First to act, he bet $300,000.

The action was now on the amateur. Behind his mirrored sunglasses, he looked at the pro, and started to move his chips forward.

"You call?" asked the dealer.

"No, I *raise*," the amateur declared emphatically. "Five more." He pushed $800,000 toward the pot. As the camera revealed his hole cards, we could see that he held the K♠7♥. He had an open-ended straight draw and a king-high flush draw, but really all he had was king-high. Without improvement, his hand would be worthless.

The action was back on the pro, and he called the extra $500,000 without hesitation. "We said it's going to be over soon," he said with a hint of a smile. He was trying to get a reaction out of his opponent, but the amateur just sat there as if he were made out of stone.

The river card was the 3♥, for a final board of

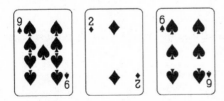 

The pro studied the board intently; he still had top pair with a decent kicker. If his hand was good on the turn, then chances were it was still the best hand. The 3♥ wasn't likely to have helped the amateur. The pro tilted his head inquisitively and checked.

Of course, the 3♥ *didn't* help the amateur. He missed his flush and his straight draws, and was stuck on the river with nothing but king-high. No matter. He waited only a second before making a motion toward his chips and declaring, "I'm all in." The pro had $2.5 million left, and the amateur had enough to cover him. The fate of the tournament now rested squarely on the pro's shoulders.

"This would be a tough, tough call," declared ESPN commentator Norman Chad. "He would have to put all of his chips in, and if he lost this pot he'd be out of the tournament."

A few moments passed. "You must have missed your flush, eh?" asked the pro, looking at his adversary. In fact, that was exactly what happened. Another few moments passed. "I could make a crazy call on you. It could be the best hand," he continued, flashing a smile at the amateur, who continued to stare straight ahead.

The pro thought about the hand for what seemed like forever. Finally, he looked across at the amateur, looked down at his hand—the winning hand—and *folded*.

The crowd went wild.

"Considering the situation—and I know we're early in the century—but that's the bluff of the century!" exclaimed Chad. "What a play!"

The pro never recovered. Less than an hour later he was eliminated, and the amateur won. In a game that is full of big bluffs, this one might have been the biggest of them all.

♣ ♦ ♥ ♠

Undoubtedly, most of you recognize that hand. The amateur was Chris Moneymaker, the pro was Sammy Farha, and the tournament was the 2003 World Series of Poker. That bluff was one of the most exciting moments in poker history, and it helped bring the game the popularity that it enjoys today.

It would be nice if poker were always that exciting. Alas, to a large extent, winning poker is usually boring poker. Sit there for hours, wait for the handful of strong hands that you can expect to receive, play them aggressively, and hope to generate a modest win. Go home, come back the next day, and play the same waiting game for the same modest profit. That's what most poker books train you to do: become a robot, play like a robot, and make about as much money as a well-trained robot.

Hey, if that playing style is for you, that's your business. As a professional poker player, I know that playing that way would bore me to tears. I also know that you can play winning poker while also being creative, innovative, and artistic.

Artistic poker? Why not? Bluffing is a form of artistry, and as far as I'm concerned, it's the most beautiful thing about poker. When you bluff successfully, you make your opponent fold the best hand. The money that should rightfully be his is now yours. Some might even call it stealing, but there's a big difference. When you steal, you forcefully take from someone against his will. When you bluff, you convince someone to voluntarily give you what would have been his. In the grand scheme of things, stealing is a lot easier.

Bluffs are also the "sex appeal" of poker. Nothing gives a player more satisfaction than a well-timed, well-executed bluff. In fact, there is even a saying: "What is more fun than winning with a straight flush? Winning with 7-2 offsuit." In the long run, every player will find his equal share of full houses, and it doesn't require any skill to win with them. On the other hand, every player will also find his equal share of garbage hands. Not every player can take those hands and, under the right circumstances, turn them into winners by bluffing successfully. Not only is it more gratifying, it is the skill that earns you the most respect from your peers.

Above all else, bluffs are really the heart and soul of poker. If nobody ever bluffed, poker wouldn't be much of a game. We might as well be playing with our cards faceup! Bluffing is what separates poker from all other card games. It's not just a matter of having the best hand. Sometimes nobody has a decent hand, which then makes the game a battle of wills. Whoever displays the better show of strength can take the pot. It's a race to be the aggressor, to assert yourself as the player entitled to the money. Poker is a game of people—it just happens to be played with cards.

♣ ♦ ♥ ♠

Bluffing is one of the most important elements of poker, and I've written this book to teach you about it. To date, shockingly, there is no other poker book that focuses on it. For that matter, hardly any poker books direct your attention to your opponents. Usually it's all about *your* cards, *your* attitude, *your* discipline, *your* bankroll, *you, you, you*. Everybody seems to forget that your opponents have the money you're after, and you need to be focusing on *them*.

First published in 1984, *Caro's Book of Tells* continues to be one of the best-selling poker books of all time. To date, it's the only meaningful poker book that focuses solely on your opponents rather than on yourself. Mike filled his book with photos of players in action, and told us what to look for in their movements, gestures, and facial expressions (i.e., their tells). Through his instruction, we could learn whether an opponent was truly confident or just pretending to be. With surprising accuracy, we could tell whether his hand was strong or weak. For a bunch of the photos, Mike even used the caption "Is this player bluffing?"

But as great as his book is, there is clearly a void. He told us how to spot a player who is bluffing, but not how to bluff! In fact, many players never learn the correct way to bluff, which is why it's easy to pick up their tells. Their timing is off, they pick their spots poorly, and their attempts to control their actions and facial expressions are weak. Once those players read this book, and they improve the quality of their bluffs, they won't be as easy to beat as when Mike wrote his book.

Despite our different approaches, Mike and I both make the same central point: To win at poker, you have to outplay your opponents. How well you play is meaningless unless you relate it to how well your opponents play. You have to force them to make mistakes. Many of your opponents make plenty of mistakes as it is; winning their money is not so difficult.

But other opponents need a little more encouragement. You need to induce them to slip up—to make bad plays when you're in the pot with them—and this book will help you accomplish that goal. It will make you ask yourself, "How can I outplay my opponents?" They want to be handed the pot without a struggle; you want to create that struggle. They want to encounter no resistance when they have marginal hands; you want to personify and magnify that resistance. You want them to know that every time they bluff at the pot, you're going to be there to make sure they don't get away with it.

Conversely, when you decide to lay claim to a pot, you want to be confident that everyone *will* get out of your way, regardless of your hand. Even if they haven't yielded in the past, this book will show you how to make them give way now. With the correct timing, experience, and artistry, it will become a common occurrence.

In short, I'm here to do for bluffs what Mike Caro did for tells—bring them to the forefront of the poker consciousness. I've devoted an entire book to one of the most important facets of the game, which up until this point has somehow been overlooked.

♣ ♦ ♥ ♠

The beauty of this book is that it will pay for itself, even if you are a low-limit player. If you learn something from this book that leads you to steal a $30 pot—a pot that you wouldn't have otherwise won—then the book just turned a profit. But that's just the beginning. Surely you'll end up stealing more than just one pot. If this book takes you from being a nonbluffer to a successful one, then in the long run, the concepts described here could easily be worth thousands of dollars.

My goal is to get you thinking *constantly* about bluffing. It should be on your mind during every hand, even if you choose not to do it. I want to stimulate your creative bluffing juices, to the point where you'll be anxiously awaiting your next chance to try one. You'll know how to pick the right opportunities, and you'll be ready when they arrive.

For the most part, you will learn by example. Forty-nine sample bluffs are the meat of this book. You probably won't be involved in a hand identical to one of them, but similar situations will arise. When they do, I want you to remember and apply what you read here.

A few of the sample bluffs, especially the earlier ones, are generic descriptions of bluffing situations. The rest of the sample bluffs were taken from actual games, and I personally witnessed most of them. Other times the bluffer, or someone at his table, told me the story. Occasionally, I was the bluffer. No matter how I knew about the bluff, I did not include it here unless I was sure that my knowledge and description of it were accurate. Finally, I used the bluffers' real names only in the final two chapters and for any other WSOP bluffs. Otherwise, the names of the participants have been changed.

I have assigned three ratings to each bluff. These ratings are by no means an exact science. They are simply my estimates of the following criteria:

1. **Degree of Difficulty:** Each bluff is rated on a difficulty scale of 1 to 10, with 1 being the easiest.
2. **Rate of Success:** Graded on a scale from Very Low to Very High, it estimates how often you could expect the bluff to succeed. As I said before, you'll hardly ever find yourself in a situation identical to the one recounted. However, you'll encounter similar circumstances, and this rating estimates your chances for success in those instances.
3. **Frequency:** Also graded from Very Low to Very High, it estimates how often you should attempt similar bluffs. Many people mistakenly believe that if a bluff's Rate of Success is high, it should be attempted often, but that is not always the case.

For example, let's say you are risking $1,000 on a bluff that could win you $5. It will almost always succeed, but that doesn't mean you should be doing it. Even if it works 100 times, and then fails the 101st time, you'll be a $500 loser. The Rate of Success would be Very High, but the Frequency rating would be Very Low.

Or you could have the exact opposite situation. If you were risking $5 to win $1,000, your Rate of Success would probably be Very Low. But if you had any chance at all of stealing the pot, then it would be well worth attempting, and that would make the Frequency rating Very High.

Finally, many bluffs have a high Rate of Success specifically because they are attempted so infrequently. If you suddenly started to attempt the same bluff repeatedly, it would no longer enjoy the same high success rate.

In many cases, the Rate of Success and Frequency are similar. But when they're not, the more important rating for your purposes is the Frequency. If you're going to commit any of the sample bluffs to memory, you should start with the ones that have a High Frequency rating. Since you will be looking to attempt those bluffs most often, you need to have them in mind so you can be fully prepared when similar situations arise.

♣ ♦ ♥ ♠

I'm ready to get started. But before we begin, let me change the topic and briefly discuss a matter of great importance.

Some people seem to believe that because poker is a game of skill, it does not qualify as gambling. In fact, many professional players have been quoted as saying that poker is not gambling. I don't know what they are smoking, but I would like some of it for myself. Poker *is* gambling, and, if you're wondering why I'm bringing this up here, keep reading.

Over the long run, if you consistently make good plays, you can expect to make money. An excellent player can show a significant profit from poker. However, even excellent players go through losing streaks. It's not as if the money falls into their lap on a daily basis. They suffer days in which nothing goes right, and they go home talking to themselves. Sometimes their bankroll isn't big enough to withstand the inevitable losing streaks that occur, and they have to quit playing until they get back on their feet again. That would be a good time to ask them if they still think poker is not gambling.

Beyond that, the majority of players are not as good as they think they are. They expect to make an easy stream of money, when in fact they might just be break-even players at best. They need to make adjustments in order to become winning players, and many of those adjustments involve taking more close gambles. A good poker player does not shy away from close gambles, as long as they are in his favor. So, just in that regard alone, it's ludicrous to say that a poker player is not a gambler.

Now, let me relate this concept to the book, and to my personal situation. I am a professional poker player. As such, I have to use all the different plays at my disposal to try to maximize my profit. Every play involves a certain degree of risk. Bluffs, which I use more than the average player, are among the riskiest plays in my arsenal. Every bluff is a gamble, sometimes in more ways than one (as you'll soon see). Therefore, if I play poker for a living, I cannot deny that I spend my life gambling.

Obviously, the same holds true for you, and please understand that while you are reading this book. Whenever you play poker, you are gambling, but whenever you bluff, you are *really* gambling! You are gambling that your opponent will lay his hand down. Your senses told you his hand was weak; now you are gambling that your senses were correct, and that his hand is so weak he cannot call.

Let's get more specific. If you read your opponent for a busted draw, you are gambling on your read being correct. If you put him on a small pair, you are gambling not only that your read is correct, but that he will lay that pair down. Last but not least, no matter what he has, you are gambling that he doesn't see your bluff for what it is, and play back at you. How can all of this not be gambling? Bluffing *personifies* the idea that poker is gambling!

If you are one of the people who try to take gambling out of poker, I can tell you two things. The first is that you'll never reach your potential as a player. The second is that this book is not for you. You must recognize that poker is gambling, and it's just a game of trying to make the best possible gambles time and time again. Many of those involve bluffing, which cause you to make bigger gambles than usual, but also provide opportunities for the biggest payoffs. You *are* gambling, and if you somehow thought you weren't, you'd better recognize it starting right now.

Abbreviations and Terminology

This book assumes you have a basic understanding of poker rules and terminology, for hold 'em as well as seven-card stud and Omaha. If you need help in that regard, I recommend *Poker for Dummies* by Lou Krieger.

The following abbreviations will be used throughout the book:

Positions:

      SB — small blind
      BB — big blind
    UTG — under the gun (the first player to act after the BB)
  cutoff — the player to the right of the button
 button — the dealer; the last player to act in each round

Games:

     NL — no-limit
     PL — pot-limit
   NLH — no-limit hold 'em
   PLH — pot-limit hold 'em
   PLO — pot-limit Omaha
  stud — seven-card stud
   H/L — high-low split
  SNG — sit 'n' go tournament; the online version of a single-table satellite

Other Abbreviations and Terminology:

 B&M — brick and mortar; a real-world cardroom as opposed to an online one
   BP — Betting Pattern
   CP — Calling Pattern (BPs and CPs are both discussed in Chapter 2)

rainbow — different suits (a rainbow flop would contain cards of three different suits)

UPC — Ultimate Poker Challenge

WPT — World Poker Tour

WSOP — World Series of Poker

CHAPTER ONE

General Bluffing Thoughts

Most of this book will focus on specific situations. This chapter will discuss some of the concepts that relate to bluffing as a whole.

Twelve Bluffing Proverbs

You will see many of these proverbs repeated, and they will be italicized for emphasis. You must understand them, remember them, and appreciate their importance:

1. There are only two ways to win a pot: You can show down the best hand, or bluff with the worst one.

If you don't bluff, you are throwing away half of your pot-winning potential. Yes, you can beat certain games by simply biding your time, showing down the best hand as often as possible, and trying to fold early when you sense you are beaten. But it's foolish to think you'll never bluff.

In many games, failure to bluff well can be the difference between winning and losing. That includes, but is not limited to: tournaments, tight games, shorthanded games, and games in which your opponents give your bets too much respect. Later on, we'll discuss those games in more detail.

Bluffing is vital in all higher-limit games. If you're a low-limit player looking to move up, you'd better have as many ways to win as you can. You'll be against many players who already understand the importance of bluffing, and if you fail to recognize that importance, you'll be at a distinct disadvantage. It'll be like entering a battle with a water pistol against a platoon armed with assault weapons.

2. If you never get called, you can never lose.

Many players are obsessed with getting paid off when they have a strong hand. I've seen some of them get amazingly agitated when they had pocket aces and won only a small pot. I hope you don't fit that description. As far as I'm concerned, that's a ridiculous reaction, for two reasons. First, it's always better to win a small pot than lose a big one. Second, rather than dwell on the small size of the pot, you should be thinking about what it means that no one gave you action. If you were able to win uncontested with A-A, it stands to reason that you could've won in the exact same manner with 7-2. If the timing is right, and you can play your junk hands in the same manner as your monsters, there's no reason why you can't win uncontested with 7-2 just as easily.

This is an especially vital concept in tournaments, where survival is the name of the game. You're hoping to accumulate chips, but that's not nearly as important as staying alive. If you can consistently win small pots without a struggle, you'll avoid elimination. The key is not to generate action on your good hands; it's to avoid getting action on *any* of your hands. How can you get knocked out if no one ever calls you? You must choose the right opponents and the proper times to go on the attack, so you can win uncontested pots as often as possible.

3. Loose players look for reasons to call, while tight players look for reasons to fold.

Tight players are obviously easier to bluff than loose ones, and you should never forget that. Before attempting any bluff, ask yourself if your opponent will be looking for a reason to call or to fold.

For example, you're playing NLH, and on the river you miss your flush draw. There's $200 in the pot, and you decide to bluff, since you've made up your mind that your opponent has a marginal hand at best. If you make a pot-sized bet, a loose opponent could easily talk himself into calling. He will think, "Wow, this guy might have me beat, but if I call and win, I can take down a big pot. That could make me a winner for the night! I've gotta go for it."

Meanwhile, a tight player might tell himself, "I think I could have the best hand, but I don't want to spend another $200 to find out. That's a lot of money. I don't want to risk losing so much when I'm not sure whether or not I have the best hand."

See the difference? The loose player saw the large bet as a positive, while the tight player viewed the exact same bet as a negative. It's hardly ever your actions by themselves that determine the success of a bluff; what truly matters is against whom you make those actions.

4. Poker is a game of information.

Winning players gather vital information about their opponents' hands without divulging information about their own. Just as that is the key to winning poker, it is also the path to successful bluffing. Anytime you make an uninformed bluff, you're merely guessing. You are taking a shot in the dark, just hoping that your opponents can't call.

You'll never enjoy long-term bluffing success that way. You need to make every effort to gather information about your opponents' hands and playing styles. If you can determine that at least one of them has a strong hand, you can save your bluffs for another time. But if you sense that everyone is weak, you can profitably attack.

Meanwhile, you have to be careful what kind of information your opponents are gathering. If you're bluffing, you can't allow them to pick up on the weakness of your hand. If anything, send out false information. Through your betting, give them reason to believe that you have a monster, when in fact you have rags.

If you can give out either false information or none at all, while simultaneously picking up accurate information about your opponents, you will unquestionably become a successful bluffer.

5. Your opponents' mistakes become your profit.

It's impossible to play error-free poker, but the biggest long-term winners will be the players who make the fewest mistakes. Your goal is not only to avoid making mistakes, but to induce as many as possible from your opponents. Whenever you have the winning hand and your opponent calls, he made a mistake. He could've folded and saved a bet, but instead that bet becomes part of your profit.

A well-executed bluff causes your opponent to make a far worse mistake. If you can get him to fold the winning hand, he will have cost himself the entire pot. Now the whole pot represents your profit, since you were rightfully entitled to none of it. It's not easy to get someone to fold a winner, but that's what makes bluffing such a valuable skill.

6. Good position makes everything easier.

You always want to act last. Since poker is a game of information, having everyone else act first gives you information about their hands. You can then use that information to help determine your correct play. Whatever you choose to do, you will be making an informed decision.

On the other hand, your opponents are forced to make uninformed decisions. They don't know what you plan on doing, so they have to make their best guess at your intentions. They're forced to guess, but you're not. You have the advantage. For that reason, all bluffs become easier from the button than from anywhere else.

Don't get me wrong. Bluffing from out of position is fine, as several of the ones in this book will demonstrate. However, don't ever kid yourself that you'll find better opportunities from the blinds than on the button. The button should become one of your best friends in the poker world, if it isn't already.

7. Indecisiveness leads to failure.

When attempting a bluff, you must be decisive. You must appear strong. Any indecisiveness will work against you. Against many players, if you take more than a few seconds to figure out if a bluff is worth attempting, you've missed your chance. They will assume that you needed time because you did not have a clear-cut decision, and they will call. You'd be better off cutting your losses, and focusing on being more prepared for the next time a bluffing opportunity comes around.

8. A good bluff tells a story that the victim believes and understands.[1]

When I say that *indecisiveness leads to failure,* it is a two-way street. The same way that you must act certain, you have to also make your opponent feel certain—certain that he is doing the right thing by folding. You don't want to leave any doubt in his mind. Let him remain confident in his fold, because creating confusion in your opponent's mind is counterproductive. Confusion leads to curiosity. Curiosity often leads to calls.

9. A good bluff should be misleading, but not confusing.

There is a tremendous difference between the two. When you successfully mislead your opponent, you control him. You get him to do exactly what you want. If you need him to fold, then you mislead him into thinking that you have the best hand.

On the other hand, when you confuse your opponent, he is not sure what to think. Instead of specifically planting the idea in his mind that you have a strong hand, you've made him wonder what you have. As I just said, confusion leads to curiosity, and curious players will spend the money to find out what you have, especially in limit games. In no-limit, a big bet might keep someone from calling. Their prudence might outweigh their curiosity. But in a limit game, players often take the easy way out by calling a single bet, just to find out what you had so they don't need to remain confused.

I've always thought of that action as a "peace of mind" call, and I've made plenty of them. I was really unsure what my opponent had, so I called a single bet just so I could see their hand, and I could sleep easier that night. Sometimes they had the best hand and sometimes they were bluffing, but I was usually glad I made the call.

---

1. Noted poker author Jim Brier gets credit for this phrase. He used it in one of our conversations, and I thought it was so good that I told him I absolutely had to use it.

Many other players make that same call when their opponents confuse them. If you avoid getting your opponents confused, you won't have to deal with their "peace of mind" calls, and all your bluffs will stand a much greater chance of success.

10. Chances are, the flop won't help.

Unless a player has a big pocket pair, he probably doesn't feel good about his hand unless the flop improves it. A-K doesn't look so hot once the flop comes 8-9-10. 6-6 looks okay before the flop, but becomes drastically worse once the flop comes A-Q-8. With everything other than big pocket pairs, players need some help from the flop to feel confident. That works to your advantage because, more often than not, that help won't arrive.

A player without a pocket pair is almost a 2-to-1 underdog to flop a pair or better. Someone with a low pocket pair is in much worse shape; he is about a 7-to-1 underdog to flop a set. In either case, your opponent will probably receive a useless flop. If you put significant pressure on him, he will then be faced with a tough decision.

Sure, the flop probably won't help you either, but that's the point. Many times, the flop misses both of you. Then it's up to you to be the aggressor, because the person who bluffs first stands a good chance of winning. You don't want to be put on the defensive, looking for help from the flop in order to win. Put your opponent in that situation. Whenever possible, make him think you have the big pocket pair that doesn't need to improve. Or else, make him think that the flop that didn't hit him helped you instead.

You'd rather have a reliable read on your opponent—some more concrete knowledge that the flop missed him. But in the absence of that kind of information, as a backup plan you can always play the percentages. Those percentages strongly suggest that the flop was no help.

11. You can't be afraid of running a failed bluff.

Some people avoid bluffing for fear of embarrassment. If you fit that description, you are probably worried about getting caught and then having to show a garbage hand. Hey, I know how you feel. It's not a fun experience. But the more often you play, the more you should come to realize that it is simply part of the game. There is absolutely nothing wrong with bluffing unsuccessfully. On the other hand, there *is* something wrong with letting a perfectly good bluffing opportunity pass because of a fear of getting caught. *That* is a problem. You have to get over that fear, because if you're going to play optimal poker, you will have plenty of bluffs that fail.

There is no way that all your bluffs will work. In fact, if you are anywhere close to a 100 percent success rate, it shows a flaw in your overall strategy. It's good to know that your bluffs are working, but it also means that you are bluffing *way* too infrequently. Since you are succeeding so often, you should increase your number of attempts. Even if you reach the point where only 50 percent of your bluffs work, that is still a fantastic success rate. Most of your bluffs will involve risking an amount much smaller than the size of the total pot. Therefore, any success rate that approaches 50 percent will show a very significant profit.

What matters is not the number or percentage of bluffs that succeed, but how much money you make from your successful attempts, compared to the money you lose from your failed ones. Sure, you can attempt two bluffs, be successful both times, and be able to say that you have a 100 percent success rate. But you should enjoy much greater prosperity if you bluff twenty times and win ten of them.

Even the world's greatest bluffers have many of them go bad; it doesn't mean they were bad bluffs. As long as you picked a good spot and executed well, don't let a failed bluff get you down. Simply brush it off, and get right back to your A game.

12. No matter who your opponent is, there will always be times that you will have a chance to bluff him.

It doesn't matter if he is a novice or an expert, a tight player or a loose one, the opportunities will be there. Against a tight opponent, those opportunities might arise once per hour; against a loose player they might come once per month. Obviously, this book will have more practical application against the tight player, so he should receive the bulk of your bluffing attention.

But don't tell me that a particular player cannot be bluffed. It's just that the opportunities appear more frequently against some than others. In general, you'll make most of your profit against the players who are easier prey, but don't close your eyes to the possibility of bluffing against anyone and everyone. Just as we are all potential bluffers, we are also all potential victims.

Bluffing Is Never Impossible

Let's continue with that last point, because many players believe that bluffing is impossible in loose games. However, they are wrong. Is it difficult? Yes. Will your opportunities be slim? Yes. But is it impossible? Never! No matter the game, sooner or later, a good bluffing opportunity will present itself.

In general, the fewer opponents who are contesting each pot, the easier it becomes to bluff. As you'll see, many of the sample bluffs in this book take place against a single opponent, because bluffs are most often successful in heads-up situations. Some of them involve two or three opponents. Very few of them involve four or more, since you shouldn't try bluffing very often against more than three players. It's possible, but usually not worth attempting, since it won't succeed often enough to be profitable.

So if you're in a loose hold 'em game in which seven or eight players are seeing the flop, you can dismiss the idea of bluffing *before the flop* or *on the flop*. With so many players, it would just be a waste of money. But then, you have to watch what happens *after the flop*. Do most of the players fold once they see a flop that completely misses them? If so, then you might have only a couple of players seeing the turn, and bluffing becomes a possibility.

On the other hand, maybe most of them call the small bet on the flop, even with nothing, but then fold for the larger bet on the turn if they haven't improved. In that case, you're limited in your ability to bluff on the flop and on the turn but, once the field gets narrowed down, you might find an opportunity *on the river*.

Here's my point: Just because seven or eight players call before the flop, don't automatically assume that you'll never have a chance to bluff. What if most of them fold once they flop nothing? And then, the ones who stay in are drawing for flushes and straights that don't arrive? It won't happen often, but sooner or later it *will* happen, so always keep your mind open to that possibility.

Most players do just the opposite. They correctly figure that they can win without bluffing, so they follow a rigid pattern. They play boring, straightforward poker. They exercise tons of patience while waiting for strong starting hands, and then hope those hands hold up. To a large extent, their strategy is correct. In the long run they should come out ahead, so they see no reason to add anything to their game plan.

They don't realize that the occasional well-timed bluff could help them win even more. They have turned their brains off to the possibility of bluffing. You never want to do that, otherwise you'll never recognize your full potential. No matter the game, the chance to bluff profitably will always come. If you're in a loose-passive game—one that is relatively easy to beat—then it won't significantly hurt your results if you miss that opportunity. But believe me, not only will it feel great when you discover it, it will open your eyes to strategies you never considered before, and your game will reach a new level.

Different Types of "Good" Games

Most of us have an image of what constitutes a "good" game. We usually envision a table full of players who see every flop and throw their chips around as if they are mere pieces of clay, not really caring if they win or lose, just looking to enjoy themselves. If given the option, we would all probably take a seat in that type of game. We know that by playing in a tight, boring manner, we could expect to win in the long run.

While that is true, the short-term luck factor is tremendous. You are at the mercy of your cards. If you get a good rush of premium hands, and they hold up, you can expect to book a nice win. But if you run card-dead, or if you get your good hands chased down, you will lose, no matter how "good" the game is. And just as you have the potential to book a nice win, some of your biggest losses will come in that type of game.

For those reasons, I find tighter games to be just as good, if not better. They are more stable, plus I'm not at the mercy of my cards. In a tighter game, if I get below-average cards, I can still pull out a win with some well-timed bluffs. And if I get a good rush of cards, I can win both by bluffing and by producing the best hand. As far as I'm concerned, that's a much better position than being in a game full of crazies, having to wait for pocket aces or kings, and then praying they hold up.

Don't get me wrong. Poker should be fun, and it's nice to play with people who are clearly enjoying themselves. The problem is that in order to beat such players, you must avoid having the same kind of fun as them. You can't play the same marginal hands that they do, otherwise you will no longer be playing profitably. Basically, you have to play A-B-C poker, and not get out of line.

Is that really what you want to do? Personally, I think it's a drag to have to play boring and tight to win. Poker is supposed to be fun, and I don't think sitting around waiting for the nuts is much fun, especially when they never come. That's why playing against a group of tighter players can make for just as good a game as any other. It lets you adopt a profitable *and* enjoyable strategy that gives you a greater chance of winning regularly. It's in those games that this book's concepts become pure gold.

Control Yourself

For those of you who strictly play online, none of this next discussion applies to you. For all I care, you can attempt a bluff and then stand up and shout at the screen, "Fold, already! Come on, you dummy! Get out of my pot!" Of course, you're not exactly playing the part of the levelheaded poker player, plus your spouse or kids might look at you a little strangely. But it's not going to affect that bluff's chances of success.

For those of you who play in B&M cardrooms, you have an added chore. Not only do you have to bluff when the situation and timing are right, you also have to keep tabs on your entire body. You must control every motion you make. Your eyes, nose, mouth, hands, even your legs—none of them can betray you.

When you make a move, everyone involved in the pot is watching. Some are watching more closely than others, and some are better than others at knowing exactly how to interpret your movements, but you should assume that everyone has an eye on you. Sure, you might be against unobservant and unknowledgeable opponents, but why risk it? Always play as if you are under constant scrutiny, because in most cases, you are.

Here are some good guidelines to keep in mind:

1. Don't start talking.

You should keep your table talk to a minimum at all times, but that is doubly true when you are bluffing. The only time you should say anything is if you have some strong reason to believe that your words will cause your opponent to fold. That is rarely the case, so for the most part, don't chance it.

There's a fine line between misleading your opponent and confusing him. If you don't successfully mislead him, then your talking will probably serve to confuse him. And, as we discussed earlier, a confused opponent is more likely to call.

2. Don't do anything out of the ordinary.

For example, if you usually bet in a smooth motion, don't suddenly slam your chips down when you bluff, thinking that will scare everyone out. Very few opponents will actually be intimidated. Most of them will find it suspicious that you acted so differently, and if they have anything at all, they will probably look you up.

Another example: If you normally look straight ahead or toward the board when you bet, don't suddenly lock eyes with your opponent and stare him down. I know that every movie would have you believe you need to do it when you bluff, but rarely will it help your cause. Most times, your opponent will realize that you've never engaged anyone in a staredown before, and he'll wonder why you're doing it this time. His curiosity will kill your bluff.

3. Don't suddenly become motionless.

Chances are that you do not normally become a statue after you bet a strong hand, so don't do it when you're bluffing either. You should be aware of what actions you normally take. For instance, where does your betting hand usually end up after you've bet? Many players let their betting hand unconsciously drift toward their stack after they bet, and it's perfectly fine if you do that, but make sure you do it consistently. After a bluff, don't suddenly let your hand freeze on the felt after the chips have left it.

Are you a chip shuffler? No problem. Just make sure you continue to shuffle your chips whether you have a real hand or you're bluffing. And then, you have to make sure that you do not suddenly start shuffling your chips twice as fast during a bluff.

Your opponents are usually more observant than you give them credit for. Even if they cannot explicitly say what is different about your actions, they are likely to pick up something subconsciously. For instance, they might not realize that it's the sound of shuffling chips that had sped up, but they can tell that something is different. That detection leads to uncertainty, and *uncertainty leads to failure*. By keeping your actions constant, you don't give your opponents any reason to wonder why you're acting a certain way.

So, in a nutshell, *be consistent*. Your physical movements should remain the same whether you have a monster, a mediocre hand, or pure garbage. Don't betray yourself through your words, your actions, or your lack thereof.

The Risk/Reward Ratio

The Risk/Reward Ratio (or RRR) is one of poker's most important concepts, and it should influence almost all of your decisions. It requires you to consider three issues:

1. How much does it cost you to take a particular action?
2. How much will you win if that action succeeds?
3. What are your chances of success?

If you know all three, then you are guaranteed to make the correct play, but unfortunately that is never the case. As far as #1 goes, you always know how much it costs you to bet, call, or raise at any given time.

#2 is often known as well. You should always know approximately how much is in the pot. Even if you haven't been keeping track of it, it's sitting right in front of you, so you can easily estimate how much you stand to win. One of the nice things about playing online is that the site always tells you the pot size. It's also a nice perk of playing pot-limit poker; the dealer is required to tell you the pot size whenever you ask. But even if you're not in one of those two situations, you should always be able to accurately estimate the pot size.

Alas, #3 is almost always unknown. You'll never be able to calculate your exact chances of success, since you do not have all the information necessary to determine it. You must make your best estimate. The more accurate it is, the better you can apply the RRR, and the better your results will be.

The RRR applies to all facets of poker. It helps you decide what to do with a strong hand, a drawing hand, or one that can beat only a bluff. We could shape an entire poker book simply around the importance of the RRR. But this is, after all, *The Book of Bluffs*.

So let's talk bluffing.

The RRR helps you to decide whether a bluff is worth attempting. Sometimes the answer is clear. Let's say you're in the main event of the WSOP. You start with $10,000 and the blinds are $25–$50. If you move all-in on the very first hand, you are almost guaranteed to win the blinds unless someone has pocket aces. Should you do it? Of course not! You are risking $10,000 and your tournament life to win a measly $75. The chances of success are about 25-to-1 in your favor, but the reward is simply not worth the risk.

At the other extreme, let's say there's a $500 pot up for grabs, and you have $10 left that can be used to bluff. Your bluff attempt will fail most of the time. But as long as you think you have a 1-in-50 chance of pulling it off, you should go for it. It won't work often, but when it does, the payoff will make it worthwhile.

Those two examples were somewhat extreme. Here's a more common situation. Let's say you are contesting a $60 pot. On the river, you have to decide whether or not to make a $20 bluff attempt. If you think the bluff will succeed more than one in four times, then it is worth trying.[2] Can you see why? If you do that same bluff three times and lose, you'll lose $20 x 3 = $60. But then, if it succeeds the fourth time, you'll win the $60 back. So a success rate of one-in-four is your break-even point. If you think it will succeed more than that, it is worth attempting. If not, then save your money for a better spot.

In general, when contemplating a bluff, the question to ask yourself is: "In this situation, will I win more money from my successful bluffs than I will lose from my failed ones?"

Other RRR Factors Must Be Considered

When applying the RRR, you can't focus on just your immediate action; you must also take into account how your current action affects future events. I've already listed the three central issues of the RRR, but here are four other things to keep in mind when deciding whether or not to bluff:

1. As I mentioned earlier, it's impossible to calculate the odds that your bluff will succeed. In our last example, we determined that your break-even point is when the bluff attempt has a one-in-four chance of success, but you can't possibly know your actual chances of success. It makes sense in theory, but not in practice. Any number you come up with is a guess, and all you can do is make as good a guess as possible.

2. A common mistake is to think that you'll break even in the long run if the bluff succeeds one out of *three* times. In fact, if betting $20 gives you a one-in-three chance of winning $60, it is worth $6.67 to you in expected value, because you'll win $20 for every three times that you attempt the bluff.

However, you cannot spend excessive time trying to formulate your guess. The very act of trying to calculate your chances of success will lower them. If you sit there and look like you are doing mental calculations, your opponents will catch on, and then you'll never be able to bluff successfully. That's why you can't sit around trying to figure out if a bluff is worth making; you have to go with your gut instincts. If a bluff feels right, then do it! Bluffing does not have to be an exact science, but it must be a decisive one. *Indecisiveness leads to failure.* If your instincts are wrong, it's no big deal. Take comfort in the knowledge that they will get better over time.

I know that is not much comfort, especially if you do not consider yourself an instinctual player. Unfortunately, I know of no better way to make your bluffing decisions than by going with what you feel is right. If you make a mistake, so what? We all make them. Just do your best not to repeat them. If you endure enough failed bluff attempts, sooner or later you will realize that your instincts need to be altered, and that is why I say you'll get better over time. Just be sure you are making a concerted effort to improve your bluffing skills, by making a mental note of your successes and failures, and analyzing the causes for them.

2. The first consideration of the RRR—how much it costs you to take a given action—is known for sure only if you're on the river. If a decision comes up earlier, then your cost could change dramatically by the time the hand is over. For instance, it might cost you $10 to call a bet on the flop, but how much more will you have to spend in order to make it to showdown?

   With respect to bluffing, let's say you raise pre-flop from the button as a bluff, only to have the BB call you. You're probably not going to abandon the bluff attempt immediately, so how much more might you spend before the hand is over? There's simply no way to know for sure.

3. Unless your action is being made on the river, the second consideration of the RRR—how much you stand to win—is also

constantly changing. If you bet the flop, the amount you stand to win will have changed dramatically by the time the hand goes to showdown. When considering the RRR, you must take into account not only the current pot size, but also any additional bets that it might contain before you're finished.

When bluffing before the river, don't ignore the possibility of money being made (or lost) on later streets. The section "Calling Patterns" makes this point clear. Sometimes you bet, knowing that the player will call, but hoping he will lay down later. If you just looked at your chances of success on the first bet, it would seem like a nonsensical play, since there is practically no chance that your opponent will fold then. It's only when you combine the first bet with follow-up bets that it makes sense, since they work together to increase your chances of success.

4. The money won or lost in a single bluff attempt won't usually cause you to win or lose for the entire day. However, the effect it has on *future* hands can potentially influence your outcome for the entire session. Every time you successfully push someone out of a pot, you assert yourself toward future pots against that opponent, plus you create a more intimidating table image in everyone else's eyes. In turn, that gives you a greater chance for success in future confrontations. You are constantly changing your success rate with each passing hand. Don't ignore the effects a given hand can have on future ones.

Players that ignore these four facets of the RRR are limiting their view of the game. They see only one bet being made toward one pot. They need to see the hand as a whole, the session as a whole, and they need to play more instinctively and less mathematically. My intentions are to lead you toward those goals.

CHAPTER TWO

Uncovering Patterns

What is your favorite type of opponent? A maniac who bets every hand? A rock who never calls? How about a beginner who never bluffs? As far as I'm concerned, they're all good, and here's why: *All good opponents fall into predictable, easily identifiable patterns.*

We will examine several types in this chapter. Some players are predictable in their manner of betting, others follow a regular routine of calling. Still others exhibit predictable physical patterns, such as the way they hold their cards or their chips. From the moment you sit down, you should be studying your opponents to try to uncover any such patterns, because once you find one, you'll own that player. You'll know what it means when he takes a particular action, and you'll counter with the correct play.

Strong players mix up their strategies. They are tough precisely because they don't fall into any predictable patterns. If you study an opponent and cannot find any patterns, you know he is better than your average player. As such, he is probably not a good candidate to be bluffed. If a favorable bluffing situation comes up, and he happens to be in the pot, then take your shot. But don't go out of your way to encounter him. Instead, look to take advantage of weaker opponents, since you will be better able to exploit their predictability.

Don't kid yourself that a player is following a pattern when he has done something only once. Just because you see a player raise on the flop with a flush draw doesn't mean he always does that. A good guideline is to see if a player does the same thing three times. Then you can treat his tendency as a pattern, and play accordingly. It's nice when a player follows a pattern, but don't create one that isn't there.

Finally, don't be afraid to admit that you initially read a player's pattern incorrectly. For instance, if you've pegged someone as a completely straightforward player, and then he suddenly bluffs out of nowhere, don't treat the bluff as an anomaly. Instead, you should assume that your initial classification of that opponent was incorrect, and go from there.

Calling Patterns (CPs)

At one end of the Calling Pattern scale, you have extremely tight players known as "rocks." They rarely call pre-flop, except when they have a strong starting hand, and they won't give any further action unless they think they have the best hand. They are good candidates for bluff attempts.

At the other end of the spectrum are the extremely loose players, known as "calling stations." They will play anything and will call almost all the time, even if they stand little chance of winning. Attempting to bluff them is usually a waste of money. In a nutshell, rocks call fewer bets than anyone, while calling stations make it a contest to see who can call most often.

Those two categories are the extremes, and they are often discussed in poker literature. Unfortunately, not many players fit those descriptions. If they did, classifying your opponents would be a piece of cake. Instead, the vast majority of your opponents fall somewhere in the middle, so that's where we need to focus our attention. I have listed five categories to help identify your opposition.

Specifically, you have players who:

1. Fold before the flop unless they have strong starting cards (rocks, or CP#1)
2. Often call before the flop, but fold if they don't like the flop (CP#2).
3. Often call before and on the flop, since it costs them only a small bet each time. But if they don't improve on the turn, they will usually fold when the limits double (CP#3).
4. Often call until the river card, because they want to see all five community cards. However, they will fold on the river if they haven't made a decent hand (CP#4).

5. Call all the way, including on the river, even with a hand that stands very little chance of winning (calling stations, or CP#5).

Those categories are for hold 'em. Similar groupings can be outlined for seven-card stud. You have players who:

1. **Fold** on third street unless they have strong starting cards (rocks, or CP#1).
2. Often **call** on third street, but fold if the fourth street card is no help (CP#2).
3. Often **call** the small bets on third and fourth streets, but then if they haven't improved, they'll usually fold when the limits double on fifth street (CP#3).
4. **Call** until the river, because they want to see all seven cards. However, if they don't end up with a decent hand, they fold (CP#4).
5. **Call** all the way, plus they often call a bet on the end, even with a hand that stands very little chance of winning (calling stations, or CP#5).

These categories, though simplified, are an extremely effective way of grouping your opponents. As I said before, many opponents will not conveniently fall into a category, and you shouldn't try to classify someone who doesn't follow a set pattern. But against those opponents that do, you will have a tremendous advantage. Among other things, you'll know whether or not bluffing is a reasonable option.

Generally speaking, you shouldn't try bluffing a loose player, but that's true only if the player is extremely loose, such as a calling station. Otherwise, it becomes a matter of determining just how loose the player is. Players that follow CP#3 and CP#4 would definitely be considered loose, but they are also extremely bluffable. The two are not mutually exclusive.

Here's an example: The field checks the flop to you, and you choose to attempt a bluff from the button. Only two players call. If you've identified one of those players by his Calling Pattern, you'll have a much better idea of whether or not to continue your bluff attempt, because you've identified that player's personal moment of truth.

Let's say you've pegged that player as following CP#2. In that case, you should lean toward checking the turn. As a CP#2 player, he would not have called unless the flop helped him. It's likely that he flopped at least a pair, and as such, it will probably be difficult to get him out of the pot. The flop was his moment of truth, so as the player trying to bluff him, it also becomes your moment of truth. If he had folded, you could have breathed easy, but since he called, you have to assume your chances of success just got a lot worse.

On the other hand, let's say that same player follows CP#3 instead. Now his call on the flop is practically meaningless. You've already classified him as someone who calls on the flop even when it's no help. So his call tells you nothing about the strength of his hand, or about the chances that a continued bluff attempt will work. If you thought the situation was right to bluff on the flop, then bluffing on the turn will usually be just as correct. You must bet again to find out where he stands. The turn is the moment of truth for both of you. You're hoping he lays down, but if he calls, at least now you know you should check the river and surrender, because he wouldn't have called on the turn without a hand.

As you see from this example, you can have two identical situations with the only difference being each opponent's Calling Pattern, and that by itself can be enough to change the way you play a given hand. For our purposes, Calling Patterns will be most important when you are attempting bluffs prior to the river and someone calls. If that player follows a specific Calling Pattern, you'll be able to make an informed decision of whether or not to continue bluffing, and for how long.

Betting Patterns (BPs)

Here are the four most common Betting Patterns and a brief look at how they affect your bluffing strategies.

1. A completely straightforward player (BP#1)

He always bets when he has a good hand and always checks when he doesn't. You'll usually find him in lower-limit games, and occasionally in higher-limit ones. His best quality is that he never bluffs. Since you have no qualms about running the (ahem) occasional bluff, you have a clear advantage over him, and you can exploit it often.

Anytime you are heads-up with him, and he acts first and checks, you should be ready to pounce. He checks, you bet. He checks, you bet. Repeat as often as necessary. There's no need to fear a check-raise, since the straightforward player wouldn't dream of doing that. Don't feel bad for him. He's going to lose his money eventually; it might as well go to you.

If you have to act first and you have nothing, you should simply check to him. Why attempt an uninformed bluff when he will give you straightforward information through his actions? Sure, other players might take advantage of your show of weakness, but he won't. He'll bet if he has something, and then you can throw your rags away. If he checks, then you'll know he also has nothing, and you can come out betting on the next card. There's always the chance that the free card will help him, but the odds strongly suggest that it won't. Fire into him, and expect him to lay down.

Clearly, there is an advantage to acting behind him, just as there is in most bluffing situations. *Good position makes everything easier.* Having to act before him cuts into your success rate a bit, but not enough to change your strategy against him. Through his actions, let him tell you whether or not he has a good hand, and then make the proper response.

2. A completely contrary player (BP#2)

He is essentially the opposite of BP#1. If he bets, it's either a bluff or a relatively weak hand. He never bets his strongest hands; he either looks to check-raise (if he acts first) or to raise on the next card (by checking in last position and hoping it induces you to bet). Some might look at this player and think he is trickier than BP#1. In the most basic sense he is, but both are equally predictable, and as such neither one should be considered tricky.

Your strategy against him is equally clear. If he checks, you have to be more wary than you would be against the average player. You can't interpret his check as weakness, so don't instinctively shift into bluffing mode. Conversely, if he bets, it should not scare you. Instead, you should be prepared to attack after he bets. Often a raise on the flop will slow him down, and then a bet on the turn will seal the deal. Or you could just call on the flop, and then if he bets into you again on the turn, raise him as a bluff. You know he doesn't have a strong hand, so many times he will respect your raise and lay down his mediocre hand.

If you are first to act, then you should look to check-raise with any decent holding, and sometimes even without anything decent. You know that someone who follows BP#2 can't often resist betting when his opponent checks to him, so you should hit him with a healthy dose of check-raises.[3] If you check and he checks behind you, don't automatically assume weakness. As a contrary player, he is much more likely to have a strong hand than would normally be the case.

3. A super-aggressive player (BP#3)

Another way to describe him is a "predictable maniac." Whenever the action is checked to him, he bets. When someone in front of him bets, he often raises. People generally seem to love having such a player at their table, and I can understand their enthusiasm. He generates lots of action. He gambles it up, and he gets others at the table to gamble with him. And he'll probably lose in the process.

But, from a bluffer's perspective, he takes away a lot of your weapons. Yes, he will probably lose money, but he will also have

---

3. In general, he is following a good strategy by being aggressive when his opponent shows weakness. However, he cannot do that every time. That is when it becomes a predictable pattern. Smart opponents will catch on, and they will look to check-raise him with almost anything. He will be forced either to vary his play or suffer the consequences.

control of the table. You are often at the mercy of the cards, and not just your cards. His are equally as important, because to win any pot, you'll have to get through him. You will usually have to produce the best hand to win in a game with a BP#3 player.

4. An ultra-passive player (BP#4)

He is basically the opposite of BP#3. He hates to make an aggressive action. He will never bet his own hand. If someone else bets, he will usually either call or fold, but hardly ever raise. While a BP#3 player is usually the most visible player at his table, a BP#4 player is a lot tougher to spot. You must exercise excellent observational skills to identify all the different types of players described here, but that is especially true for the ultra-passive player.

Notice that BP#3 and BP#4 players don't give you clues about the strength of their hands. The BP#3 player is aggressive no matter what he has, whereas the BP#4 player checks with both his strong and his weak hands. That's why it's so important to identify who's who as quickly as you can. Actions carry a lot more information when you know the type of player making those actions. A bet that would slow you down if made by a BP#1 player should hardly faze you if it comes from a BP#3 player.

The presence of a BP#3 player will often change the complexion of an entire game. He causes everyone to loosen up, making bluffing much more difficult, since there are more large, multiway pots. Also, everyone knows that the BP#3 player is betting anything, so they fall into a calling mode. Even though they start out by loosening their calling requirements against only the maniac, they eventually start making more loose calls against everyone. By no means should you leave that game, but make sure you recognize what is happening, and cut down on your bluffing frequency.

Daniel Negreanu, one of the world's best players, wrote an excellent article about going into a low-stakes game and playing like a complete maniac as a learning tool.[4] Even if you lose money for that session,

---

4. "Nutbar," *Card Player Magazine,* Volume 14, Issue 26.

you gain a whole new insight into the game. You see how it feels to control the table, you get to see how other players react to you, and now that you've seen the game from the maniac's point of view, you will be better prepared to counter him when he sits down in your game.

Not only do I fully agree with Daniel's suggestion, I'd take it a step further. He says to be a maniac for an entire session, which entails following BP#3. I'd suggest playing four different sessions, and following every extreme Betting Pattern for an entire session. Play in a low-stakes game, so that you won't be putting too much at risk. You're not doing this exercise to try to make an immediate profit; you're doing it to get into the mind-sets of your various opponents, which will hopefully improve your results in future games.

For instance, see how it feels to be a super-passive player. Go through an entire session without making a bet or a raise. If you win, that's great. Take your money. But when it doesn't work, ask yourself how your opponents used your passivity against you. Among other things, did they try bluffing you more often, figuring that you were always weak when you checked? How many bluffing opportunities did you miss because you weren't allowed to make a bet?

Maybe this exercise sounds strange, but I promise you, any money you lose will be worth it in terms of the insight you gain. The more thoroughly you understand your opponents' ways of thinking, the more prepared you will be to counter them.

Other Patterns (Looking to Your Left)

One of the best ways to improve your game is to habitually look at the opponents to your left before taking action. Don't swivel your head or make it obvious. Simply glance to your left out of the corner of your eye before making a move, to pick up information on what the players behind you plan to do. It is an indispensable habit. If you don't yet do it, start today.

We've established that position is vitally important. Being the button is a tremendous advantage because everyone has to act before you. They're forced to give you information relative to their hands, which you can then use when deciding what action to take. But if the players to your left give away that information prematurely, it's almost as if you are acting after them. In effect, you have gained position on them. You just need to make sure that you correctly interpret that information.

Here are some things you might catch a player doing:

Preparing to fold

From a bluffer's perspective, you love to see an impatient folder. He looks at his cards, decides they're unplayable, and holds them in such a way that he is ready to toss them in the second the action reaches him. He figures he's not giving any valuable information away. Since he's not going to play the hand anyway, what does he care if everyone knows he's folding?

He doesn't realize what a crucial long-term mistake he is making. If he telegraphs the times he folds, then it stands to reason he also telegraphs the times he *doesn't* fold. When he doesn't hold his cards as if he is ready to toss them, you'll know he's prepared to play, and you'll act accordingly. Simply put, you should always be ready to strike, but before you do, look to your left and see if that player is giving you the green or the red light.

If he's giving you the green, you can repeatedly exploit him. Let's say that everyone folds to you in the cutoff seat. If you look to your left and see that the button is in folding mode, you have essentially become the button. You can now raise without fear of being reraised by someone with position on you. It's like having the button twice every round, an incredible advantage.

Sometimes multiple players telegraph their intentions to fold, and then you can play hands from way out of position, not just the cutoff seat. *Card Player* columnist Michael Weisenberg described a perfect example from a lowball game, and you don't need to be a lowball player to appreciate it. He won a hand he would not normally have played.

> *I was first or second to act, and had something like . . . a pat 10. Normally, I would not open with that hand any earlier than from the cutoff position. But I could see that both Sally*

*and Jim [sitting behind me] were going to fold. I also could
see the cutoff spreading his cards so that the button could see
that he held what was presumably a fistful of facecards,
while the button was doing the same thing. They wouldn't be
showing their cards if they were going to play. Thus, I could
open from first position with what was only a last-position
hand—because I knew that the four players to my left were
all going to fold.[5]*

Clearly, you should switch seats to try to get premature folders
on your left. Players who hold their cards a certain way when they
intend to fold are absolute gold mines, but if they are seated to your
right, they become worthless.

Reaching for chips

Many players look at their cards, decide they are prepared to play
them, and instantly reach for their chips, even if there are three or
four players ahead of them. Once you see someone do that, your next
job is to determine if he is following a reliable pattern. Does that
player always reach for chips when he intends to play, or is it sometimes a meaningless scare tactic?

Assuming that player is not being tricky, and is simply impatient
when he has a strong hand, you now know when not to bluff. If you
look to your left and see someone reaching for chips, chances are
that player is not going anywhere, and you can save your bluffs for
another time.

The impatient bettor is just as valuable to you as the impatient
folder. If he routinely telegraphs when he intends to play by grab-
bing his chips, then it stands to reason that he telegraphs the times he
will fold when he *doesn't* reach for his chips. Thus, you know not
only when to avoid him, but also when to exploit him.

Believe it or not, many players don't just reach for their chips;
they reach for the exact number of chips they plan to use. With a

5. "Where to Sit in Lowball," *Card Player Magazine,* Volume 15, Issue 17.

quick glance to your left, you can see how many chips a player has in his hand, and thus whether he intends to call or raise. If he's ready to raise, then you know to play only your very strongest starting hands.

If he plans on only calling, then you should play any hand you were prepared to play anyway, since you know he doesn't have a monster starting hand. Furthermore, you can use that information to your advantage later on if you flop nothing but decide to bluff. Since he presumably does not have a big pocket pair, he is looking for the flop to improve his hand, but *chances are, the flop won't help him,* just as it didn't help you.

Changing posture

Many poker players slouch in their seats, but sit up straight when they are involved in a hand. Some of them routinely jump the gun and sit upright before the action reaches them, knowing they are about to get involved in the action.

If you have a player like that to your left, you are in luck. If you see him lean forward a bit, or he appears taller, or he makes some other similar, obvious change in posture, you know that he is prepared to play, and you can act accordingly. On the other hand, if the player remains slouched, you can assume he has no interest in playing the hand, and that he's given you the green light to ignore him.

Showing disinterest

If a player looks at his cards and thinks he might play, he usually pays attention to the action in front of him. So when a player isn't following the action, it's often a reliable telegraph that he doesn't plan to get involved. If he looks at his cards and then looks at the TV, looks for a waitress, turns to a friend, or does anything other than watch the action taking place, you can expect him to fold. Whatever action you take, assume that he won't be a threat.

All of these tells assume that, pre-flop, the player in question looks at his cards ahead of time. If, instead, he waits until the action reaches him before looking, he won't give anything away.[6] Maybe after the flop he will betray some information, but you'd prefer an opponent who follows one of these patterns both before and after the flop. That's why the first thing you should note when you look to your left is whether or not those players look at their cards before you act.

If they don't, they're not much good to you. So instead, look around the table to see if any other players look at their cards early, and whether they give off any clues about their hand. In fact, that should be one of your jobs within the first few minutes of sitting down at a new table. See who is telegraphing their actions both before and after the flop, and then try getting a seat to their right. They will serve you well.

One final note

Most players who follow these patterns do them subconsciously, and as such, they are reliable indicators. Some players, however, become compulsively misleading. For instance, certain players grab for their chips when they intend to fold. Others pretend to be watching TV when in fact they are paying close attention to the action. They are often being deceptive without knowing exactly why, and it shouldn't cause you any problem. If the same player always grabs for his chips and then folds, you know to look for that particular tell from that player.

As we discussed previously, anytime your opponent follows a reliable pattern, you stand to benefit. It's just a question of identifying that pattern. Once you note that a player consistently makes the same motion, it does not matter what the motion is; you now have vital information. And for as long as that player remains to your left, you will have a tremendous advantage over him without his even realizing it.

---

6. That's why waiting until the action reaches you before looking at your cards is often a good idea. Even if you're pretty sure that you don't give off any premature tells, this way you can be absolutely certain.

Drawing Hands

A vital component to successful bluffing is being able to identify the players who are on a draw. You want to bluff at players who are weak, and drawing hands are among the weakest hands your opponents will play. If a player misses his draw, he is usually left with little or nothing, and then you are in perfect position to steal on the river.

The question is, how can you tell when a player is on a draw? Obviously you can't always know, but very often a player's pattern will give you hints that he doesn't have a made hand. As an observant player, your job is to gather those hints, so that you can tell what a particular player usually does when he's on a draw. For example:

1. Sometimes his Calling Pattern gives it away. Let's say a player checks from early position. Then there is a bet and a raise behind him, and when the action comes back around, he calls two bets cold. That usually signals a drawing hand. After all, if his hand was strong enough to call two bets, why wasn't it strong enough for him to bet it? Yes, he could be slow-playing a big hand, but that is the less likely scenario. Chances are he doesn't have anything yet, just good potential.

   Generally speaking, when you see a player call all bets without thinking of raising, there's a good chance he is drawing. Whenever possible, you want to try to get heads-up with him. Then, as long as his apparent draw never gets there, you can attack and claim the pot.

2. Sometimes his Betting Pattern gives it away. A common pattern is for a player to get aggressive on the flop, going to war with bets and raises, but then to back off on the turn if his draw doesn't immediately materialize. When you see someone who is willing to raise and reraise on the flop, but then doesn't bet the turn, a drawing hand is a distinct possibility.

   Some particularly aggressive players never stop betting their draw, even when it misses. If your opponent seemingly follows that pattern, you have two courses of action. If your hand can beat a bluff, then you can simply call him down. Or if your hand is so bad that the player with the busted draw could be bluffing with the best hand, then you must look to bet or bluff-raise him on the river, assuming the river card doesn't appear to complete his draw. If you correctly decide that he missed, then it would be extremely difficult for him to call any bets or raises on the river.

It's on you to identify what type of player you are against. But whatever he does, you must observe him, and identify his Betting Pattern on a draw. Then wait for him to do it again, and attack.

3. Sometimes his body language gives it away. Many players do amazingly stupid things when they miss their draws. They shake their head in disgust, or flash their missed draw to their neighbor. Some even openly admit that they were looking for a club on the river, and only this "rotten dealer" would put a diamond up there instead.

Just like the player who folds out of turn and figures he's not giving away any information, the player who misses his draw and makes no effort to hide it doesn't realize what a mistake he is making. He figures he cannot win anyway, so what is the point of masking his frustration? For one thing, if he habitually shows his frustration when he misses, then he probably stays silent when his draw hits. If you suspect that player is on a draw, and then he doesn't have a negative reaction to the river card, it stands to reason that he made a hand, and you can pass on the possibility of bluffing.

But when he does react negatively, you can take advantage of it. Maybe you started out betting as a bluff, or you had a worse draw, and the player with the busted draw would actually win a showdown. Now he has given you the green light to take the pot that is rightfully his. Stealing a pot from a player who missed his draw doesn't have to happen all that often to have a significant positive impact on your bottom line.

As you can see from everything we've discussed, true players don't slack off between hands. If you want to be the best, you have to put in the effort. Even when you fold early on, you have to watch your opponents and pick up information. You must recognize as many of their patterns as possible, and take advantage of them in future confrontations. I am very critical of players who tell me they are bored between hands, because I know they cannot possibly be exercising their poker minds to the fullest. Don't be one of those players. Stay alert and attentive, whether you're involved in the hand or not.

CHAPTER THREE

Basic Bluffs

This book contains some really intricate and complicated bluffs. But you'll find that the simplest bluffs are usually the most effective, and they are the ones used most often. Don't look to make complicated plays when simple ones will do.

Bluff #1. Hold 'em's Most Basic Bluff

The scenario: Any hold 'em game.

The bluff: You're on the button. Everyone folds to you pre-flop. You raise, and the blinds fold.

Degree of Difficulty: 1
Rate of Success: Medium/High
Frequency: Very High

Why this bluff works: Notice that I did not specify whether the game is limit or no-limit, high-stakes or low-stakes. Most important, I didn't specify what your cards are. It doesn't matter. With the right type of opponents in the blinds, this play will show a long-term profit no matter what you have. Do not make the mistake of folding just because you have a completely trash hand. *The cards are not important; the opponents in the blinds are.*

If your opponents are straightforward, predictable, and relatively tight, then you should raise with any two cards. You can be confident of where you stand based on their actions. You know that they will reraise with their very strong hands, call with above-average hands, and fold if they have an average or below-average hand, and that knowledge makes it easy for you to respond effectively.

Most of the time they will fold, and that is the simplest of results. When they call, you have position on them throughout the hand, and you will almost always have an opportunity to bluff at them again (more on that later). If they reraise, then you can throw your hand away after the flop, unless you happen to have a premium hand or hit a lucky flop. That doesn't sound like fun, but keep in mind that with the type of opponent I described, that result won't occur too often. One of the blinds would need to come up with a very strong hand, and that won't happen often enough to stop you from raising them regularly.

When to back off: If your opponents are particularly tricky, and are likely to play back at you with a wide range of hands. In that case, you should raise with surprisingly few hands from the button. You'd rather have either a premium hand, in which case you're happy to see a reraise, or a completely trash hand, so you can have no qualms about folding if you miss the flop.

Cards like A-4 offsuit and K-6 suited—hands that are very marginal—are not what you want against aggressive opposition. Considering that I seem to be advocating very loose play from the button, mucking those hands may appear abnormally tight. But that's the point I'm trying to make. Ninety percent of your decision of whether or not to raise should be based on who is sitting in the blinds. Only 10 percent of your decision should be based on what cards you hold.

Seat selection: If you have particularly tricky players sitting one or two to your left, then you're in the wrong seat, and possibly even in the wrong game. If you're in a tournament, then you have no choice but to deal with them. But if you're in a live game, you definitely want to reconsider where you are sitting.

You want *predictable* opponents to your left. If another seat opens up, where the tricky players can be on your right, and you can see what they are going to do before you act on your own hand, then move there. But in general, I would consider switching games altogether.

You want to be the tricky, unpredictable player at the table. Don't let anyone else take that distinction away from you.

Trading places: In order to bluff successfully, you sometimes have to put yourself in the position of the one being bluffed. That is an exercise that we will use often, so let's start here.

Pretend *you* are the one in the blind, and the button raises you. There are many reasons why you might fold. Just to name a few:

1. You have a below-average hand and don't want to spend any more money on it.
2. You know that if you call, the button will probably continue to show aggression throughout the hand, which will put you on the defensive for the remaining betting rounds.
3. You know that the button will have position on you throughout the hand, which makes it easier for him to outplay you if you both flop nothing.
4. You might suspect that the button is raising any two cards, but there is always the chance he stumbled on to a strong hand, and it could cost you a lot of money to find out.

Now it should be clearer why we want tight players in the blinds when we raise them. *Loose players look for reasons to call, while tight players look for reasons to fold.* If you raise on the button, and you have tight players in the blinds, they will consider all of the things I listed above. Usually it will lead them to the tight answer (often not the right answer) of folding.

They want to take the easy way out. It's up to you to give it to them. They want to fold and move on to the next hand. You should be more than happy to oblige them. Raise and take their blinds. They won't miss them. They're already looking forward to playing the next hand instead.

Bluff #1A. Playing Past the Flop

It's the exact same situation as above. Everyone folds to you pre-flop. You raise with a weak hand hoping to steal the blinds, except this time the BB calls. The flop provides no help for you, your opponent checks, and now it's your move.

This is an extremely common scenario. You chose to be aggressive from the button, but the BB chose to see the flop. Since there is still some poker to be played, there are now three things you want to know about him:

1. Is he tricky or straightforward?
2. (Closely related to #1) What is his typical Betting Pattern?
3. What is his typical Calling Pattern?

If you've never played with him before, then obviously you won't have any answers to those questions. In that case, go with the assumption that he is capable of being bluffed until you learn otherwise. After all, if he is unbluffable, there wasn't much point in raising from the button to win the blinds. The blinds need to fold more than half the time to make that by itself a profitable play, and unless they are tight players, that won't be the case.

Let's start with #1. If he is tricky, then raising with a weak hand was not a good idea to begin with. We want to pick on predictable players. If you've never played with him before, then you're excused because you had no way of knowing his usual tendencies. However, if he check-raises you, or in some way puts you on the defensive, then you know for the future that he is not easy pickings. Assuming he does neither of those things, he should qualify as an acceptable bluff victim. So we'll continue under the assumption that he is not overly tricky.

Let's look at question #2. The BB merely called your raise and then checked to you on the flop, so he cannot be a BP#3 player (super-aggressive). If he follows BP#2 (contrary), then you should be wary of his check, since he might look to check-raise. But if he follows either BP#1 (straightforward) or BP#4 (super-passive), then you clearly must bet the flop. In the case of a BP#1 player, his check is a clear sign of weakness, and you should assume that the flop missed him. A BP#4 player would check to you no matter what, but *chances are, the flop didn't help,* so you must bet and give him a chance to fold.

If he folds, then end of story, take the pot. But if he calls, you now have to look at question #3. Did he call because he flopped something (CP#2), or because he always calls the small bet on the flop (CP#3 or higher)? Your knowledge of his Calling Pattern dictates how far you should go with your bluff. If he follows CP#2, then you should shut down once he calls your flop bet. If he follows CP#3, then it's imperative to bet the turn as well, since that is his moment of truth. However, if he calls you a second time, you should then check the river and cut your losses.

If he follows CP#4, then you have to follow through with bets the entire way, and look for him to possibly fold on the river. You might think you are investing a lot of money on a simple bluff attempt, but if he is truly a CP#4 player, then his calls on the flop and turn were relatively meaningless. There is still a decent chance he will fold on the end, and while you've invested a healthy amount, you also stand to win several bets from that opponent, so it becomes worthwhile. And finally, if he follows CP#5 (calling station) then you shouldn't have been bluffing him to begin with.

Your default strategy: Many players have no problem raising from the button, but then are at a loss for what to do next. Typically, if one of the blinds calls and then checks the flop, the button always bets. But then, if he gets called, he usually checks the turn unless he makes a hand. Essentially, his opponent's call on the flop causes him to shut down his bluff attempt. He gives no consideration at all to his opponent's Betting or Calling Patterns.

If you're on the button, and this is your first encounter against the player who called you from the blinds, this is not a terrible default strategy. On the plus side, you were able to make two bluff attempts (before the flop and on the flop), and thus you gave your opponent two chances to fold. Also, your bluffs were made on the two cheaper betting rounds, thus limiting your potential cost.

The downside is that you haven't learned if your opponent could have been bluffed out with a bet on the turn and/or river. Therefore, if you decide on that course of action, then it is *imperative* that the next time you go against that same opponent in the same situation, you must follow through with bets on the turn and, if necessary, the river. He will almost certainly call a flop bet, in the expectation that you will check on the turn if you have nothing, just like you did the last time you faced him. That's why you have to change gears and surprise him. If you fall into a predictable Betting Pattern, you have no hope of controlling your table.

What if both blinds call you pre-flop? Clearly that cuts down on your chances of success, but your potential reward has gone up too. I would never recommend following a specific Betting Pattern. However, here is a good default strategy for you to follow:

1. If either opponent bets on the flop, or check-raises, or somehow shows an aggressive action, then continue only if you think you might have the best hand.
2. If they check to you on the flop, go ahead and bet. If they both fold, then your job is done.
3. If you get called in both places, then lean toward checking the turn.
4. If only one of them calls, then you are essentially in the same situation as we discussed previously. Treat the rest of the hand as if only one player had called pre-flop, and base your actions on his calling tendencies.

Please recognize that this is an overly simplistic framework. For instance, if you folded every time you had no pair and one of them bet, you could never win. Once they recognized what you were doing, they would always call your pre-flop raise and come out betting. You would become a perpetual bluff victim. So clearly, you have to sometimes raise the flop with nothing. Just as your opponents become easy victims once they fall into a pattern, you can easily turn into one too, so make sure you avoid becoming predictable.

You should only follow a default strategy when you have no information on a particular opponent. And generally speaking, your default strategy should be to remain aggressive. However, you have to mix up that aggression based on anything you learn about your opponents. Knowledge of their Betting or Calling Patterns should cause you to vary your play. That way, not only will you stand a better chance of success in that specific instance, but your opponents won't be able to define a set pattern that you follow, so your chances for success in future hands will go up as well.

From the right of the button: Bluffs #1 and #1A specify that you are on the button, but you don't necessarily have to be. We talked about the importance of looking to your left. Now you can put that suggestion to good use. Let's say you are in the cutoff seat, and everyone to your right folds. You look to your left and see that the button is also prepared to fold. You can now raise, knowing that you will "become the button." The same holds true if you are two seats to the right of the button, but you look left and see both of the next two players preparing to fold.

In either case, assuming that you correctly determined that the players behind you will fold, it will be just you against the blinds. Plus, your raise will have an added bonus. Your pre-flop raise will carry a little more weight to observant opponents. They might see you raise on the button and instinctively think you are stealing. But when you make the raise from one or two positions to the right of the button, they might assume you have a strong hand, not just a stealing one.

Any time you have a reliable read on the players to your left, you have the potential to make this simple bluff more than once per round, plus you get to make it from a more convincing position.

Bluff #2. Stud's Most Basic Bluff

The scenario: Any seven-card stud game with an ante involved.

The bluff: The first three cards are dealt, and the player to your left is the low card on board. He makes the required bring-in bet. Everyone else folds, you complete the bring-in (i.e., you raise), and the low card surrenders.

Degree of Difficulty: 1
Rate of Success: High
Frequency: Always

The analysis: Clearly this play has a lot in common with Bluff #1. Both represent the most basic bluff for their respective games, and both involve using your position and aggression to try to steal a small pot. However, four key differences should be noted:

1. In hold 'em, you have to worry about both the SB and BB. In stud, you have to beat only one player.
2. In hold 'em, the SB and BB have two completely random hands. In stud the low card, by definition, has at least one bad card in his hand, thus his hand rates to be worse than average. In both hold 'em and stud, you could unknowingly be bluffing with the best hand, but it is more likely the case in stud, since you already have at least one card higher than your opponent's.
3. In hold 'em, when you raise pre-flop from the button, you are typically risking four units to win three. For example, in a $2–$4 game, the blinds are $1 and $2. You would raise to $4 from the button in order to win the $3 in blind money. In $10–$20 hold 'em the blinds are $5 and $10, so you'd be raising to $20 in order to win $15. Anytime the SB is half of the BB, and the pre-flop raise doubles the BB, you are betting four units to win three.

In stud, as long as an ante is involved, you'll usually get a better ratio than that. It depends on how many players are at the table (and thus how many antes you are gunning for), but you will usually stand to win more than the amount you are raising. For example, in a typical $4–$8 stud game, the antes are $.50 and the low card starts the action for $1. If there were eight players dealt in, then there were $4 in antes plus the $1 for the low card. When everyone in front of you folds, you can complete the bring-in to $4. Therefore, you are betting $4 to win $5. Although the ratio in stud varies at different limits, it will typically be in that general range when you have a full table, and it will worsen slightly for each empty seat.

4. In hold 'em, you know that, when you raise from the button, you will have the privilege of acting last on all future betting rounds. However, in stud, you're guaranteed to be "in position" only on third street. After that, it depends on who catches higher upcards, since the player with the highest board acts first. Since you are starting with a higher card on third street, odds are that you will have to act first on fourth street, and there's a chance you'll be first to act on every card, giving your opponent the more favorable position.

I listed these differences in what I determined as their order of importance, with #1 being the most important. As you can see, #4 is the only factor that might make the stud bluff more difficult. #1 and #2 clearly indicate that it is much easier to steal the pot on the first betting round in stud rather than hold 'em. #3 shows why you'd rather steal the antes in stud than the blinds in hold 'em.

You cannot ask for a much better situation than the one laid out here. You have only one opponent, a decent chance of having the best hand anyway, plus attractive pot odds. Combined, those factors make this play not only one of the simplest, but also one of the most favorable plays you can make.

If you are lucky enough to have the low card to your left, and everyone folds around to you, you should always complete the bring-in. It doesn't matter what kind of player he is, what cards you have, or how often the situation comes up. Show no mercy to the player with the low card. *Raise him every time.* Chances are he will fold, and you will win the pot. That, of course, is the desired result. But even if he stays in, all is not lost. Now you have to determine whether or not to follow through on your bluff attempt, and the more you know about your opponent, the easier your decision will be.

Looking to your left: I won't rehash everything from the hold 'em example. Just remember that the low card doesn't always need to be in the seat to your immediate left for you to make this play. If he is two seats to your left, but you can tell that the player in front of him will fold, then you can complete the bring-in with anything. You know it will just be you against the low card, and it becomes an automatic raising situation.

Bluff #2A. Playing Past Third Street

It's the exact same situation as above. The low card brings it in to your left, and everyone folds to you. You raise with a weak hand hoping to steal the antes, except this time the bring-in calls. Fourth street provides no help, and now you must decide how long to continue your bluff attempt.

Again, I won't rehash everything I said in Bluff #1A, but understand that all the same concepts apply. Your knowledge of his Betting and Calling Patterns will play a large part in how you play the remainder of the hand. However, stud has a few specific differences:

1. You might have to act first on fourth street. In that case, you won't know for sure if the fourth street card helped your opponent, but betting in that spot is still mandatory. You have to give him a second chance to fold. If he calls, and then you remain high man on board throughout the hand, you have to try to base every subsequent decision on his action the previous round. Keep in mind that his hand usually won't be that good if you continue to have him high-carded. Typically, you

should continue betting as long as he isn't making obvious improvement to his hand. Assuming he isn't a calling station (in which case you should back off if you truly have nothing), he will fold often enough for you to show a profit.

If he becomes high man on board anywhere along the way, he'll have to act first. You can then let his actions dictate yours, in the same manner as in Bluff #1A. However, keep in mind that your success rate is lower once his is the higher board. Chances are, unless your visible cards work toward a straight or a flush, they won't be that intimidating as the lower board.

2. He could make a substantial, visible improvement somewhere along the way. He could catch an open pair, or have three suited cards showing on fifth street, or he could simply have threatening high cards. If any of those happen, and you still have nothing, you can back off and cut your losses.

   In fact, that is one of the advantages of bluffing in stud. You can usually tell from your opponent's board cards whether or not his hand continues to be weak. If it does, then you can remain on the attack. But if he clearly improves his hand, no problem, just let him have the pot. Besides, your opponents will not know whether or not you were on an outright bluff. They could easily assume that you had a decent hand, but felt threatened by your opponent's strong board. Thus, you can make a credible fold, and you have nothing stopping you from running a similar bluff again.

3. Your board could visibly improve, in which case your bluff should become a lot easier. If you make an open pair and bet, it will usually be enough to win. However, you should definitely become wary if your opponent continues to call you down. Chances are, he can either beat your open pair, or he has a strong draw that he refuses to part with. I'm not necessarily suggesting that you stop betting. Just be sure to proceed with caution.

Bluff #3. Raising After You Post

The scenario: In most cardrooms, you cannot join a hold 'em game and get dealt in for free. You either have to come in as the BB, or else post the BB from somewhere behind the button. Your best choice is to wait for the button to pass you, and then post when it is directly to your left.[7] Let us assume that you are joining a game and posting in that manner.

The bluff: If everyone folds to you pre-flop, you should raise with any two cards.

> **Degree of Difficulty:** 1
> **Rate of Success:** Medium/High
> **Frequency:** Always

From a mathematical standpoint: The money you've posted is no longer yours, so don't think of it as such. It belongs to the pot now, and the only way you're getting it back is to win the pot. When everyone folds to you, there are 2.5 small bets in the pot (the SB, BB, and your post), and it's costing you only one small bet to try to steal them. At those odds, you have to make the attempt. Consider Bluff #1, in which you are risking two small bets to win one and a half. If that play is worth making, then clearly this one is too.

But there are two differences from Bluff #1: First, you have the player on the button to worry about. If he folds, then there's no problem. You have essentially bought the button, which puts you in the same situation as Bluff #1. But if he calls or reraises, you should

---

7. We are assuming a full game, or close to it, in which case posting behind the button lets you play more hands for less money. You're paying only the BB instead of both blinds, and you're seeing almost an entire round of hands. Plus, you are posting in late position, which is more favorable than having to post in the early-position BB. If instead you were in a shorthanded game, it would make more sense to come in as the BB than to post behind the button.

consider abandoning the bluff attempt unless you happen to have a strong hand and/or hit a good flop. Otherwise, it could get too expensive trying to force out an opponent that has position on you. It cost you only one small bet to attempt the bluff; if you meet resistance, don't be afraid to accept failure and cut your losses.

The second difference is that in Bluff #1, we said the most important thing is knowing what type of players are in the blinds. You should be more inclined to raise from the button if they are tight and/or predictable. But in this case, unless you've played with the same players before, you don't know what types of players they are. After all, this is your first hand.

But that's part of the reason you should always make this play. Not only will it win you the blinds a good percentage of the time, but you'll begin to learn what types of players are sitting to your left. If they are tight, then you'll be able to get them out, and you've set the tone for the remainder of your session. Plus, you'll start out a winner on your very first hand, and that can't be bad. However, if they end up being too stubborn and/or aggressive, then you can consider switching seats so you can get more predictable opponents on your left. Whether or not the bluff wins you the pot, it provides you with valuable information about your opposition.

Unfortunately, this situation doesn't come up too often, so make sure you take advantage of it whenever it does.

Bluff #4. The Field Checks Twice

The scenario: $3–$6 hold 'em.

The bluff: One player limps pre-flop from middle position, and you limp from the button with J♣10♣. The blinds call, so four of you see the flop, which comes

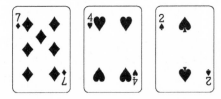

Everyone checks to you, and you check along. The turn card is the 7♣. Everyone checks to you again, but this time you bet, and you win the $12 pot uncontested.

Degree of Difficulty: 1
Rate of Success: Very High
Frequency: Very High

The analysis: This type of situation comes up fairly often. You're last to act, and the field checks to you twice. No matter what type of game it is, what cards you have, or what the board is, you have a very likely bluffing situation.

After all, what do you have to be afraid of?

1. Someone was slow-playing a big hand by checking it twice? It's incredibly unlikely. First, players don't often have hands strong enough to slow-play. Second, very few opponents check a big hand twice. It requires more discipline than most players have, especially at lower limits.

2. Will the other players suspect you have nothing? Sure, maybe they will. That is a much more realistic worry. But with what can they call you? Anyone with a pair would probably have bet already. Maybe someone with bottom pair chose not to bet, but that means someone would need to have bottom pair (or some other weak made hand), and he would need to call your turn bet and potential river bet as well.

   The typical player won't bother to make those calls. He'll figure that he's only spent one small bet on his hand so far, and there's really not much incentive to then spend two large bets on such a marginal hand. Usually, he'll be content to simply fold and move on to the next hand, and you're giving him the opportunity to do that.

3. Will someone put you on a steal and attempt a re-steal by check-raising with nothing? Believe it or not, if that thought crossed your mind, it makes me happy. It means that you are thinking about creative bluffs, and I hold high hopes for your

future as a bluffer. Having said that, you won't often see someone attempt that play. It comes up so infrequently that you should barely even consider it.

Sure, any of those three things could be true, but none of them should stop you from making the correct play of betting from last position when everyone has checked twice. In this specific example, you're betting $6 to win a $12 pot. In other words, you are getting 2-to-1 on your bet, and the chances that someone would call are not even close to that.

You can't be afraid of running a failed bluff. It happens. You still need to make this play, because your opponents have shown so much weakness that it would be a crime not to take advantage of it.

Bluff #5. The Field Checks Once

The scenario: $3–$6 hold 'em.

The bluff: One player limps pre-flop from middle position, and you limp from the button with Q♣10♥. The blinds call, so four of you see the flop, which comes

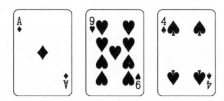

Your opponents all check the flop, you bet and take the pot.

Degree of Difficulty: 1
Rate of Success: Medium/High
Frequency: Medium/High

The analysis: Hopefully you noticed that the Rate of Success and Frequency both dropped two levels from the previous bluff. In general, this is a good play, and you stand to make money in the long run. However, it's not as profitable as Bluff #4. Here are three key differences to note:

1. Your opponents have shown weakness by checking once, but not nearly as much weakness as if they checked twice. For instance, with a board of A♦9♥4♠, one of the blinds would probably check the flop with a pair of nines, or even an ace with a weak kicker, but would then bet the turn if a harmless card came. But you'll never know that, because you bet before he had the chance. Once he checks twice, you can be more confident that he doesn't have either top or middle pair.

2. Your best-case scenario is to win the pot with your first bet. However, that won't happen nearly as much when you make your initial bluff attempt on the flop. It will cost your opponents only $3 to stay in rather than $6, and many of them will call the flop with a wide variety of hands. They could have anything from an ace with a weak kicker to a gutshot straight draw or worse.

   Now, you need to have a good knowledge of their Calling Patterns to have a clear idea of where everyone stands. Otherwise, you are pretty much guessing at what they might have, and then you are bluffing in the dark, so to speak. A continued bluff attempt could work, but you'd rather have a clearer idea of just how weak your opponents' hands are, rather than having to guess at it.

3. You run the risk that someone was slow-playing a strong hand. It's still not likely, but it's much more probable that someone checked once in order to slow-play rather than twice. He would have bet his strong hand on the turn, but now you'll never know.

Again, keep in mind that I am merely noting what makes this play worse than Bluff #4. That doesn't mean it's a bad play. You are risking $3 to win $12, and that initial bet will win you the pot more than once every five times. Even when it doesn't, you will have taken control of the hand. Your opponents will usually check to you on the turn, and you can then decide what your best option is. Sometimes a continued bluff attempt will work. Other times you can check the turn if you suspect that someone will call you down, and you will have invested only $3 in your bluff attempt. Plus, you could always pair one of your cards on the turn or river, which could give you enough to win.

It's often correct to show strength when your opponents show weakness. The next chapter will be devoted to that concept. I'm just reminding you that the more weakness they demonstrate, the greater your chances of success will be.

Bluff #6. I Could Have Anything, I'm in the Big Blind

Good position makes everything easier. Bluffs from out of position are inherently more difficult, and usually don't succeed as often. However, there are exceptions, as these next two simple bluffs demonstrate.

The scenario: $3–$6 hold 'em.

The bluff: Two players limp, the SB limps, and you check your option to raise from the BB with 10♠2♠. Four-handed, the flop comes

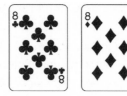

The SB checks, you bet, and your opponents fold.

> **Degree of Difficulty:** 1
> **Rate of Success:** High
> **Frequency:** High

Why you should attempt this bluff:
1. The texture of the flop is very favorable for bluffing. It contains a medium pair, no straight draw, and no flush draw. When you bet, there are not many things your opponents can have that will lead them to call. A sensible player would either need an eight, a three, or perhaps a pocket pair to stay in. Chances are that among three opponents, none of them will have any of those things, so there is a good chance all of them will clear out.
2. Some timid opponents might even lay down a three or a low pocket pair, fearing that you have trips. They know that if you have an eight, and all they have is a three, they are drawing dead no matter what comes on the turn and river. Since they have invested only one small bet, they would prefer to cut their losses, rather than call bets all the way to potentially see that they were drawing dead.
3. They know that you were in the unraised BB, and therefore could have anything. If a late-position player bet at this flop, opponents might wonder how likely it is that he called in late position with an eight or a three. But since you essentially have two random cards, opponents will have no problem believing that the flop hit you.
4. You are getting a very good return on your investment. There are four small bets in the pot, and you are risking only one. You are getting 4-to-1 odds on your bluff attempt, and your rate of success is typically much better than 20 percent.
5. Your opponents have very little invested in the hand, both financially and psychologically. When they see you bet, their attitude is often, "Let's get this hand over with and play the next one." Of course, you are more than happy to oblige them.

What opponents would you prefer? Knowing your opponents' Calling Patterns is important for this bluff. Ideally, you want opponents who follow CP#2, meaning if they don't catch a piece of the flop, they fold. That way, your bluff will work a high percentage of the time, since they won't have an eight or a three very often. And the times that someone calls your flop bet, you know they must have a part of the flop, and you'll be able to cut your losses by abandoning your bluff attempt, unless you happen to catch a lucky turn card. CP#2 opponents will make your life easier.

On the other hand, opponents who follow CP#3 or higher—ones that will call on the flop with as little as two overcards—will make it difficult for your bluff to succeed. Not only will you rarely win the pot on the flop, but you also won't know if you should bet again on the turn. You don't know if their call means that they have trip eights, a pair of threes, or something like Q-J offsuit. You'd rather have a better idea of your opponents' cards before you invest multiple bets in a bluff attempt.

When bluffing with position, it's a lot more acceptable to have your opponent(s) call your bluff attempt on the flop. You are in a much better position to make follow-up bluffs on the turn and the river if necessary. When bluffing from out of position, it's more important to get your opponent(s) to lay down on the flop. You do not want to have to make follow-up bluff attempts as first to act. Your chances of success will be significantly lower.

Final notes: You can use this bluff in pot-limit or no-limit games, but it generally works best in limit, since one of the advantages is that you spend only one small bet. In big-bet poker, if you lead with a small bet, it will often appear weak, and your bluff won't stand much of a chance. On the other hand, if you make a pot-sized bet, you'll need the bluff to work more than half the time in order for it to be worthwhile, and you won't necessarily achieve that high a success rate.

This bluff works best in low-limit games. Higher-limit players recognize the above scenario as a typical bluffing situation, and they will be more likely to raise you, just because they suspect you might be out of line (and of course they'd be right).

Bluff #7. The Field Checks Once, You're in the Blinds

The scenario: $3–$6 hold 'em.

The bluff: Three players limp, the SB folds, and you check your option to raise from the BB with 7♦6♣. Four-handed, the flop comes

You check, and everyone checks behind you. The turn is the 2♣. You come out betting, and no one calls.

> **Degree of Difficulty:** 1
> **Rate of Success:** High
> **Frequency:** Very High

The analysis: This is very similar to Bluff #5, in that your opponents made one show of weakness before you went on the attack. The obvious difference is your position, but in some ways it works to your advantage. Just as we described previously, many players in first position will check the flop with middle pair, top pair/weak kicker, or a big hand with which they had hoped to check-raise.

Therefore, when you come out betting on the turn, your opponents must consider that you might have checked the flop with one of those hands. Since your check on the flop does not demonstrate the same degree of weakness as it would if you checked from the button, your turn bet should get some respect.

The key to this bluff: The nature of the turn card. I listed the Rate of Success as High only because the turn card was the harmless 2♣. If it were any card nine or higher, or any spade, your success rate would drop dramatically. There would be a much greater chance that one of your opponents would either pick up a pair or a draw of some sort, and your bluff would meet resistance.

Ideally, you want the turn card to be lower than anything on the flop, or else you want it to pair the board. In either case, it would be unlikely to help anyone, and you could expect a high success rate.

Bluff #8. Richie Bluffs from the SB

Even though I started you off with some generic bluffing situations, I've taken most of my bluffs, including this one, from actual hands.

The scenario: $6–$12 hold 'em with $4–$6 blinds.

The bluff: Two players limped, then the button raised. Richie called from the SB with 6♣5♦, the BB folded, and the two limpers called. Four-handed, the flop came

Everyone checked to the raiser, and to Richie's surprise, he also checked. The turn card was the A♦. Richie came out betting, hoping to represent either an ace or a flush. The first limper folded, but then the second limper and the pre-flop raiser both called. The river was the 4♣, for a final board of

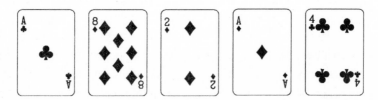

Since there was now a decent-sized pot at stake, Richie bet in the hopes that both of his opponents were drawing and missed. Sure enough, the first limper mucked, later admitting that he had the K♦. Unfortunately for Richie, the pre-flop raiser called and showed 9♣ 9♠ to claim the pot.

The analysis: We can usually learn more from our failures than our successes, which is why this book will contain some failed bluffs scattered throughout. I put this hand here to compare it to the previous one. In both cases the bluffer was in first position, everyone checked the flop, and then he bet on the turn. However, we should consider a few key differences:

1. In Bluff #7, you were in the unraised BB. In this one, Richie had to call an extra $8 with 6♣5♦, and that's hard to justify. He chose a bad spot to bluff, but if he had correctly folded pre-flop, he would have never had the chance to make further mistakes.

2. Since there was no pre-flop raise in Bluff #7, the pot was small and thus relatively easy to steal. Also, everyone involved had invested only one small bet, so nobody felt any strong attachment to the pot.

   In this bluff, the pre-flop raise changed the complexion of the hand significantly. Since everyone had contributed two small bets rather than one, they all felt a greater attachment to the pot, making them more likely to call. The bigger pot made it more worthwhile for Richie to attempt a bluff, but it also gave his opponents more reason to contest him; thus his chances of success were much worse.

3. As we said earlier, in order for a bluff attempt from the blinds to be worthwhile, there must be a strong likelihood that everyone will fold to your initial bet. You don't want to be put in the position of needing to make further bets from out of position.

   However, the nature of the board made it very unlikely that Richie would win the pot with a single turn bet. He could expect anyone with a big diamond to call in the hopes of catching a flush on the river. But even more importantly, other players might see the three diamonds on board and suspect that Richie was betting a flush draw. That would lead them to call with some surprisingly weak hands. Then, if a diamond didn't arrive on the river, they would call in the hopes that Richie missed his flush draw. *Loose players look for reasons to call,* and in this hand they could find an excellent reason.

4. Assuming that the pre-flop raiser had a legitimate raising hand, Richie had to wonder why he would check an ace-high flop from last position. In all likelihood, the raiser was either slow-playing a big hand, or else he had a pocket pair and was respecting the ace. If the raiser was slow-playing, then Richie had no hope. If he had the pocket pair, then Richie could try to push him off it, but the raiser surely felt better about his pair once he saw a second ace on board. That made it less likely that someone had an ace, and suddenly his two pair looked a lot stronger.

   Also, keep in mind that there's a big difference between respecting the ace and fearing it. Many players are smart enough to check the flop in that situation, but that doesn't mean they're smart enough to lay their pair down when someone represents an ace by betting into them.

Richie made a poor pre-flop call, and followed it with two poor bluff attempts. The pre-flop raise (signaling an opponent had a strong hand), the resulting larger pot, and the dangerous turn card all suggested that his bluff was destined to fail. Keep in mind what gave Bluff #7 a high rate of success: the absence of a pre-flop raise, a smaller pot, and an innocuous turn card. You need all those things to hold true in order for similar bluffs to be profitable.

Bluff #9. We All Started Somewhere

Even though this hand took place four years ago, I still remember it clearly, mainly because my friend's reaction was so genuine. It reminded me what a great feeling it is to discover something new at the poker table.

The scenario: Mario, the focus of this hand, had been playing poker for only a couple of weeks, but he wanted to seriously learn the game. He smartly stuck to $1–$5 spread-limit seven-card stud, the smallest game offered in our local cardroom.

The bluff: Mario started the hand with the J♣ showing and 10♦9♦ in the hole. He called the opening $1 bring-in bet, as did three other players. By fifth street, his board was J♣4♣2♣. No one had a pair showing, and the player to his left was high with an ace. He checked, and everyone checked around to Mario. He checked along. On sixth street he caught the 6♣. Everyone checked to Mario again, and finally he pulled the trigger and made a bet. They all folded in rapid succession, and he took down the modest pot with jack-high.

> **Degree of Difficulty:** 1
> **Rate of Success:** Very High
> **Frequency:** Very High

The aftermath: After the hand Mario ran across the cardroom and found me. He described how the hand played out, and then told me, "Matt, that was the first time I've ever bluffed."

"Really? It felt good, didn't it?"

"Actually, I was scared as hell! When everyone checked to me on fifth street, I started to grasp the idea that they were afraid of my hand. I know this might sound silly, but that was kind of a new feeling for me."

"It's not silly at all. I know what you mean."

"Yeah, so, I could tell they thought I might have a flush, but I still didn't feel right betting. I just figured I should take the free card, since I didn't have anything."

"There's nothing wrong with that."

"Yeah, but then, when I caught a fourth club, and everyone checked to me again, they all looked so dreary! It was like they were all resigned to losing the hand. I figured I had to give it a shot. Plus, I could have caught a fifth club on the river, right?"

"Absolutely. You played it just right. And hey, you popped your cherry. Good job, man."

"Ha ha, yeah. I'm not sure how often I'll do that again. It's kind of nerve-wracking to bluff. But it was kind of fun too."

Now it's four years later. Mario is an extremely solid mid-limit player who bluffs as much as the next guy, if not more. And, more often than not, he picks the right times to do it.

The analysis: I believe that one of the rites of passage to becoming a good poker player is running your first successful bluff. If you're an experienced player, you know that bluffing is part of any typical poker session. In fact, half of your bluffs are probably so second-nature that you barely have to think about them.

I mean, let's say you were in Mario's shoes. If you were the one with four clubs showing on sixth street in seven-card stud, you wouldn't hesitate. You'd bet the four-flush, everyone would fold, and you'd take the pot. That would come naturally to almost every stud player, and you probably wouldn't give it a second thought, nor would you feel the need to pat yourself on the back for such a play. Rather, the alternative of checking and possibly (gasp!) folding would be so cowardly and foolish that you would never forgive yourself for abandoning claim to the pot that should have been yours.

But you might be surprised at how many beginners are terrified to run that bluff. They are afraid they will get called, afraid of the embarrassment at having to show a garbage hand. Even you experienced players should be able to remember what that once felt like. It takes guts to pull the trigger on a bluff, especially when you are just starting to learn the game.

To the beginners reading this book, you might recognize the emotions that Mario experienced. They are not at all unusual, so don't be discouraged. All of the great players you read about and see on TV had to start somewhere, right? At some point along the way, they had to become comfortable bluffing regularly. If you haven't reached that point yet, don't worry. It will come, and this book will help it come a little sooner.

No Quitting Allowed

In this chapter, we discussed several bluffs in which your hole cards are irrelevant. Hopefully, you've begun to realize that any hand can become a winner. As such, you should never mentally concede a hand just because you look down and see trash cards. Unforeseen opportunities will often arise, and you should be prepared for them.

In every form of poker there are times in which you are in the hand whether you want to be or not. In hold 'em, Omaha, or Omaha H/L, you have to post the BB. In stud or stud H/L, you have to start the action as the low card. Often you have such a poor hand that you wouldn't give it to your worst enemy. Even so, you still need to pay attention to the action. If no one raises on the first betting round, then you're in the game, poor hand or not. And if the right cards come on the flop (or fourth street), an opportunity for a bluff might present itself.

Let's look at quick examples from all five games that I mentioned:

Hold 'em: One player limps, the SB calls, and you check from the BB with J♥2♣. The flop is 8-7-6 rainbow. Everyone checks. The turn pairs the 8, and the SB checks again.

Omaha or Omaha H/L: One player limps, the SB calls, and you check from the BB with K♣8♥5♠3♣. The flop is J-10-9 rainbow. Everyone checks. The turn is a 2, and the SB checks again.

Stud or Stud H/L: You start the action as the low card with the 4♥ showing and Q♣9♠ in the hole. The player to your left calls with the 4♠, and everyone else folds. On fourth street you catch the A♥, he catches the 9♣, and you're first to act.

In all of those situations, betting is virtually mandatory. It doesn't matter how poor your hole cards are. Ignore them, and simply focus on the hand from an observer's perspective. You'll discover that you shouldn't even consider checking. In the first two examples, your opponents have demonstrated weakness and no desire to claim the pot. In the third example, your board is several times stronger than your opponent's. In all cases, the pot is there for the taking.

You might wonder why you should even care about such a small pot. The thing is, your opponents won't care about it either. If they see bad cards on the flop or fourth street, and such a small pot at stake, they often mentally concede.

Hey, *someone* has to win it. If they have lost interest, you might as well take them out of their misery. Small pots like these can do wonders for your win rate, and they sometimes spell the difference between winning and losing.

Lesser players don't even pay attention to the action once they see a bad hand. They refuse to spend another dime, figuring they could only cost themselves more money. Ironically, what costs them money is their failure to take advantage of these overwhelmingly favorable situations. If you're going to be a top player, you can't do that. Sure, most of the times that you get stiffed as the low card or the BB, you will simply check and fold. But you must always be ready for the possibility of a steal.

The "How Can I Win This Hand?" Game

Let's talk some more about the possibilities of bluffing with garbage hands. In Chapter 2, I gave you lots of things to do when you're not involved in a hand. But let's assume you've been playing at the same table for a while, and you've uncovered most of your opponents' patterns. I'll give you one other thing you can do. Play a game in your mind. In this game, pretend that you're still in the action, and you have the worst hand possible. Now, ask yourself: "How can I win this hand without going to showdown?"

This is a great bluffer's exercise, and it will make you wonder if you've been putting too much emphasis on your cards, and not enough emphasis on the situation. Of course, in many cases, you would need to have the best hand to win. But through what you've learned by studying your opponents, and by coming up with creative ways to represent a strong hand, you can invent strategies to use at the proper times.

Once you've played this mind game a few times, you'll realize how often nobody has anything they are too proud of. It can be quite a revelation. Then you have to decide how you would best take advantage of everyone's weakness, because it's your opponents' weakness that will be the key to many of your bluffs.

CHAPTER FOUR

Attacking Weakness
(Drawing Hands)

There are two keys to consistent, successful bluffing. One is attacking when your opponents are weak. The other is convincingly representing strength through your betting. Every winning bluff needs some element of both, although they are rarely in equal proportions. It would be nice if you could always represent a monster hand every time your opponents have next to nothing. Unfortunately, it is hardly ever that easy.

Between the two, identifying and attacking weakness is far more important than representing strength. Players usually fall into the habit of focusing on their own hand rather than yours. If theirs is weak, they couldn't care less what you have. They just want to move along to the next deal, and hopefully pick up something better. If you can simultaneously represent a strong hand, that's just icing on the cake. Many times, it isn't even necessary.

In these next two chapters, the focus will be entirely on whether your opponents' hands are sufficiently weak for you to attempt a bluff. You won't always be able to convince your opponents that you have the strong hand that you're representing. However, if their hands are weak enough, it usually won't matter. Even if your bluff did not convince them, very few opponents have the guts to call you down with a truly poor hand, or to play back at you with rags.

Have you ever heard an opponent say, "I know you've got nothing," but then he folds? It's pretty illogical, yet I've heard it often. If he "knows" you have nothing, why doesn't he call? As much as he may hate to do it, he folds because his hand is so weak that he can't even keep you honest. Of course, he could, but he just doesn't realize it. For you, it means that you didn't do a good job of representing a strong hand, and you need to work on that. Whatever you were pre-

tending to have, he didn't believe you. However, you correctly identified his hand as being extremely weak, and thankfully, that's often
all it takes to bluff successfully.

Words of wisdom: On page 422 of his famous poker bible,
Super/System, Doyle Brunson says, "You should never start out
bluffing at a pot and keep bluffing at it without an out." I completely
agree with him, as I'm sure most players do. I find it interesting,
though, that his statement focuses on the strength of the bluffer's
hand. Essentially, he is saying, "Don't bluff with a hand so weak that
it has no chance to become the best hand."

As I've said, I prefer to keep the focus on your opponent's hand,
and that's what these next two chapters will do. Very often, the
strength of your hand is irrelevant. When you're bluffing, you don't
intend to ever show your hand, so your cards don't matter. The more
important thing is to accurately gauge your opponent's strength, or
lack thereof.

So, when I read Brunson's words, I see them as having a double
meaning. You should have outs to make the best hand, not just because your hand has some strength, but because your opponent's
hand doesn't. In other words, "Don't bluff when your opponent has a
hand strong enough to have you drawing dead." After all, if your opponent's hand is that strong, you probably shouldn't be bluffing in
the first place.

The ultimate weakness: Your opponent's hand doesn't get any
weaker than a missed draw. You usually won't need to bluff in those
situations, since you can probably beat a busted draw. But if you
have a lower draw, or some other weak hand, then you can't let the
hand go to showdown. You have to identify and take advantage of
those situations because they can provide you with some of your easiest and most profitable bluffing opportunities.

Bluff #10. There's No Worse Feeling

The scenario: $6–$12 hold 'em.

The bluff: Kevin and another player limped from middle position, and Susie limped from the cutoff with Q♣J♣. The button and both blinds called, so there was six-way action. The flop came

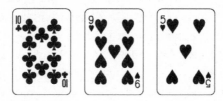

Both blinds checked and Kevin bet. The next player folded, and Susie raised. Everyone folded to Kevin, who called. Heads-up, the turn was the 7♠. Kevin checked and called Susie's bet. The river was the 10♠ for a final board of

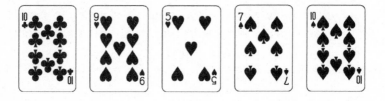

Kevin checked, Susie reached for her chips, and before she could even complete her action, she heard Kevin say, "Don't bother. I missed," as he flashed his K♦J♦ before tossing it in.

Degree of Difficulty: 3
Rate of Success: Dependent on your opponent's hand. If it's a missed draw, then Very High, otherwise Low/Medium.
Frequency: High

The analysis: One of the toughest decisions in poker is deciding whether to play a drawing hand passively or aggressively. If you are against a large field of opponents, then playing it passively makes sense for two reasons:

1. It would be nearly impossible to win without hitting your draw. Since you'd have to convince every opponent that you have the best hand, a bluff would rarely work, and aggression would be somewhat pointless.
2. You don't want to force anyone out. Since you'll have to hit your draw to win, you may as well get paid off by as many opponents as possible if your card arrives.

However, let's say you are against one or two opponents. Or perhaps, as in Susie's case, you think an early bet or raise could narrow the field. In those situations, you should often look to take the initiative. Unless you are absolutely convinced that one of your opponents has a strong made hand, you should do everything in your power to try to win the hand without having to hit your draw.

Susie did not know exactly what Kevin had. But with two hearts on the flop and the potential straight draw presented by the 10♣9♥, she figured there was a decent chance that Kevin was also on a draw. Thus, she decided to take the offensive, hoping she could get heads-up with Kevin, and then win the pot whether she made her hand or not.

The key point in the hand was the action that followed her flop raise. If multiple players had called, or if someone had reraised, then her best play would have been to back off. It would have been unlikely that she could win without making a hand, so she would have been correct to become passive. But when everyone folded to Kevin, and he merely called, Susie's chances of success improved tremendously.

Her continued aggression throughout the hand was vital. Unless Kevin had bet an extremely weak hand on the flop, there was little chance that he would fold once the 7♠ came on the turn, but Susie did not bet the turn expecting him to fold. Rather, she knew her bet was crucial to the success of the bluff as a whole. Checking the turn would have shown extreme weakness that could have easily cost her the pot. Kevin would have probably bet his busted draw on the river, correctly sensing that Susie was also on a missed draw. For her to make a realistic bluff attempt on the river, she had to maintain her aggressive stance on the flop and turn.

He who bluffs first bluffs best: There will come times when you and your opponent both miss your draws, and it will become a question of who pulls the trigger and bluffs the river first. You must always be ready to fire that bullet, because there's no worse feeling than checking the river with a missed draw, having your opponent also check while saying, "I missed," but then he turns over a higher draw than you. There is no excuse for losing a pot that way.

Having said that, I've seen it happen all too often. It usually occurs when a player abandons his bluff attempt on the river, discouraged by the fact that his opponent called on the turn. If the texture of the board is such that your opponent can't be on a draw, then checking the river makes sense. His call on the turn means he will probably call the river too. But if there is any reasonable chance that your opponent is drawing, and you can't beat even a busted draw, then betting the river is crucial.

That was the case here, and Susie was smart enough to make the necessary river bet. She didn't back down simply because Kevin called on the turn. After all, what was the worst thing that could happen? If he called or check-raised, then she lost an extra bet. That's no big deal. The much greater mistake would have been to save that last bet, which would have cost her the entire pot.

Semi-bluffing

On page 91 of *The Theory of Poker,* David Sklansky defines a semi-bluff as "a bet with a hand which, if called, does not figure to be the best hand at the moment, but has a reasonable chance to outdraw those hands that initially called it." In the previous bluff, Susie's hand would fit that description. Queen-high could not realistically hope to be the best hand, but she certainly had ways to make the best hand even if she was called.

Semi-bluffing, or bluffing with outs, is a recognized and accepted strategy. However, I feel that people overuse the concept and try to bluff at pots that they have no chance of stealing. Their only hope is to hit their draw, but they use the pretense of semi-bluffing to explain why they got so aggressive with their drawing hand.

Strictly speaking, your purpose is to get your opponent to fold. If you have outs to make the best hand in case you get called, they are simply your backup plan. It's a perfectly good idea to have backup in case your bluff fails. Your main objective is to win, so any outs that increase your chances of winning are a big plus.

However, our goal here is to get your bluffs to succeed. And if they don't, then we should focus on what caused them to fail. Focusing on the outs you might have if your bluff fails is not central to our goal. For that reason, this book won't explicitly discuss semi-bluffing any further.

An example: Let's say you semi-bluff with a straight draw and it gets there on the river. Now you bet your straight, and your opponent calls. On the one hand, you'll win the pot. On the other hand, you'll know that as a bluff, your play was a failure. If you hadn't made your hand, your opponent would have called and you would have lost. Winning the pot is a misleading result. Players usually pat themselves on the back for winning with their semi-bluff, but they are missing the key point. It was a bluff. As such, you're supposed to pick situations in which your opponents are too weak to call. Since your opponent called, you clearly read the situation incorrectly. He was stronger than you thought. It's okay to be happy that you won the pot, as long as you are also critical of your play. Try to figure out why your opponent paid you off, and what you could have done differently to get him to fold if you had missed.

Conversely, let's say you make your straight, you bet it, and your opponent folds. You might argue that you wanted to get paid off, but is that really true? Sure, you lost an extra bet, but you can take comfort in the fact that you picked the right time to bluff. It was irrelevant that you made your straight. Unless your opponent somehow detected that you made a hand on the end, his fold tells you that your river bet would have won you the hand regardless. As a bluffer, that gives you reason to be proud. You didn't need to fall back on your possible outs. Whether you had a straight or pure garbage, the pot was yours. *That* is the result you are striving for.

Bluff #11. Roy Doesn't Draw the Line with His Draw

The scenario: $6–$12 hold 'em

The bluff: Roy was in the BB with the K♣10♣. Everyone folded to Lisa, a fairly straightforward player in the cutoff seat, who raised. The button and SB folded, and Roy called. Heads-up, the flop came

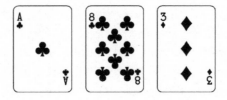

Roy flopped the nut flush draw and came out betting. Lisa immediately raised, Roy came back with a reraise, and Lisa called. The turn was the 5♥. Roy bet and Lisa called. The river was the 3♠, for a final board of

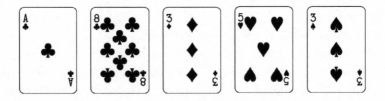

Roy bet, Lisa called, Roy announced, "King high," and Lisa produced the winning hand to take the pot.

Why this bluff *did not* work: Don't worry about what Lisa had just yet. Instead, let's break this hand down step by step.

Before the flop, calling a raise with K-10 suited is fine. It doesn't thrill me to be out of position in a heads-up pot with a marginal hand, but it's worthwhile to call just in the hopes of flopping something good. If the flop misses Roy completely, he can check and fold, and move on to the next hand.

After the flop, Roy played his hand in a justifiably aggressive manner. He had only one opponent and a draw to the nuts, so checking and calling would have been way too weak. I completely agree with betting out. Check-raising would have been an equally good play. Either way, as long as Roy is taking an aggressive action, I agree with it. If Lisa has any pocket pair or a K-Q type of hand, Roy stands a good chance of taking the pot without having to make a real hand.

However, let's say Roy knows that Lisa wouldn't raise on the flop without an ace. If that's the case, then there's no point in reraising. He can't possibly get Lisa to lay down an ace if no club comes. The board is just too disconnected and nonthreatening. The only thing to do is call Lisa's raise and hope that the flush comes. Sometimes bluffing just isn't an option.

But let's assume that Lisa is capable of raising on the flop with something like 10-10 or J-J (a pocket pair that can beat middle pair but not top pair). Then Roy's reraise on the flop is good poker. Roy can bet the turn, and there's a decent chance Lisa will lay down. So far so good.

But then, on the turn, Roy bet and Lisa called. As far as I'm concerned, at that point the bluff attempt is over. If Lisa calls the turn, she is calling the river with any hand that can beat Roy, and that's all there is to it. There is only one possible hand she could have that Roy could beat, and that is a lower flush draw. Since Lisa is a straightforward player, it's not very likely that she raised pre-flop with lower clubs. Plus, even if she has a worse flush draw, a bet on the river is still pointless, since Roy's king-high would win a showdown.

When Lisa calls the turn, her most likely hand is a big ace. Even if she has a medium pocket pair and is making a loose turn call, her actions signify that she's made up her mind to pay off Roy. The call on the turn signals a call on the river. At that point Roy must recognize the situation for what it is, and save his money on the river.

By the way, Lisa showed A♠J♠ to win the hand. The main point of this discussion, though, is that it really didn't matter what she had. You have to be able to reevaluate your position on the fly. It often pays to follow through with a bluff attempt for the entirety of the hand. But sometimes you need to back off. This was one of those times.

Lesson to be learned: When you attempt a bluff on the turn, and your opponent calls with a hand whose strength is unlikely to change on the river, then that player is probably prepared to go to showdown. In this example, Lisa called the turn with an A♣8♣3♦5♥ board after having raised pre-flop. It's tough to imagine that she had some sort of draw rather than a made hand. That means the strength of her hand was unlikely to be affected by the river card, so a call was to be expected.

On the other hand, if the board had been 9♣8♣7♥4♥ when she called on the turn, then a river bet by Roy would have made much more sense. Maybe she had a made hand, but with that board, there would have been a much greater chance that she was drawing. Whether his river bluff would have succeeded or not, it would have been worth making.

But with a board that presents no obvious draws, you should usually give your opponent credit for having a made hand when he calls on the turn, and save your money on the river.

Bluff #12. Alex's Busted Straight Draw

The scenario: $15–$30 hold 'em

The bluff: Two players limped pre-flop from early position, and Alex limped from the button. The SB called, and the BB checked his option, so there was five-way action. The flop came

The SB checked, and the BB came out firing. One player called, the other folded, and then Alex raised. The SB folded, while both other players called. Three-handed, the turn was the 4♦. It was checked to Alex, and he bet again. The BB folded, while the other player called. Heads up, the river was the 2♠, for a final board of

It was checked to Alex, and again he bet with confidence. His opponent disgustedly showed his Q♥10♥ before mucking it. Alex then flipped up his 6♣5♣ and asked the table, "Do you think we're playing tiddlywinks?" The BB acknowledged that he had 10-9 off-suit, and had bet on the flop with only a gutshot, but even *he* could have won the pot with his ten-high had he stayed in.

Degree of Difficulty: 5
Rate of Success: Medium
Frequency: Medium

The analysis: I like Alex's call pre-flop on the button with 6♣5♣ in a multiway pot. I also like his raise on the flop. He wasn't going to fold an open-ended straight to a single bet, so he might as well raise and take control of the hand. Then, once his opponents flat-called the raise on the flop and checked to him on the turn, he knew his raise was a success. He had the choice to take a free card or to remain aggressive, but either way the hand was going to be played on his terms.

Then came the moment of truth. It would not have been such a bad play if Alex had decided to check and take the free card. If either opponent had a jack, or even a seven with a decent kicker, they were probably not going anywhere. But Alex took the chance that they had neither. He committed himself with a full-out turn-and-river bluff. Obviously, if we look at the hands that his opponents held, he clearly made the correct play, but he couldn't have known that for sure.

Having said that, there were definite clues that his play might work. The player in the unraised BB could have had any two cards, and he didn't need much to come out firing. He could have been betting almost on a whim, just hoping the flop missed everyone. A weak draw or a low pair were distinct possibilities. Then the next player just called, which indicated that he probably wasn't very strong either. If he had something like top pair, he probably would have raised, to try to shut everyone else out and leave him heads-up with the BB. From the action that took place, Alex correctly decided that there was a good chance he could steal the pot if he missed his draw. Notice how having the button made it so much easier for Alex to make educated guesses about his opponents' hands. This bluff would have been a lot tougher if he had players acting behind him.

Don't be a halfway crook: Alex chose between taking a free card and bluffing. He understood that he couldn't do both. In other words, you can't check the turn in last position and then expect to bluff on the river. If Alex had checked the turn, his bluff attempt was essentially over. He would have shown too much weakness to make a bet on the river believable. It would have reeked of desperation. He would have had to either make the straight or give up.

Mobb Deep, a well-known rap duo, said it best: "Ain't no such things as halfway crooks." You usually either have to commit yourself fully to a bluff attempt or abandon it completely. Don't leave yourself in the middle. Otherwise, you'll have opponents calling you on the river with as little as ace-high. They know you would have bet the turn with any decent hand, so they'll want to keep you honest with almost anything.

Ironically, this is one of the rare times a half-assed river bluff might have worked, because his opponents' hands were unusually weak. They didn't even have an ace-high that could keep him honest! However, once he displayed weakness on the turn, somebody would have probably bet right into him on the river. Then he would have folded, giving the pot to someone else with a busted draw. His mistake would have resulted in their profit. Instead, it was the other way around; they played their draws passively, so he took the initiative and picked up a nice pot.

Have a reason for showing a bluff: When the hand ended, should Alex have turned his cards up and talked smack? I would say no. He just wanted to stroke his ego a little. There was really nothing to be gained (except for me—I gained the use of his bluff in my book). He made a good read and a good play, and both his opponents knew it. They weren't going to go on tilt for folding queen-high or ten-high, so he did not benefit from showing his bluff.

However, he cost himself the chance to make a similar bluff later. If they played their drawing hands so meekly the first time around, who is to say they wouldn't do it again? Now, they knew better than to repeat that mistake. The more professional move would have been for Alex to muck his cards quietly, and wait for another good bluffing opportunity to arise.

Should You Show Your Bluffs?

Let's discuss this issue in more general terms. You've just bluffed successfully. Now you have the choice of either showing your cards or mucking them. Even though I have my personal preference, I'll provide arguments for both.

Reasons to show a bluff:
1. If it is an excellent bluff, you could gain psychological dominance over your opponents. They might think to themselves, "Wow, I could never pull off a bluff like that! This guy is good!" Then they will respect your future actions, which is

exactly what you want. Instead of opponents calling more often (which is usually the case when you show a bluff), it could cause them to avoid confrontations with you, letting you continue to bluff. However, you really need to know what constitutes an excellent bluff. The quality of the bluff is what draws the line between impressing your opponents and irritating them.

2. If the player you've bluffed is prone to going on tilt, then showing him how he got bluffed might tilt him. He could become so upset about folding a winner that he will play off-balance for a while, and in turn he will almost certainly lose.

3. If there were an audience present, such as at a WPT or WSOP event, I would show a bluff. Televised poker is interesting, but sitting in a live audience and watching it can be boring. That audience wants something to cheer for. If you show a good bluff, not only will they cheer your play, you'll probably become the fan favorite. Having the crowd on your side will give you a good psychological advantage over your opponents.

Reasons *not* to show a bluff:

1. You are confident in your abilities, and don't need acknowledgment from the rest of the table. The players who most often show bluffs are the ones who are insecure about their poker skills, and need to show everyone that they were capable of making a good play. Now their ego is stroked, and they feel better about themselves, but they've hurt their chances of making similar bluffs again.

2. By showing a bluff, you unnecessarily give your opponents free information, and you should know better than to do that. You'd rather let your bluff victim think he did the right thing. Personally, I will even go so far as to tell my opponent, "Good laydown." Hey, I'm not lying when I say that! It *was* a good laydown . . . for me. Whatever it takes, you want to convince your opponent that folding was correct.

3. You want your opponents to continue folding when you bet. In the grand scheme of things, you don't want callers. *If you*

never get called, you can never lose. Showing a bluff encourages them to call, so for your purposes, it is counterproductive.

4. You know that the whole idea of advertising a bluff is garbage. Many players seem to think that they should show a bluff, and that way they'll get paid off when they have a monster. Sure, they'll get action on future hands, but now they had better hope to get some cards! Otherwise, they've just shot themselves in the foot. *There are only two ways to win: producing the best hand or bluffing with the worst one.* If you show everyone your bluff, and now they continually keep you honest, you've just lost one of those ways.

5. You don't want the bluff victim to suddenly become focused on you. Many players take it personally when you show them a bluff, and now they become more determined to outplay you. That hurts their overall chances of winning, but it helps the other players at the table more than it helps you. The monster you've created will begin to forget about everyone else, so those players will have the opportunities to get the best of him.

   Meanwhile, he's going to be focused on your actions. You won't be able to breathe without him trying to stop you. It's silly to put yourself in that situation. If you keep the bluff to yourself, you won't be under anyone's scrutiny, and you'll have more freedom to bluff profitably again in later hands.

My preference: I think if you pull an excellent bluff, against a player who is likely to go on tilt, in front of a live audience, then you should show it. Okay, maybe you don't need all three of those to be the case, but at least one of them should hold true. Otherwise, I am a big proponent of keeping my bluffs to myself. Yes, I've shown a few bluffs, but that's out of the thousands that I've done. The cons of showing a bluff simply outweigh the pros.

Bottom line: You bluffed successfully once. There is no reason why you can't do it again, as long as you don't flaunt it. Once you do, your opponents probably won't allow you to bluff again for a while, and during that time you have to produce the best hand to win. Even though you'll get paid off when you do, you'll have put yourself at the mercy of the cards. If you learn one thing from this book, it's that you don't want to rely on good cards to win. You want to be able to win with anything. Showing a bluff restricts your ability to do that, so don't do it. Don't hurt your bankroll just to help your ego.

Betting After Your Opponent Checks the Turn

Let's assume all of the following are true:

1. On the turn, just you and one opponent are left.
2. He has position on you.
3. When the turn card comes, you check, and he checks behind you.
4. You expect your hand cannot win a showdown.

If you are playing limit poker, I recommend betting the river *every time*. I usually don't like formulaic poker. I rarely suggest making the same play every time in a given scenario, but this is an exception. Your opponent has shown extreme weakness, and you simply can't ignore it.

Even if a scary-looking card arrives, such as a third suited card, you should still bet. If the river gave him a flush, then you'll lose a bet. That's not a big deal. However, if he wasn't on a flush draw, then the river will look as scary to him as it does to you. If he has something such as bottom pair—a hand with which he would typically check the turn—then it would be very difficult for him to call.

He obviously won't fold every time, but he will *definitely* fold often enough to make betting a profitable play. You are risking only one large bet to win the pot. Even if the pot is small, your bluff doesn't have to succeed very often to make it worthwhile.

Notice that I specified limit poker. In NL or PL, this play won't work nearly as often. Many good players check on the button with a strong hand, waiting for you to bet on the river. They are confident in their hand, but not so confident that they want to fully commit themselves with one card still to come. So they will simply check behind you on the turn, and be ready to snap you off on the river.

Not only will you get called down more often, it will cost you more to bet on the river than it would in limit poker. Your Risk/Reward Ratio is nowhere near as good as in limit hold 'em. So while I recommend always betting the river in limit, I suggest you pick your spots more carefully in big-bet poker. If you detect significant weakness in your opponent, but can't beat even the weak hand you suspect he has, then go for it. But if your opponent tends to check semistrong hands in position (a very common practice in big-bet poker), then don't waste your money.

Generally speaking, you don't want to find yourself in a heads-up pot, out of position, with a hand that can't win a showdown. Hopefully you figured that out on your own. But once you're in that spot, do your best to make the most of it, as Steve did in this next bluff.

Bluff #13. Steve Takes the Initiative

The scenario: $6–$12 hold 'em

The bluff: Steve limped from early position with J♠10♠. The player to his left called, Jason called on the button, and the blinds made it five-way action. The flop came

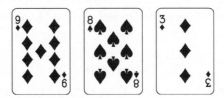

The blinds checked to Steve, and he decided to bet his open-ended straight draw, backdoor flush draw, and overcards. The next player folded, but Jason raised. The blinds folded and Steve called, leaving him heads-up and out of position.

The turn was the 4♣. Steve checked, and Jason checked behind him. The river was the 8♣, for a final board of

Steve fired in a bet, Jason turned his A♦6♦ face-up and declared to anyone who would listen, "I never hit a flush! I've been missing all day!" He folded, while Steve nodded sympathetically and scooped the pot, inwardly smiling because Jason's ace-high was good enough to win.

Degree of Difficulty: 3
Rate of Success: Very High
Frequency: Very High

The analysis: When Jason raised Steve's flop bet, Steve had a choice. Instead of playing his hand the way he did, he could have reraised and become the aggressor with his draw. A reraise followed by bets on the turn and river would have worked well, since Jason was on a draw and missed. Even if Jason had raised the flop with a hand like A♥9♥, Steve would still have had a lot of outs and wouldn't have lost much equity with his reraise.

If I were playing the hand, I probably would have chosen that course of action, but Steve decided to take the more cautious approach. He knew that Jason's raise could mean anything from a weak drawing hand to top pair or better, so he chose to flat-call and see what came on the turn.

Then came the important point in the hand. Many players in Steve's position, once they choose to just call on the flop, take the attitude that they'll either hit their hand or else check and fold on the river. They voluntarily give up the initiative. You should only take that mind-set if you are confident that your opponent has a very powerful hand. That's not the case too often, and it definitely wasn't the case here. Instead, you should be looking for ways to bet him out.

In the preceding section, we talked about how it's mandatory to bet the river in Steve's shoes. Now you can see why. Once Steve showed weakness by checking the turn, Jason would have bet any decent made hand, since the turn card seemed so harmless. But he checked, so then it became open season on him. He either had a drawing hand, or something so weak that he probably couldn't even call a single bet on the river. Either way, he should not be allowed to reach showdown for free. It's your job to make sure he doesn't.

Jason's mistake cost him the pot. If he followed through with bets on the turn and river, he would have won the pot. *His mistake becomes your profit.* But you have to be prepared to take advantage of your opponents' mistakes, or you'll never see that profit. Jason checked the turn—mistake. Steve bet the river—profit. If Steve had checked the river, that would have been *his* mistake, and it would have resulted in Jason's profit.

Bluff #14. Leon Puts Jimmy on a Draw

The scenario: NLH with $5–$10 blinds. Leon had bought in for $1,000, as had most of the other players. But by the time this hand came up, he had gone on a bad run, and was down to about $400.

The bluff: Jimmy and another player limped in from middle position. The SB limped, and Leon checked his option in the BB. Four-handed, the flop came

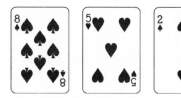

The SB checked, and Leon decided that flop wasn't likely to have hit anyone. He bet $40. Jimmy doubled the bet to $80. Everyone folded around to Leon, who had a decision to make. He was familiar with Jimmy's tendencies, having played with him many times before. He knew that whenever Jimmy doubled the bet like that, he was on a draw and trying to get a free card on the turn. Based on that information, he decided that Jimmy's most likely hand was a spade draw. So he decided to call the raise, and then attack if no spade came on the next card.

The turn was the 2♣, and Leon moved all-in for his remaining $320. Jimmy called for time and starting counting his chips, seeing how much he would have left if he called and lost. He then looked Leon over, looked back at his cards a couple of times, and finally said, "Okay, I need to get lucky," while pushing forward the $320 to call.

The river was the J♦. "I missed," groaned Jimmy, as he turned over the K♠10♠. Leon mucked his cards in disgust and went for a long walk. While walking away from the table, he could hear the other players' disbelief. "King-high is good? What the heck did he have? How could he bet $320 and not beat king-high?" Since several players demanded to see his cards, the dealer tapped the muck and flipped over Leon's 9♥3♥. Leon took a solid week off before showing his face in that game again.

Why this bluff *did not* work: I can hear you. You're asking, "Why was Leon getting involved with 9♥3♥? Why didn't he simply check and fold?" Yes, of course he could have done that. But if he thought it was a good time to bluff, then more power to him. As for bluffing with a 9♥3♥, since he had made up his mind to win the hand before the river, his cards were pretty much irrelevant. After all, he had no plans to show them. Unfortunately for him, the bluff didn't work. I don't fault him for making the effort, but I do think he could have improved on his execution.

Let's start with what Leon did correctly:
   1. He picked a fairly decent spot to attempt a bluff. Since he was in the unraised BB, essentially holding two random cards, a

flop of 8♠5♥2♠ could easily have hit him. At the same time, unless someone flopped a set, it was unlikely that they were playing hands containing any of those cards. I wouldn't necessarily run a naked bluff into three opponents just based on the structure of the flop, but it certainly made more sense than bluffing into a flop such as K♥Q♠J♠.

2. His read of Jimmy was dead-on. Having seen Jimmy make the same play several times before, he decided that the minimum raise meant Jimmy was drawing. He put Jimmy on spades, the most likely draw, and he was absolutely correct.

3. When the spade didn't come on the turn, he put Jimmy to a tough decision, which is generally a good thing to do to your opponents. By making such a large bet, he gave Jimmy the incorrect odds to draw at his hand. Then it became a question of whether or not Jimmy would recognize that fact, and lay his hand down.

Strictly speaking, Jimmy made a bad call. Even if he optimistically thought that he had fifteen outs to win (the nine remaining spades plus three kings and three tens), out of the forty-four remaining cards, then that gave him a little better than a 2-to-1 chance of winning. However, Leon was forcing him to call $320 into a pot that only contained $520. The pot odds were not there for him to make that call. So even though Jimmy might walk away thinking that his call with king-high was a great play based on the results, he would lose money in the long run if he always made that call.

What did Leon do wrong?
1. He counted on Jimmy to make the "correct" play. He should have remembered D.A.I.—Don't Assume Intelligence. He thought that Jimmy would be smart enough to recognize the poor pot odds he was getting. But since Jimmy called, we know that Leon gauged him incorrectly.

2. He chose to bluff when he was relatively short-stacked. He would have been better off bluffing when he had more chips, and thus more potential heat to put on Jimmy.

3. He had been running badly, and thus his table image was not too strong. Psychologically that might have affected Jimmy's decision to call.

   When opponents see that you haven't been winning, they suddenly feel like they can beat you with whatever they have. It doesn't necessarily make logical sense, but if it influences their thinking, then you should be aware of it. Leon should have realized that his table image was poor and waited for a better opportunity.

4. His biggest mistake was going all-in prior to the river. He put Jimmy to the test on the turn, but at that point Jimmy still had hopes of making a strong hand. A bluff has a lot more power when your opponent has little or no chance of improving and is resigned to the weakness of his hand.

What are the two ways Leon could have won the hand?

1. Since Leon correctly put Jimmy on a flush draw, and concluded that Jimmy wanted a free card on the turn, he could've simply let him have that free card. Then if the flush did not come on the river, Leon could win with a bet. If Jimmy missed his draw and was left with king-high, he couldn't possibly call a bet on the river.

2. Leon could have bet small on the turn, and then pushed all-in on the river. That way, not only does he stand a greater chance of chasing Jimmy out, he can build a bigger pot before doing so! Let's say Leon had bet $100 on the turn. Jimmy would have called, figuring he needed to improve in order to win. Then when the river card was no help, Leon would have still had $220 to push in, Jimmy would have folded, and Leon would have built himself a nice-sized bluff pot.

If your opponent is able to show down a busted draw and beat you, then somehow you made the mistake of not betting on the river. In Leon's case that mistake arose because he fired all of his bullets on the turn. One way or another, Leon should have saved some ammunition for the river.

I am not saying that either of those plays would have been fool-proof. Both would have been calculated risks, since Jimmy could still make his flush or pair one of his cards. However, Leon would have abandoned his bluff attempt if a spade came, and would have been in a bad spot only if a king or ten came, which comprised only six out of the possible forty-four river cards. Regardless of the results, it would have been a risk worth taking for Leon, and an effective way to take advantage of his good read.

CHAPTER FIVE

Attacking Weakness (Other Hands)

It's easiest to bluff an opponent who has a busted draw, but you can pick on plenty of other weak hands too. Anytime someone has unimproved high cards, you should be able to muscle him out with comparative ease. Even if he has a small pair, a solid bluff should convince him to fold. Or, perhaps your opponent is simply trying to represent strength, but you're able to sense that he's lying. The more accurately you can identify those situations, the easier your bluffing life will be.

Bluff #15. Dropping the All-in Bomb

When playing a no-limit hold 'em tournament, you hardly ever want to limp into the pot with a marginal hand. Pre-flop, it's usually either raise or fold. The reason is that you will run into aggressive players who will sense the weakness of your call and try to raise you off your hand no matter what they have. Hmm. Sounds like smart, aggressive poker to me.

The scenario: The middle stages of a multi-table no-limit hold 'em tournament. Roughly half the field has been eliminated.

The bluff: Three or more players limp pre-flop. You are either on the button or in one of the blinds. You go all-in, everyone folds, and you pick up the blinds plus some nice dead money.

> **Degree of Difficulty:** 2
> **Rate of Success:** High
> **Frequency:** Low

Basic Premise: Players don't typically limp in with strong hands. Their limps demonstrate weakness; now it's on you to demonstrate strength. If their hands aren't strong enough to raise coming in, then how can they be strong enough to call an all-in raise? They're not. Put them to the test. Chances are, they won't pass.

Important points:
1. This is strictly a tournament play. In live games players are a lot more prone to limping in with big starting hands. Your all-in raise could easily run into A-A or K-K, and then you're sunk. Plus, you really don't want to risk your entire stack in a live game unless you are supremely confident that you will win. Tournaments are different. As a famous tournament player once said, "In a no-limit tournament, you have to be willing to die in order to live."[8] Sooner or later, you have to put all of your chips at risk. You might as well do it when you stand little chance of being called, and therefore little chance of going broke.
2. I purposely chose the middle stages of a tournament. At the early stages, you'll probably see many players limp in, but the risk is not worth the reward. The blinds will be so low that it won't be worth betting your entire stack just to pick up a little dead money. In the later stages, it would be nice to be able to make this play, but then you'll rarely see multiple players limp in.

   That's why the middle stages are best for this move. Weaker players will still be limping in pre-flop, and the amount of dead money they contribute will make it worthwhile to attempt a steal.
3. Make sure you drop the all-in bomb only against opponents who have habitually limped pre-flop. If someone has raised nearly every time, and he suddenly limps into the pot, a warning bell should go off in your head. Maybe he is simply mix-

---

8. Amir Vahedi used this quote on a 2003 ESPN broadcast, but he was not the first to say it. Dr. Max Stern is generally given credit for coining the phrase. Either way, it's a good one.

ing up his play, but there's also a decent chance he now has a big hand. Many players raise with everything except when they have A-A or K-K, and then they will limp in hoping to trap someone. Please don't fall for their overly simple trap.

During the early stages of the tournament, make a mental note of who likes to limp. Don't pick on them yet; just make a note of them. Then, once you get deeper into the tournament, and several of them limp in together, you've got them where you want them.

4. I chose three or more players on purpose. You could do it with only one or two limpers, but you won't win as much, and your risk is almost the same. You might as well wait until your potential reward is highest.

   You want to make sure that the first player into the pot is absolutely a habitual limper. He is the one you need to worry about the most. Once you get past him, each successive limper is less and less likely to be trapping with a monster hand. Think about it. If you had a big hand, maybe you'd limp in occasionally, to try to trap someone. But would you do it once one or more players have limped in front of you? Probably not. You'd rather raise and charge the limpers to see the flop with inferior hands.

   That's why, when multiple players limp, it's a sign that some of them are trying to sneak into the pot with subpar holdings. They are just holding their breath, hoping no one will raise. How foolish of them. Lower the boom, and show them how the game is played.

5. The BB is the best place from which to make this play, followed by the SB and then the button. As the BB, you've seen everyone act on their hand, so there are no surprises waiting behind you. If you're on the button, you've got the blinds to worry about, and they can't be totally ignored. Either one of them could wake up with a big hand, and since you've passed the point of no return, there's nothing you can do. Still, the chances of that happening are low enough that you should be willing to make this play from the button if you've got the requisite three limpers.

From any position to the right of the button, you should become more hesitant. Unless you have a tell that the players to your left will fold, there are too many of them to worry about. Wait until you are in the correct position to attempt this play.

6. The low frequency is what allows the rate of success to be high. If opponents see you make this play more than once, they will catch on. Then there's a good chance that one of them will limp in front of you with a big hand, hoping that you will again drop the all-in bomb, and he'll be ready for it.

   That's why you must make this play when your opponents are not expecting it. If you overdo it, you lose the element of surprise, and then you might be the one that gets a rude awakening when a player limps in with A-A and nails you.

7. Again, we have another bluff in which your cards are irrelevant. Ideally, it would help to have an ace in your hand. That makes it less likely that someone has pocket aces. Plus, you'll always have a decent number of outs against someone who decides to call you with something other than aces. But when making this play, you don't expect to get called very often, so this is only a secondary concern. Generally speaking, any two cards will do.

♣ ♦ ♥ ♠

Similar to the "All-in Bomb," these next three bluffs are not ones that you should necessarily try all that often. However, they are good examples of what you can do when you sense that your opponent is full of it. You can call his bluff by pulling out a bluff of your own.

Bluff #16. Randall Smells Weakness

The scenario: $6–$12 hold 'em.

The bluff: Five players limped pre-flop. The SB folded, and Randall checked his BB option with 10♣3♠. Six-handed, the flop came

Randall checked, obviously intending to fold. However, the action got checked around, so he got to see the turn for free, which was the 2♥. He checked again. This time the action got checked to the button, a solid regular named Jerry, who bet $12. Even though Randall had no hand, no draw, and no reason to stay in, he felt that Jerry's bet was extremely suspicious. He check-raised, making it $24 to go. Everyone folded around to Jerry, who called. The river was the 5♦. Randall bet, Jerry folded, and Randall picked up a nice little pot with his garbage hand.

Degree of Difficulty: 5
Rate of Success: Medium/High
Frequency: Low

The analysis: For most of the hand, Randall had absolutely no intention of bluffing. Trying to run a bluff through five players is usually a losing proposition. However, once Jerry came out betting on the turn, Randall immediately saw an opportunity. By replaying the hand in his mind, he came to four conclusions:

1. As last to act, Jerry would almost certainly have bet a flush draw on the flop. Therefore, it was extremely unlikely that the 2♥ gave him a flush. At best, it might have given him a flush draw with one card to come.
2. It was highly unlikely that the deuce helped Jerry in any other way.
3. Jerry would have bet any decent hand on the flop once everyone checked to him, so it was hard to give him credit for top or middle pair.
4. He was probably just taking advantage of his position and the fact that everyone checked twice, indicating that they didn't have much of anything.

Therefore, Randall decided the time was right to attempt a re-steal. He didn't think any of his other opponents would give him any trouble, since they had checked twice and had clearly lost interest in the hand. Once they folded around to Jerry, Randall expected one of two things to happen. If Jerry truly had nothing, he would fold. If he called, then he probably had a heart draw, and Randall was prepared to abandon his bluff attempt if a fourth heart came. Instead, the board paired, and Randall was home free with a final bet on the river.

Note the low frequency: You really don't want to overdo this type of play. Just as Jerry's bet was suspicious, Randall's raise had to look equally suspicious. After all, what could he have that he would check twice, yet it was strong enough for a check-raise? Randall had to be confident that Jerry's hand was weak, and he was. But he also had to hope that Jerry, or any of his other opponents, wouldn't have the nerve to put him to the test with a three-bet, figuring that he was on an outright steal. Thankfully, they didn't.

If you have a strong conviction that you can win the hand with a bluff, as Randall did, then it's tough to stop yourself from attempting it. And yet, sometimes that is what you must do, because that's what helps keep the Rate of Success at what I estimate as Medium/High. The success rate is inversely correlated to the frequency; the less often you attempt such bluffs, the more likely they are to work. Once you start check-raising every time you sense weakness, your opponents will begin to suspect that you are out of line, and eventually they will pick you off.

Bluff #17. Paul Bluffs a SAP

The scenario: $6–$12 hold 'em.

The bluff: One player limped pre-flop, then a super-aggressive player (a SAP, no pun intended), raised from the cutoff. Paul called on the button with J♠10♠. The BB called and the limper called, so there was four-way action. The flop came

Everyone checked to the SAP, who bet as expected. Paul raised! Everyone folded around to the SAP, who looked at Paul, looked back at his cards, and folded, not looking too happy about it. Paul took down a decent-sized pot, especially considering the hand never reached the turn.

Degree of Difficulty: 3
Rate of Success: Medium
Frequency: Low

The analysis: Are bluffs like this a necessary part of your game? Not at all. Against a SAP, there's no need to get fancy. You can simply wait until you flop something good, and then get involved with him.

Then why did I include this bluff here? Because all too often, I've heard the adage that you can't bluff a maniac, and that's not entirely true. Maybe you don't *need* to bluff a maniac, but that's different. It *can* be done and, if you want to maximize your earning potential, it *should* be done. You just have to pick your spots carefully. For your best chances of success, several things have to be true:

1. The SAP always bets when everyone checks to him, but once someone raises him, he'll slow down if he doesn't have anything.
2. You are the first person to act after he bets.
3. You are in a spot in which, if the SAP wasn't there, you'd have a good bluffing opportunity.
4. The flop is unlikely to have helped him in any way.

#1 is the most important, because it forms a distinction between two different breeds of SAPs: the controlled maniac and the out-of-control maniac. An out-of-control maniac permanently refuses to re-linquish control of a hand. He will put in every possible bet or raise, no matter what. Even if he has no hand, no draw, and no chance of chasing everyone out, there is no getting rid of him. This player is practically impossible to bluff, and if you ever try, I will find you and chastise you properly.

If you're going to pick on either of them, it has to be the con-trolled maniac. He'll bet anytime the action is checked to him, but he knows when to throw on the brakes. When no one makes a move at the pot, he will stake his claim. But if he meets resistance, he is smart enough to back off and wait for a better spot. In the long run, he will do many times better than the out-of-control maniac. But if the situa-tion is right, he is the one that can be bluffed.

Then it becomes a matter of satisfying the other criteria. In Paul's case, he was sitting directly behind the SAP, the rest of the field had checked, and unless someone had a king or three, the flop wasn't to their liking. If there was ever a time to bluff a maniac, Paul found it.

For all we know, he may have been bluffing with the best hand. The SAP might not have been able to beat jack-high! Even if that was the case, Paul certainly couldn't call with an unimproved J♠10♠, just hoping he had the best hand. It was either time to fold or, since he felt the bettor had nothing, give him a little test.

Put yourself in the SAP's mind: With a flop like K-3-3 rainbow, you feel good about your chances of stealing the pot. But once you get raised, how can you realistically expect to force your opponent off his hand? After all, what could he have? It must be a king or a three; there's nothing else out there! And with either of those, it's hard to imagine a situation where you could cause him to fold.

With that in mind, even a maniac will sometimes back off, real-izing that he would only be wasting money trying to win the hand. Little does he know that he got outplayed.

Bluff #18. Todd's Bluff at the UPC

The scenario: Thirty players were left in a $1,000 NLH tournament at the Ultimate Poker Challenge. Todd and the player to his right both had about $4,000, which was slightly above average, and the blinds were $50–$100.

The bluff: Todd was on the button. The action was folded around to the loose-aggressive player (LAP) to Todd's right. He pointed directly at the short-stacked BB and asked him, "How much you got left?" The BB counted his chips and found that he had $700 in addition to the $100 he had posted as the blind. The LAP then deliberately counted out $800 worth of chips and fired them in.

Todd pretended to look at his hand, but didn't really care what he had. Without knowing his cards, Todd made it $3,300 to go! The blinds folded, and the LAP disgustedly threw his cards in the muck, almost instantly! Todd picked up $950 without having to see a flop.

Degree of Difficulty: 4
Rate of Success: Medium/High
Frequency: Medium

The analysis: Pre-flop, I never look at my cards until the action gets to me. One of the reasons is that bluffing scenarios become much clearer when you ignore your own cards. In other words, you might think to yourself that you're in a good position to steal the pot, but then you look down and see 7-2 offsuit and start reconsidering. If the timing seems right, then don't talk yourself out of a good bluff! By not looking at your cards, you won't be discouraged by the fact that you have a weak hand. Just concentrate on doing what it takes for your opponents to fold.[9]

---

9. Obviously, I'm not suggesting that you make a habit of ignoring your cards. But if you strongly sense weakness in your opponent, then you want to pay as little attention to your own hand as possible. Your focus should be on what he has, not what you have.

Also, if you ever decide not to look at your cards, make sure that you at least give the appearance of looking at them. Don't ever let your opponents know that you

That is what Todd did here. It might seem silly for him not to look at his own cards, but he was so sure that the LAP had a weak hand that he didn't want to consider anything other than reraising. The LAP's raise was based purely on intimidation. He pointed directly at the BB, as if he were a target. The LAP was essentially saying, "Look man, you'd better not call this raise, 'cause you're gonna be all-in if you do."

Think about it. If the LAP truly had a strong hand, why would he want to intimidate the BB? Wouldn't he want to get some action instead? Along the same line, why would he want to raise to eight times the BB? Wouldn't he prefer to make a more reasonable raise, and possibly get a caller? When Todd watched the LAP in motion, he saw a lot of bluff and bluster, and not much substance. He was confident in his read that the LAP was weak, and he backed that read with a substantial reraise that, if he were wrong, could have cost him the tournament. But the fact that the LAP folded without hesitation showed that Todd's instincts were dead-on.

Besides winning the pot, Todd's bluff had ramifications toward future hands. The LAP had been focusing entirely on the BB, as if no one else mattered. Todd's reraise sent a clear message: "Hey, I'm here too. If you forget about me, I'm gonna make you pay." The LAP was visibly thrown off his game, and was the next player eliminated at the table, even sooner than the short-stacked BB! It demonstrated beautifully why there's nothing like exerting dominance over a LAP to throw him off-balance, and a well-timed bluff can do just that.

Bluff #19. From Gutshot to Glory

The scenario: NLH with $1–$2 blinds. Everyone involved had at least $400 to begin the hand.

The bluff: Amy was the BB with 9♣8♦. Two players limped in along with the blinds, so there was four-way action. The flop came

---

didn't look at them. Todd snapped the corners of his cards and lowered his eyes toward them, so at least his opponents didn't know that he was playing blind.

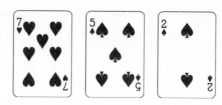

It gave Amy a gutshot straight draw with two overcards. She decided to take a $6 stab at the pot, hoping to win it right there. Unfortunately, the next player made it $20 to go, and the player after him cold-called the $20 without hesitation. The SB folded, and it was Amy's turn to act.

She could have taken the easy way out and folded. But she was able to read her opponents so confidently that she wanted to take advantage of it. She was almost certain that the player who made it $20 to go had a medium pocket pair such as eights or nines, and after seeing a favorable flop, was hoping to protect that pair with a raise. Meanwhile, the player who cold-called the $20 was clearly on a draw, since he didn't even consider raising or folding. Amy was pretty sure that player needed a spade, so sensing that she knew exactly where she stood in the hand, she called the extra $14.

The turn card was the 10♦, making Amy open-ended. She felt a bet would not accomplish anything, so she checked. The next player again bet $20, and again the button called rather quickly. Amy sensed that the $20 bet was neither here nor there, since it clearly wasn't big enough to get anyone to fold. She felt that the player didn't want to convey total weakness by checking, but didn't have enough confidence in his hand to make a strong bet. Based on that information, Amy's read on both players remained unchanged. However, she wanted to take control of the hand to set up a bluff on the river, so she made it $60 to go. The first player called, but didn't look too happy, and the second player flat-called for the third time in the hand, ending any doubts that he was on a draw.

The river card was the 5♣, creating a final board of

Amy was sure that it didn't help either player, but she also knew that she had to bet enough to get past the initial bettor, since she was extremely confident that the second player had nothing and could not call. Amy came out with a $250 bet. The first player groaned, glanced back at his cards, and mucked them. The second player did exactly the same thing. He looked at the board, groaned, looked back at his cards, shrugged, and mucked them. Amy took down the pot with nine-high, and the best part was that she built the pot nicely with her raise on the turn, to make it a pot worth stealing.

Degree of Difficulty: 9
Rate of Success: Medium
Frequency: Low/Medium

The analysis: Amy combined her good reads with a good Betting Pattern to create a truly magnificent play. Furthermore, she avoided the biggest mistake made by many players in her position. Namely, when they see the 10♦ on the turn, they instinctively bet out, thinking that their hand has improved somewhat, and they might as well take a second chance at stealing the pot. While that is not a terrible play, it has several faults:

1. A check-raise carries much more power than a lead bet on the turn. Leading out when the 10♦ hits is not nearly as convincing as check-raising the turn and *then* leading out on the river.
2. If you bet too little, opponents might (correctly) read you as weak, and raise just to test you.
3. If you bet too much, your opponents might commit themselves to the pot, which is the last thing you want.

#3 is the biggest thing to worry about. If you are an overaggressive bluffer, you might push all-in on the turn in Amy's shoes. That works fine if your opponents fold, but the risk far exceeds the reward. The pot has $68, and everyone has over $400, so why overbet the pot so drastically?

Strictly speaking, the drawing hand *should* fold since his pot odds are awful, but that doesn't mean that he *will* fold. D.A.I.— Don't Assume Intelligence! If he calls on the turn, you have screwed yourself royally. If everyone misses their draw, he could turn over ace-high and beat your nine-high for a monster pot.

Lesson to be learned: When you put your opponent on a draw, you have to save some ammunition for the river. There is no reason to commit yourself early if you are astute enough to put your opponent on a particular draw. Why not wait and see if he makes it? If he does, you can fold and save some money. If he doesn't, then you can bet your remaining chips and force him out.

The Weakness of the Cold-Caller

General premise: In NLH tournaments, when a player raises pre-flop, you rarely see an opponent just call behind him with a premium hand. That opponent almost always reraises. If he just calls, he probably has a marginal hand at best.

The main reason: A fear of playing past the flop. With hands like A-A and K-K, players generally want to get their money in pre-flop, because they are scared of making a mistake after the flop. They are afraid they'll see a dangerous flop and then either fold a winning hand, or go all-in with a loser. So they make a substantial reraise pre-flop, which usually keeps them from having to make a tough decision later. They want to force their opponent either to fold to the reraise, or call with what is presumably the inferior hand.

When this strategy is most prevalent (and most correct): The late stages of tournaments, specifically when you are in the money or close to it. You'd prefer to reraise with strong hands rather than risk the possibility of going broke with them. Tournament poker is about survival. Most good players know that every time you let someone see a cheap flop with a worse hand, you give them the opportunity to get lucky and bust you. Therefore, toward the end of a tournament, you will almost never see a player flat-call a pre-flop raise with a premium hand.

The player who follows this pattern most clearly: The table chip leader. Most of the time, the chip leader will use his imposing stack to try to muscle players around. If someone raises in front of him, and he decides to play against that person, he will often reraise to put their shorter stack to the test. Flat-calling usually indicates that he doesn't have a premium hand. At best, he has a marginal hand, and he simply wants to try to outflop or outplay the raiser post-flop, knowing he has the bigger stack and position on him throughout.

Let's add all this up: When a player raises pre-flop, and an opponent behind him just calls, it signals weakness. In the late stages of tournaments and/or when it's the table chip leader who calls, it's an even clearer sign of weakness. From a bluffer's perspective, this should be music to your ears.

Let's say you are at the final table of a multi-table NLH tournament. Or perhaps you are near the end of a NLH single-table satellite such as an online SNG. You are the pre-flop raiser, and someone flat-calls your raise. When the flop comes, you should be prepared to make a substantial bet whether you have a hand or not. By merely calling, your opponent is probably attempting to hit a favorable flop. *Chances are, the flop won't help.* Maybe he will get lucky and make a good hand, but poker is about playing the percentages, and bluffing in that spot is the correct play.

Now here's an even better play. Instead of being the pre-flop raiser, let's assume you are one of the players somewhere behind the cold-caller. You are in the perfect position to reraise as a bluff. When someone raises pre-flop, and another player just calls, you should at least consider reraising a substantial amount with any two cards.

The main benefit of this play: If it works, you will pick up a substantial pot without having to see a flop. Since one player raised and another called the raise, the pot contains at least five times the BB, and probably more. You are getting a bigger pot than if you had just one opponent, even though your risk is roughly the same.

How is that possible? You might be wondering how your risk could be the same when you have two opponents instead of one. As we've said, the caller of the pre-flop raise adds very little risk to your play. As a smart player, who has read this section and understood the concepts, you know he is a minimal threat.

However, the original raiser might not have that same understanding. He might have a fear of the cold-caller, even though you know better than to fear that player. When you reraise, he truly has to worry only about you, but he might think that he also has to worry about the caller. That might lead him to lay down some semistrong hands, ones that he might have called you with if it weren't for the presence of the third player. That factor essentially offsets the added risk of having the third player in the pot.

A word of caution: Cold-calling a raise with a monster hand is something that you *should* do, especially if a player behind you has shown a propensity to reraise when someone flat-calls a raise. That means he is aware of the concepts described here, and he may incorrectly smell weakness when you call. He'll reraise, and then you'll have him trapped. In poker parlance it is called playing "second hand low." It is an expert play that can be a thing of beauty when done correctly.

The thing is, not too many players have the discipline to make that play. The vast majority want to get their money in pre-flop so they can avoid any further decision-making. It's boring, it's uninspiring, but that's what they do, and that's why the reraise of the cold-caller is so reliable.

Keep in mind, though, that you're not the only one who knows these concepts, or who is reading this book. If enough people start reraising the cold-caller, then the natural progression is for more people to start cold-calling with monster hands. Maybe it will take a while before that starts to happen, but it's something you should keep in mind.

Three Cases of Reraising the Cold-Caller

At the 2003 and 2004 WSOP main event final tables, ESPN showed three instances of a player reraising the cold-caller. Not all of them worked, but they all illustrated perfectly the concepts I've discussed. In all three cases, the cold-caller was the chip leader, his hand was extremely marginal, and it could be said that all three bluffs should have worked. Maybe against lesser opponents, they would have worked. Read about them, and you can decide for yourself.

Bluff #20. Harrington Shocks the TV Audience

The scenario: Seven players were left in the 2004 WSOP Main Event. Greg Raymer was the chip leader with almost $8 million. Josh Arieh was a distant second with a little under $4 million, while Dan Harrington was sitting near the back of the pack with only $2.3 million. Raymer and Arieh had clearly been the aggressors so far, and it seemed just a matter of time before someone took a stand against them.

The bluff: The blinds were $40,000–$80,000. From UTG, Arieh opened the pot for $225,000 with K♥9♠. Raymer, sitting to his left, called with A♣2♣. It was folded around to Harrington on the button, who looked down at 6♥2♦. "Those are rags," said ESPN commentator Norman Chad matter-of-factly. Clearly he assumed there was no way Harrington would even think of playing the hand. Well, he was wrong.

"I'm gonna raise it," said Harrington, as he pushed $1.2 million toward the pot.

"Um, those are rags, Dan," said ESPN commentator Lon McEachern, as if maybe Harrington had seen his hand incorrectly.

"This is a *huge* bluff he's trying to execute here!" exclaimed Chad.

The action came around to David Williams, who looked down at A♠Q♣ in the BB! He had the best hand by far, but from the way the action had gone down, he had to assume that his hand was no good. He didn't take long in mucking his hand, and I think almost anyone in his position would have done the same thing.

Arieh then stared down Harrington for a moment or two, but it was clearly just an act. He had no intention of calling with K♥9♠. He folded, and now there was only Raymer left to contend with.

Raymer looked over at Harrington's stack to see how much he had left. Clearly Raymer was giving more thought to calling than Arieh had, but in the end, he decided that there was no way his hand could be good. "Give him the money," he said as he tossed his cards in.

"Dan Harrington adds a half a million chips to his stack bluffing with a 6-2 offsuit! Now that's poker, baby!" McEachern said admiringly.

The analysis: Arieh and Raymer were the most aggressive players at the table, and they had been playing more hands than anyone else. So they probably didn't need strong hands to get involved in the action. Raymer sensed weakness in Arieh's raise, which led to his call with only an A♣2♣. He figured that, not only might he have the best hand, but he also had the position and the chips to outplay Arieh after the flop.

However, it seemed as though he didn't consider the players behind him. Harrington not only sensed the same weakness in Arieh's raise that Raymer did, but he also sensed even greater weakness in Raymer's call! He knew that Raymer, as an aggressive player, would have reraised with any strong hand. Before even looking at his cards, Harrington had probably made up his mind to lower the boom on both of them.

Harrington also knew that his image was perfect for the play he wanted to make. He was perceived as tight, but not weak-tight. The other players at the table clearly respected his play, and they did not want to get involved in a hand with him if they could help it. Harrington knew that, and in fact he even said as much in one of his ESPN interviews. It helped that he was aware of his own image, and he took advantage of it just as any good player should.

The icing that topped this bluff off was the size of his reraise. An all-in reraise would have had a hint of desperation. It might have signaled too clearly that he did not want to be called. He knew that he was playing against top-level competition, and specifically against two players that had been making good reads all tournament; he therefore did not want them to get any idea that he might be bluffing.

So he reraised for about half of his stack, which subtly gave the impression that he had a monster hand. It almost gave the appearance that he wanted a call, and of course, that is what he wanted his opponents to think. He wanted them to assume that they were disappointing Harrington by not calling. I think it's safe to say that both Arieh and Raymer were extremely surprised when they eventually got to see what Harrington had.

To some extent, his bluff was formulaic. He saw a pre-flop raise and a cold-call, and that's often a sign that a bluff could work. But I don't want to downplay the fact that Harrington made a great read. Two players in front of him demonstrated a willingness to be involved in the hand, including a raise from UTG, which usually means a strong hand. Yet he correctly decided that he could muscle them out. He made them lay down the best hands by making a stone-cold bluff, and Lon McEachern couldn't have said it any better: Now that's poker, baby!

Bluff #21. Hughes Loses a Coin Flip

The scenario: The same event, but now only five players remained. By the time this hand came around, Raymer had extended his chip lead, and now had over $12 million. Meanwhile, Arieh had dropped to below $3 million, while Glenn Hughes, the quiet man to that point, was the short stack with about $1.5 million.

The bluff: The blinds were still at $40,000 and $80,000. Arieh opened for $225,000 with 3♣3♦. On the button, Raymer called with 5♣5♠. It was folded to Glenn Hughes in the BB, who looked down at K♠Q♦. He moved all-in for his remaining $1.5 million. Arieh quickly folded, and then the decision was on Raymer. So far, this was eerily reminiscent of Harrington's bluff.

"I think we've got a race if I call. A coin toss," said Raymer, looking Hughes over.

"Rock and roll," said Hughes. "We came to gamble."

Raymer studied him for a couple of seconds more, then announced that he would call. They turned their hands up, and the flop came

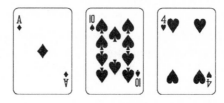

At that point, Hughes good-naturedly implored the dealer, "Give me a jack, king, or queen. A jack, king, or queen! Come on dealer, you can do it. You can do it! Give it to me!" The turn card was the 10♦, giving him the other three aces as additional outs, but the 9♥ on the river was no help. Hughes lost the hand and exited graciously, waving and smiling as he left with $1.1 million dollars for his fifth place finish.

The analysis: Part of me is hesitant to call this a bluff, because I'm sure Hughes felt there was a decent chance he had the best hand. He knew Arieh, having been the first player in the pot, could have had just about anything. He knew that Raymer would have reraised Arieh with any pair queens or higher, or A-K or A-Q; in other words, the hands that dominated K-Q. There was a good chance that Raymer had a weak ace (à la the A♣2♣ from the Harrington bluff), but he could also have had a K-J or Q-J type of hand, which Hughes would have dominated. Although this play was similar to the last one we looked at, Hughes had confidence in the strength of his hand when he pushed all-in, whereas Harrington knew he was in trouble if anyone called.

Having said that, we should ignore Hughes's cards. When looking at this hand from a bluffer's perspective, we want to know why Hughes wasn't able to win the pot without a fight. We can be pretty sure that if Hughes had a choice, he would have preferred for everyone to fold, so that he could win $500,000 without having to produce the best hand. As bluffers, we are always happy when our opponents fold without ever getting a chance to beat us.

Most people probably expected Raymer to fold rather than call another $1.3 million. After all, Hughes had just as tight an image as Harrington and had hardly played a hand all night. So why did Raymer fold to Harrington but call Hughes? I can see four reasons:

1. Obviously, 5♣5♠ was a better hand than A♣2♣. Still, he could not have been happy with it when Hughes pushed all-in. Either Hughes had two overcards, which made Raymer about an 11-to-10 favorite, or a higher pair, which made Raymer a 4-to-1 underdog. One of the first things you learn in no-limit hold 'em is never to risk a lot of chips when you are either a small favorite or a big dog. For that reason, it could be argued that Raymer made a bad call. But since Hughes had only overcards, he made the correct play. The question is, was Raymer lucky that Hughes had only overcards, or did he have reason to believe that fives were the best hand?

2. For some reason, Raymer had made up his mind that Hughes didn't have a pair. He made that clear when he said he thought it would be a coin toss if he called. Whether that was based on a strong read or optimistic thinking, we'll never know for sure. Maybe he just said it in order to get a reaction out of Hughes, and when Hughes said, "We came to gamble," Raymer got the information he wanted. Or it could simply be that he was running hot, so he put his opponent on the hand he could beat. Whatever his reasoning was, Raymer convinced himself that he had the best hand, and he was right.

3. As I said before, this was the second time around—the second time that someone tried to push Raymer off of his hand after he flat-called a pre-flop raise by Arieh. He had not amassed $12 million in chips by laying hands down! He was surely growing tired of people getting aggressive on him. He wanted to be the one in control of the table, and Harrington had already taken him off of a hand not too long ago. He didn't want it to happen again.

4. But in the end, I think the deciding factor was the amount of chips at risk. In Bluff #20, Raymer had about $8 million in chips, while Harrington had $2.3 million. If Raymer went all-in and lost, not only would he have surrendered about 30 percent of his stack, it would have gone to arguably the most dangerous player at the table. He realized that he would be risking almost a third of his chips on the slim chance that he could produce the best hand. Plus, the last thing he wanted to do was give those chips to Harrington. Folding was an easy decision.

Against Hughes, the odds were significantly better. Raymer had over $12 million to Hughes's $1.5 million. It cost Raymer only about 12 percent of his stack to call. Even if he lost, he still would have had a commanding chip lead. Plus, Hughes did not seem as much of a threat as Harrington. Of course, Raymer had no intention of doubling anyone up. But if he had to choose between the two, he'd surely rather lose a pot to Hughes, who did not have Harrington's WSOP experience or intimidating table image.

I think the combination of all those factors caused Raymer to call. However, that does not mean that Hughes made the wrong play. Raymer clearly had a marginal hand, and many players would have folded pocket fives to an all-in reraise. I'm sure Hughes has no regrets about the way he was knocked out, and if the same situation came up again, he probably wouldn't change a thing. Well, I guess he would change the flop to include some facecards. But other than that, he simply made a good play that had bad results. Raymer made a gutsy call, and that's what champions do.

Bluff #22. Benvenisti Bluffs the Wrong Guy

The scenario: Five players were left in the 2003 WSOP main event. Sammy Farha was the chip leader with $3.2 million. Chris Moneymaker wasn't too far behind with $2.45 million. Dan Harrington and Jason Lester each had just over $1 million, while Tomer Benvenisti was the short stack with $520,000.

The bluff: The blinds were $15,000–$30,000, and Harrington raised to $90,000 with 4♠4♦. Moneymaker, sitting to his left, called from the button with A♠2♠. Benvenisti then pushed $520,000 all-in from the SB with J♥10♦. Harrington folded almost instantly. Moneymaker leaned forward and stared intently at Benvenisti, who did not seem completely comfortable being under Moneymaker's scrutiny. Finally Moneymaker chunked down his chips and declared that he was calling.

The flop came

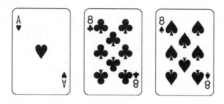

and Moneymaker pumped his fist in exhilaration. The 9♥ on the turn gave him pause, since it gave Benvenisti an open-ended straight draw, but then the harmless 9♠ fell on the river. Moneymaker took down over a million-dollar pot, and took a crucial step toward his eventual championship.

The analysis: There are many reasons that Benvenisti's bluff should have worked. He knew that Harrington was a relatively tight player and would call only if he had a particularly strong hand. He also knew that Moneymaker was the loosest player at the table, and could have called Harrington's raise with a wide array of hands. He correctly thought an all-in reraise would make Moneymaker think twice about getting involved in the hand. Benvenisti was short-stacked and needed to make a move, and it looked like he picked the right time to do it.

Furthermore, A♠2♠ was about as bad a hand as Moneymaker could have in that spot. If Benvenisti had any pocket pair or a bigger ace, then Moneymaker was about a 2-to-1 underdog *at best*. Those were, by far, the most likely hands for Benvenisti to have. Even if Benvenisti was getting out of line with a K-Q (or a J♥10♦), and A♠2♠ was the best hand, it could only be about a 60-to-40 favorite at best. The bottom line is that A♠2♠ was a terribly marginal hand, there was a good chance that it was a significant underdog, and many players would have quickly let it go.

However, Moneymaker did not immediately fold. He smartly decided that there was no harm in taking a minute to consider his options, and in the end, it was information he picked up while staring down Benvenisti that led him to make the call. In Moneymaker's own words:

> *My first thought was to follow Dan . . . into the muck, but then I thought about it some more and wondered if I could pick anything up by twiddling my thumbs for a beat or two. . . . So I checked him out, and as I did, I noticed that his arm muscles were in a kind of spasm. He's a big guy, Tomer Benvenisti, and I could really see his muscles tighten up on him, and his shirt moving fitfully underneath, which told me he was nervous. I thought, okay, is this an ace-ten kind of nervous or a two-seven kind of nervous? . . . I had to determine if Tomer's tells told me anything I could use. After a bit I saw him rock gently in his chair, back and forth, something I hadn't really seen him do to this point, and I took this as a sign that he was weak in the hand. I could have been wrong, but I didn't think so, and I started to look on this as my chance to take him out, to thin the herd by one other player, and I only had to risk another 20 percent of my stack to do so. I called.[10]*

Even though the bluff made sense in theory, when it came time to execute, Benvenisti did not control his movements well. In the ESPN footage, you can clearly see the things that Moneymaker alludes to. Benvenisti's face tightened up, he rocked back in his chair, and generally did not look confident at all. When you try to bluff the chip leader—a player who had been running well and making great reads for several days—you had damn well better put on a good game face.

10. *Moneymaker,* pp. 188–89.

Moneymaker looked for a reason to call and he found one, which shows why Benvenisti picked the wrong guy to bluff. You want to attack players who look for reasons to fold, not for reasons to call. Harrington didn't even consider calling. He mucked his hand immediately. Clearly, he was a good player to bluff. Moneymaker, on the other hand, had always taken his time before folding, and had shown a willingness to make several brave calls throughout the tournament. The last thing you want to do is to try to bluff someone like that.

Would I have made that call with the A♠2♠? Probably not. Then again, I am not a world champion. Benvenisti's bluff would have worked against me, and probably against 99 percent of players in Moneymaker's shoes. Unfortunately for Benvenisti, he tried to bluff the wrong guy at the wrong time while making the wrong physical movements. His play made intrinsic sense, and if he had managed to remain still, he just might have made it work.

In summary: Maybe I made a mistake by presenting three examples of a bluff that usually works, but only one that succeeded. Don't be turned off by the two examples that didn't work. The two players that foiled those bluffs went on to be world champions, and they made excellent reads of their opponents. Your typical opposition will not be at nearly the same level. The plays that Hughes and Benvenisti made would have worked against the overwhelming majority of players. Reraising the cold-caller is usually a great way to pick up large pots without having to see a flop. Give it a shot when you get the chance, and find out for yourself.

CHAPTER SIX

Representing Strength

As we said in Chapter 4, every bluff has some element of attacking weakness and representing strength. In this chapter, we will examine bluffs in which the latter is the dominant element. Even if your opponent has a halfway decent hand, you can still bluff successfully, as long as you can convince him that you have a stronger one. *A good bluff tells a story that the victim believes and understands.* Using your actions from start to finish, you must give him sufficient reason to believe that his hand is no good.

What strong hands can you represent? Anything from a royal flush down to ace-high. It's all relative. You want to represent whatever you think it takes to beat your opponent. If he can't even beat a pair of aces, then it's pointless to represent aces full. Simply representing a pair of aces, and having your opponent believe you, would be enough to get the job done.

Picking your spots: If you're going to run a bluff based primarily on your apparent strength, you need three things to hold true:

1. Your opponent's hand still needs a certain element of weakness. I don't care how good a job you do of representing a straight; if he has one himself, he's not exactly going to be intimidated. The threat of an ace-high flush isn't going to bother him if that's precisely what *he* has. Obviously, he can't have the very hand you're trying to represent.

   But beyond that, you'd prefer that he doesn't have any sort of semistrong hand. If you think he has one, then just wait for a better opportunity to bluff him. Rest assured, there will be plenty of them.

2. If he seems at all weak, then you need a situation that allows you to credibly represent strength. You can't just start betting and raising at random. You have to choose a time when you can most realistically portray a strong hand, and the best opportunities occur when the board looks dangerous.

Anytime there is a threat of a big hand—one that you don't think your opponent has—you can attempt to represent that hand. If there is a pair on board, make him think you have trips or a full house. If the board is 8-9-10-Q, convince him that you have the jack for the straight. And, when there are four clubs on board, make him believe you have the A♣ for the nut flush. *The better job you can do of selling your hand, the better the chance that he will buy your bluff.*

3. Finally, you need an opponent capable of laying down a halfway decent hand. There are many opponents who will give you credit for the hand you are representing, but will still call just to see it. Don't bother with them. Go after opponents who take pride in saving a bet. You'll leave them thinking they made a good laydown, but you'll be the one raking in the pot.

However, when it comes time to appear strong, you must realize that some hands are easier to represent than others.

Three important facts:
1. Among all three-of-a-kind or better hands, flushes are the easiest hands to represent.
2. Players generally fear flushes more than any other hand. Straights are a distant second.
3. You will pull off more successful bluffs representing flushes than straights.

From a mathematical perspective: The fear of a flush makes sense. I'm not saying that your average player necessarily takes into account the probabilities that I will mention here. But on some level, many players correctly have the general idea that flushes pose a more realistic threat than straights.

For instance, if you compare a suited flop, such as

and a connected flop, such as

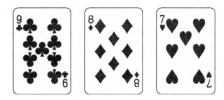

you will see that the chances of making a flush with the first flop are almost the same as the chances of making a straight with the second one.[11] However, as soon as you add a gap to the connected flop, such as

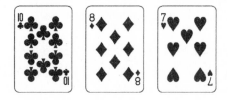

you now lose one-third of the straight possibilities from the previous flop.[12] Once you add a second gap, such as

11. With the suited board, you have ten clubs left in the deck, which can be combined into forty-five different two-card combinations. With the connected board, you have sixteen combinations each of J-10, 10-6, and 6-5. Thus, there are forty-eight possible straights with the 9♣8♦7♥ flop, and forty-five possible flushes with the K♣8♣2♣ flop.

12. Now, you only have sixteen combinations each of J-9 and 9-6, so thirty-two total straights rather than forty-eight.

you lose two-thirds of the straights from the original flop.[13] From a bluffer's perspective, you would have to convince your opponent that you have exactly 10-9. That is a hell of a lot harder than convincing him that you have any two clubs when the flop is K♣8♣2♣.

A similar phenomenon occurs on the turn. If, on the turn, the board is

nine remaining clubs could give someone a flush. If the board is

four aces or four nines complete the straight. So again, with nine flushes compared to eight straights, the chances of the two are almost the same. However, add a gap, such as

---

13. Now, only the sixteen combinations of 10-9 make a straight.

And now only the four tens complete a straight. Let's say you had the choice of trying to run a bluff with a board of Q♣9♣6♣3♣ or K♣Q♦J♥9♠, and in both cases your opponent had top pair. I *guarantee* that you will get called more often with the straight board than the flush board, and the math behind it justifies your opponents' actions. That's not to say I wouldn't attempt a bluff with a K♣Q♦ J♥9♠ board. However, I would do it with the understanding that it won't work as often as a bluff representing a flush.

From a hand selection perspective: It is common knowledge that loose players play too many starting hands, but they are especially loose when it comes to suited cards. Many loose players play any two suited cards, but wouldn't automatically play any two connected cards. Even experienced players tend to overestimate the value of suited cards. In a given position, they would fold K♣9♥ in a heartbeat, but they see K♣9♣ and suddenly it becomes a must-play. Something about seeing suited cards triggers the impulse to call. I'm not saying it's rational, or that it's the right play, because in most cases it definitely is not, but it is what many players do.

That's why, if some of your opponents have loose starting hand requirements, it makes sense to respect the flush possibility as soon as three of a suit are on board. Even with an extremely dangerous flop such as 8♣7♣6♣, chances are that no one flopped a big hand. However, a flush is a much more likely possibility than a straight, simply because the same people who wouldn't play 9-5 offsuit or even 5-4 offsuit would play any two clubs.

As a bluffer, you should recognize the flip side of this coin. Since your opponents play way too many suited hands, they naturally assume that others do the same. Hopefully, you know better than to call pre-flop with 10♣2♣, but your opponents don't know that. When they see a flop with three clubs, some of them will assume that anyone with two clubs would have stayed around for the flop. That flop will put them on the defensive, much more so than one containing three cards to a straight. As a result, you should be able to uncover some prime bluffing opportunities.

From a recognition perspective: You could almost throw out the mathematical and hand selection analyses (even though they are very true), because this is the overwhelming factor. Suited cards are simply more noticeable! It's as basic as that. Just as suited cards attract a player when he sees them in his hand, they catch his eye when he sees them on the board. Almost all players see two clubs on a flop and immediately register the possibility of a flush draw. Relatively few see 10♣9♥2♠ on a flop and think to themselves that someone has a straight draw.

When two clubs flop and a third comes on the turn, everyone takes notice. It's almost impossible to ignore that third club. As a result, checking to the possible flush has become second-nature for players of all different skill levels. One of the first things beginners learn is that once three suited cards are on board, beware of the flush possibility. Even more advanced players, who would normally be aggressive with hands like top pair, proceed with caution once the third club comes. Even if they continue betting, they cannot disregard the presence of the possible flush.

Conversely, when the board comes 10♣9♥2♠8♦, only extremely tight players immediately fear the possible straight. If a player bet with A-10 or K-10 on the flop, then he is likely to continue betting when the 8♦ comes on the turn. Only after he gets raised will he acknowledge the straight possibility.

That leads to all sorts of strategy implications, such as why you should prefer to play 6♥5♠ as opposed to A♣3♣ in a no-limit cash game. In a nutshell, you'll get paid much more often if you make a straight with the 6♥5♠ than you will if you make the nut flush with the A♣3♣. You have a much greater chance of busting your opponent. When he sees three clubs on board, his mind immediately registers the flush possibility, and he will hesitate to give any significant action without the nut flush. For you, the bluffer, that creates a wonderful opportunity to exploit.

Bottom line: A suited board is a bluffer's paradise. This section will be about representing strong hands. Don't be surprised that many of them deal with representing flushes.

Bluff #23. Bare Ace Play (#1)

The scenario: PLO with $5–$10 blinds. Wesley and Scott both had about $1,500 at the start of this hand.

The bluff: As the first player in the pot, Wesley made it $30 to go from early position with A♦A♥Q♣9♥. Scott called behind him and the BB called, so they took the flop three-handed. It came

Wesley had an overpair, a gutshot straight draw, and a backdoor flush draw. The BB checked, and Wesley bet $60. Scott called, which didn't thrill Wesley, but it was better than being raised. The BB mucked, leaving them heads-up.

The 5♦ came on the turn, putting three diamonds on board. With $215 in the pot, Wesley bet $100. Scott pondered briefly, then raised to $300. Wesley barely hesitated before announcing he was reraising the pot, which meant he was making it $1,115 to go. Scott fell deep into thought, and took at least three minutes to make his decision. Finally, even though he seemed pained to do it, he surrendered his hand, and Wesley took down the pot.

Degree of Difficulty: 8
Rate of Success: Medium/High
Frequency: High unless you get caught one time, then it becomes Medium[14]

---

14. You don't want your opponents to know that you have this play in your repertoire. As long as you never have to show your hand, they'll never know that you are capable of betting a bare ace. But once they see you do it one time, they'll know for future hands that you might be representing the nut flush while holding only the ace, and they'll be more likely to look you up.

The analysis: This is one of only two PLO bluffs in this entire book. PLO is a wonderful bluffing game, and there are dozens that would be worth mentioning, but I know not many people play it, so I'll stick mostly to hold 'em and some stud. Still, this bluff beautifully illustrates the power of the bare ace, so I couldn't pass it up.

PLO, or any form of Omaha, is a game of the nuts. If you don't have the nuts, or a draw to the nuts, you usually have little business in the pot. Aces are powerful in PLO, not just because they are the highest pair, but because you can make the nut flush if you have an ace suited with another card. A♣A♠9♣6♠ is a beautiful hand because it can make two nut flushes, whereas A♣A♠9♦6♥ is a decent hand, but not nearly as strong. However, smart players know that even with the latter hand, if three clubs or spades hit the board, they are still in a good spot to control the action.

Now let's return to the hand in question. Wesley's raise pre-flop with aces (one of them suited) is completely acceptable. On the flop, Wesley bet for several reasons. He might have the best hand (with a pair of aces), or he might get lucky (by hitting an ace for a set or a jack for the straight), plus he knew that neither of his opponents could be drawing to the nut flush, since the A♦ was in his hand. He was fully aware that if a diamond came, he might be able to win the pot with continued aggression.

On the turn, Wesley's bet had two purposes. He was hoping that Scott would fold, fearing the nut flush. Or if Scott called, he was building the pot so that he would have the option of making a big bluff on the river. He really didn't expect Scott to raise, but Scott probably sensed weakness in Wesley's $100 bet, and wanted to test him a little.

That put Wesley in an interesting situation. He knew that he was behind, and almost definitely drawing dead, so calling was not an option. Many players would have folded, but he hated the thought of folding, since he knew that Scott was bluffing, albeit with the best hand. In other words, Scott was representing the nut flush, which he couldn't possibly have, but he probably held a lower flush or a set. Reraising, and putting Scott to the test, was the only option that Wesley felt was right.

Earlier, we said that bluffing is often a matter of representing a big hand convincingly. Wesley had done that throughout the hand, and now he had to complete the job by reraising the full amount. When it came time for Scott to decide whether or not to call, he had to mentally review all of Wesley's prior actions. Added together, they painted a very convincing picture of the nut flush.

If you don't think so, pretend you're in Scott's shoes with a king-high flush—the "second nuts." You need to decide whether to call an $815 raise, so you play back the hand step by step. Your thought processes might go something like this:

1. Wesley raised pre-flop, so he probably has aces, with one or more of them suited. Thus, there's a decent chance he has the A♦ with another diamond.
2. Wesley bet $60 on the flop, which he would do with the nut flush draw. He wouldn't want to put in a pot-sized bet without a made hand, but if he flopped four diamonds, he wouldn't want to check either.
3. If he made his flush on the turn, he'd again make a relatively small bet, since he would want some action on his big hand. When I raised him, he probably thought there was a chance that I had a set, and that's why he reraised the pot. He wanted to charge me the maximum to draw to a full house. But he didn't know I had the king-high flush, otherwise he might have raised less.
4. If Wesley isn't bluffing, then I am drawing completely dead if I call.

It's that last one that would probably seal the deal. All in all, Scott really had only one decision to make: Wesley either had the nut flush, or was on a complete bluff, so which one was it? When crunch time arrived, Scott made the wrong decision, but it really wasn't his fault. Wesley did a great job of representing the nuts, and he was properly rewarded with a $425 profit.

The only flaw to Wesley's bluff: Wesley committed himself fully on the turn. If Scott had decided to call the big reraise, Scott would have won the hand, because Wesley would have had about $300 left, and it would have been pointless to attempt a $300 river bluff into a $2,400 pot. Scott would have called with any halfway decent hand, even if he thought he was beaten, simply because the pot was so big.

If Scott had something like a set of tens and decided to call, with the mentality that he had to catch a full house to win, it would have been a bad call. He would have been getting only 2-to-1 pot odds in a situation where the odds were 3.4-to-1 against improving his hand.[15] But that's not the point. You cannot always count on your opponent to make the "correct" play. To some extent, Wesley was lucky that Scott was "smart" enough, and had enough discipline, to fold.

One reason Wesley chose Scott as his bluff victim was that he knew Scott could lay down a very good hand. But he had to be $1,100 sure, and I question whether he was *that* confident Scott would fold. And, if he was wrong, he left himself no outs, since he did not have enough chips to try to muscle out Scott on the river. That was the only reason that I gave this bluff an 8, and not higher. If you want to see a "perfect 10" PLO bluff, wait for Chapter 10, and Bluff #42, "The Bare King Play."

Bluff #24. Club Fear

The scenario: $5–$10 stud

The bluff: Gene brought it in for the mandatory $2 with the 2♣. The player to his left, with the Q♥ showing, immediately completed the bet to $5. The action was called in four places, with no one having a doorcard higher than a queen. Gene looked down to see the 2♦J♠ in the hole. It was not a great hand, but there were no other deuces out, plus the action couldn't get raised behind him, so he threw in his $3.[16]

---

15. He could account for the four cards on board plus the four in his hand. Out of the remaining forty-four cards, ten would give him a full house or quads, while thirty-four would not.

16. I originally wrote about this hand in *Card Player Magazine,* Volume 16, Issue #22, p. 48.

Fourth street did not visibly help anybody. Gene caught the 7♣ for a 2♣7♣ board. The player two to his left caught an ace for an A-5 board, and as first to act he checked. Everyone checked around to Gene. There's no question that everyone expected him to check to the third street raiser, who had a board of Q-J. But a quick glance at everyone's cards and actions told Gene two things: First, nobody had anything they were too proud of; second, there was only one club out besides his two. At that point, Gene bet! He was expecting the player to his left to raise to isolate him, and that player did not disappoint. Everyone folded around to Gene, and he called.

On fifth street Gene caught the 10♣ for a 2♣7♣10♣ board, while his opponent caught the 2♠, which was extremely unlikely to have helped him. He checked, Gene bet $10, his opponent instantly folded, and Gene won the $54 pot without a fight.

Degree of Difficulty: 6

Rate of Success: Low/Medium (Assuming random cards after fourth street. But becomes Medium/High if a club comes on fifth or sixth street.)

Frequency: Medium/High

Why this bluff worked:
1. Gene's bet on fourth street was done with the expectation that the player to his left had a pair of queens and would raise. Everyone else in the hand would fold when faced with the prospect of calling two bets, and that's exactly what he wanted to happen. Gene knew he did not have the best hand with a pair of deuces, and against five players he would have had to get extremely lucky to end up with the best hand. But against this one opponent, he had two ways to win the hand. If he improved to trips or even just two pair, it might be enough to win, since there was a good chance that his opponent had only a lone pair of queens. But he was also confident that he could win if he caught a club on fifth or sixth street. He was betting a board of 2♣7♣, so surely his opponent must put him on a club draw. What else could he be betting?

2. It didn't hurt that the cards fell just right. He was lucky to catch a club on fifth street, but I think the bluff would have worked even if he caught one on sixth street. And with only one club among the other twelve cards he could account for (including his two hole cards), he had about a 46 percent chance of catching one on either fifth or sixth street.

3. As I said earlier, many players have an exaggerated fear of flushes. If you can properly represent one before the last card, you can get most players to fold before the hand reaches the river. In this hand, Gene represented a flush so well that even many expert players would have folded if they were in his opponent's shoes.

Further analysis: Gene did not enter the hand intending to bluff, but when circumstances dictated it, he was able to change on the fly. He called on third street because he was getting the right odds to try to make the winning hand, but he *bet* on fourth street because he was suddenly presented with an opportunity.

There were two other possible plays on fourth street. Checking and folding would have been a weaker play, but certainly an understandable one. On the other hand, the third option of checking and calling would have been by far the worst of the three. He would have needed at least three deuces to win against so many opponents, and he was not getting the correct odds to try to spike one. And then, even if he found a deuce, it would not guarantee a winning hand.

So if you find yourself in a similar situation, and you decide to continue with the hand on fourth street, don't fall into the routine of checking and calling. Take the initiative! Situations that let you combine the possibility of a bluff with the possibility of producing the best hand are exactly what you are looking for.

Incidentally, if you really had four clubs on fourth street, the preferable play would be to check. Otherwise the player to your left would raise as expected, he'd scare off your other opponents, and you'd lose the multiway pot that you'd want with a hand such as a flush draw. You'd be stuck in a heads-up situation on the defensive, needing to hit your flush to win. Furthermore, if you got lucky enough to hit a club right off the bat, your opponent would probably be scared away, and he wouldn't pay you off. (Keep in mind how fast Gene's opponent folded when he hit the 10♣.)

Many players, even good ones, would check Gene's pair of deuces, but they'd bet a four-card flush in the same situation. I'm telling you to consider your alternative plays in both situations. It might give you a whole new outlook on the way you play the game.

Bluff #25. Brandon's Community Card Bluff

The scenario: An extremely loose $5–$10 stud game. It was definitely not the type of game suited for bluffing. Community cards (the seventh street card shared by everyone) were a common occurrence, since so many players were frequently staying in to the end. Brandon had been playing poker for only about three months, but even he could tell that he was in a good game.

The bluff: Brandon had a very decent starting hand of (7♦A♥)7♣. He called the opening $2, as did each of the other seven players! By sixth street his board was 7♣5♥K♣5♣. Somehow he was high man on board with an open pair of fives, even though six opponents remained. The man directly to his left had A-Q-J-10 showing, and appeared to be the main threat. Brandon checked to him, and predictably, he bet $10. Everyone called around to Brandon. He held sevens and fives, and he could see one other seven on someone else's board. With two fives and a seven still remaining in the deck, a big pot at stake, and no possibility of a raise behind him, he had every intention of seeing the river card.[17]

17. I find it interesting that Brandon hardly ever bluffed, because he was a fairly new player and not yet comfortable doing so, yet he was aware of all the factors I just mentioned. Is bluffing that much more difficult a concept? Or does it take more fearlessness, which he had not yet developed? I am still amazed by how many players know the basic concepts of poker inside and out, but continue to have some phobia of bluffing. As far as I'm concerned, bluffing is among the first things you should learn. The longer you go without incorporating bluffs into your game, the tougher it becomes.

He tossed in his $10. The dealer counted the remaining cards and informed them that they would be receiving a community card. She burned, turned, and out came the 2♣. At first, Brandon was ready to grunt in disgust, but then the man to his left, who presumably had a straight, grunted in disgust himself. So Brandon began to wonder, why was he upset? The community card seemed innocent enough. Brandon looked around at the board. One player had the 2♥ showing, but he didn't appear to be a threat.

Then Brandon looked at his own board. He had three clubs showing with the pair of fives, and the 2♣ community card gave him four. How interesting! He looked around the board again and saw only one other club. Even more interesting! Obviously he didn't have a club in the hole, but what a pot this was! Could he take it with one $10 bet? He figured it was worth a shot. He bet $10.

The player with the potential straight nearly went ballistic. He stood up and shouted to the dealer, "How could you put a club up there?" And then to no one in particular he yelled, "There's not a single freaking club on the board," to which Brandon was tempted to reply, "Well, there's one . . ."

The straight man turned up the king he had in the hole that completed his straight—and mucked it! If Brandon had paid this gentleman, he couldn't have given a better performance for him. Now, naturally, no one wanted to call with any hand worse than a straight since they had already seen one folded, and like ducks in a row everyone tossed their cards into the muck. Brandon scooped a pot of over $200 in a $5–$10 game on a total bluff! He might have started the hand as a novice, but it was definitely his first step toward becoming a seasoned veteran.

Degree of Difficulty: 6
Rate of Success: Low
Frequency: Low/Medium

The analysis: The critical issue is the way Brandon adjusted on the fly. Throughout the hand, he had been carefully analyzing his chances of winning, but bluffing hadn't even crossed his mind. With six opponents in the pot, and a straight staring him in the face, all he was considering was his chance of filling up.

But he never stopped taking in as much information about the hand as he could. That led to his observation of the club possibilities and his flash of clarity. He managed to process that information quickly enough to realize suddenly that a bluffing opportunity had presented itself.

Note how time was of the essence in his decision-making process. If he had taken longer than a few seconds on the river, his bluff would have been less believable, and it would have been more likely that the straight man would have called.

It just goes to show that, even in games with loose players and multiway pots, when bluffing would seem impossible, profitable bluffing situations do arise.

Brandon's inexperience showed: While he made a great play and was able to make a last-second adjustment, he should not have had to rely on a split-second decision. Brandon was observant, much more so than the average player, but he didn't notice his three clubs (and the absence of clubs in everyone else's hand) until the community card came, when his opponent grunted in disgust.

If he had been more experienced, he would have already seen the potential to represent a club flush. He would have known that if the community card were a club, he would have four showing, and he would have immediately come out with a bet. That would have been a more convincing show, and if the straight player was thinking of calling, he would have to consider how quickly Brandon bet out when the club hit, and that might have pushed him even more toward folding.

Counting your bluff outs: Brandon called $10 on sixth street because he figured that he had three outs to make a winning full house. However, he didn't even consider that the nine remaining clubs could lead to a successful bluff. When counting your outs, you should ask yourself two questions:

1. How many of the remaining cards give me a winning hand?

2. How many cards make my hand appear strong enough that I can bluff by representing a winning hand?

In Brandon's case, there was a better than 50 percent chance that he would hit one of his actual outs or his bluff outs on the river. One could even argue that Brandon would have been correct to bet his hand on sixth street, knowing that so many of the potential river cards helped him. Or, getting more creative, he could have even check-raised the straight man and potentially gotten two bets out of everyone, in the anticipation of a favorable community card! Of course, that would have built a bigger pot, which would have made it tougher to bluff successfully, but a good poker player always considers all of his possibilities.

In this hand, Brandon's goal originally seemed very straightforward. He simply wanted to make the best hand. But once he added the possibility of bluffing into the mix, the situation became more complicated. If he had gone a step further and taken his bluff outs into account on sixth street, it would have become *much* more complicated, as he might have come up with all the different ways the hand could be played.

When a seemingly simple hand suddenly becomes full of varied, interesting possibilities, you start to appreciate the intricacies of winning poker.

Bluff #26. Bruno Shifts Gears

The scenario: $20–$40 hold 'em

The bluff: Sam limped from UTG, and a middle-position player limped behind him. Bruno called from late position with 6♣6♥. Both blinds were in, so they saw the flop five-handed, and it came

The blinds checked, and Sam came out betting. The next player folded, and Bruno seemed unsure what to do. After a brief hesitation, he chose to call. The SB called and the BB folded, so they were now three-handed.

The turn was the J♠. The SB quickly checked, while Sam took a few seconds before softly tapping the table with a check. Bruno immediately bet. The SB folded without hesitation. Sam shook his head and lamented, "That was a baaaaad turn card," as he folded his A♥9♥ faceup.

Degree of Difficulty: 4
Rate of Success: Medium/High
Frequency: High

The analysis: Before the flop, Bruno's call with 6♣6♥ from late position in a multiway pot was pretty standard. After the flop, Bruno had a tough decision, and his hesitation reflected that. He could have folded, raised, or called, and made a legitimate argument for any of the three. Let's look at each possibility:

1. Folding. At first glance, folding a pair and an open-ended straight draw for one small bet might seem unusually tight. But in actuality, Bruno's hand was pretty weak. He had a pair lower than anything on the flop, and his straight draw was to the "dummy" end of the straight, which is often a losing proposition. The six that would give him a set could easily give someone a straight, while the ten that would give him a straight would give anyone with a jack a higher straight. Plus, there's always the chance that someone flopped a straight, in which case he was all but dead. Folding would have been completely understandable.

   However, Sam was the only player that had shown strength. Bruno could easily have felt that Sam posed the only threat, in which case it made sense for him to stay in. Unless Sam had flopped the straight, Bruno's sixes had to stand some chance of winning. Either it was the best pair or his draw was live. If that were the case, then folding was not his best play.

2. Raising. Raising would have made sense in two scenarios. First, if he put Sam on a bare straight draw, such as an A-10 or K-10 type of hand, and he thought his sixes might be the best hand. Then his raise would be an attempt to narrow the field, put Sam on the defensive, and hope that his sixes could hold up.

Second, if he saw his sixes as strictly a drawing hand. If he assumed that Sam had a better made hand, then he had to improve to win. Thus, he might have raised in the hopes that Sam would check to him on the turn, and then he could take a free card. The only problem is if Sam recognized what Bruno was doing. Then, not only would Sam not give him a free card, he would probably three-bet the flop, and make it even more expensive for Bruno to make his straight. Given his aggressiveness, that is probably what would have happened.

3. Calling. Given Sam's actual hand, calling was the correct play. Bruno correctly put Sam on a semistrong made hand and knew that if he raised, Sam would have probably countered by three-betting. Calling was not only his cheapest way to see the turn, it gave him two ways to win. He could hit his straight, or he could see if a dangerous turn card caused Sam to slow down, in which case he was ready to pounce.

When the scary-looking J♠ hit and both opponents checked, Bruno acted without hesitation. Even though he had played defensively on the flop, he easily switched to the offensive on the turn. He felt pretty confident that Sam couldn't call. He wasn't as sure about the SB, but it was a risk worth taking. After all, what was the worst thing that could have happened? If he got called, he could have simply checked the river. If someone check-raised, he could have laid his hand down after spending $40. Neither one would have been a big deal. With a $160 pot up for grabs, it made sense to take a shot at it. There was clearly much better than a 4-to-1 chance that his two opponents would give him credit for a straight and lay down, and the results bore that out.

Interestingly, I believe Bruno's hesitation on the flop helped his cause. Normally, you want to make decisive actions, and any hesitation is usually interpreted as weakness. But in this case, he was able to contrast his actions on the flop and turn. He seemed unsure of himself on the flop, but acted with total confidence on the turn. That made his bluff more believable, and if Sam had been considering calling, I'm sure Bruno's lack of hesitation helped to dissuade him.

Bluff #27. A Helpful Ace on the Turn

The scenario: $5–$10 hold 'em.

The bluff: As the first player in, David called pre-flop from middle position with the J♥10♥. A couple of other players called behind him, plus the SB called, so there was five-way action. The flop came

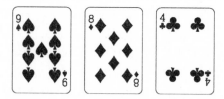

giving David an open-ended straight draw with two overcards. The SB came right out with a bet. The BB called, and David decided to raise. He wanted to try to get the players behind him out so that he could become the button. That would give him control for the remainder of the hand, plus the option to take a free card if the blinds checked to him on the turn. Obediently, the players behind him both folded, and both blinds called.

The turn card was the A♦. The blinds checked to David, and he bet again. They both folded, and David won the pot with jack-high.

Degree of Difficulty: 3
Rate of Success: Medium
Frequency: Medium/High

The analysis: As the medium Rate of Success suggests, the other players in the hand are not always as cooperative as they were here.

If either of the players behind David had called two bets cold, then it would not have been the end of the world, but he would have probably needed to make a hand in order to win. But when the only callers were the blinds, David was in the driver's seat.

If the turn card had been a nine or lower, he would have probably been better off checking and taking the free card (unless of course it was the seven that gave him a straight). If the turn was a ten, jack, or queen, he could have led the betting with what was probably the best hand (if it was the queen it was definitely the best hand). And if it was a king or an ace, he was in a prime position to steal the pot, assuming it didn't pair anyone.

Some players in David's position take the free card when the ace comes. I think that is clearly the inferior play. It's weak poker. Sure, the ace is a scary card, but it's just as scary to your opponents. If they have a pair of eights, or even a nine with a weak kicker, it will be tough for them to call bets on the turn and river. If they have a draw they might call, but then you have put them in the position of needing to hit their draw to win, instead of the other way around. The ace presents you with an opportunity, and you must be ready to pounce on it.

Bluff #28. Jeez, What a River! (#1)

The scenario: $8–$16 hold 'em.

The bluff: Everyone folded to Jack, who raised in late position with 7♣7♠. Only the blinds called. Three-handed, the flop came

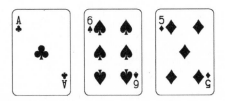

They checked to Jack, and he bet, hoping that neither player had an ace. The SB folded, but the BB called. The turn was the 4♥, giving

Jack an open-ended straight draw. The BB checked and Jack bet again. This time the BB check-raised, and Jack called without giving it much thought. He figured he was behind, but there was still a chance he could win by hitting his straight. The river was the 5♠, for a final board of

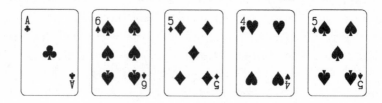

When the river card hit, the BB was visibly upset. He checked in disgust, and Jack did not think he was putting on an act, so he tried to decide what the BB had. At first, Jack thought that the BB had a straight, and was upset because the board paired, possibly giving Jack a full house. But then, Jack figured it would be awfully pessimistic of the BB to automatically assume that a straight was no good.

As he thought about it further, Jack suddenly realized that the BB almost certainly had A-4. He check-raised with two pair, and now he was upset because his second pair was counterfeited. Jack was sure that 7♣7♠ couldn't win a showdown, but he didn't want to check and give up either, so he fired in $16. The BB sighed loudly as he grabbed $16 from his stack.

"A-4 no good," Jack made a last desperate attempt to keep the BB from calling.

"Yeah, yeah," the BB grumbled as he tossed in his $16, "show me ace-king."

Jack smiled ruefully as he produced 7♣7♠.

"Hey, don't do that! I thought that five killed me!" The BB showed his A♦4♦ and took the pot, suddenly not looking so upset anymore.

Bluff #29. Jeez, What a River! (#2)

The scenario: $10–$20 hold 'em.

The bluff: Hal, a solid player, raised pre-flop from middle position. Everyone folded to the SB, who called, and Diane also called from the BB with 8♦7♦. Three-handed, the flop came

The SB checked and Diane checked, intending to fold. But, to her surprise, Hal checked as well. The turn was the 10♦, giving Diane a flush draw. The SB checked, and now Diane decided to take a stab at the pot. She figured the SB had clearly lost interest and was not a threat. She hoped that Hal had raised with something like 8-8 or 7-7 and would give it up. And then, she figured even if Hal called, she could still make a flush and win.

Alas, almost immediately after Diane's $20 went in, Hal raised. The SB folded, and Diane called for time as she tried to determine whether she should call. It seemed likely that Hal had been slow-playing a big hand on the flop, but which big hand was it? After some brief thought, Diane came to the following conclusions:

1. She didn't think Hal, as a knowledgeable player, would slow-play two pair or a set with a dangerous flop such as that. Since any ace, king, nine, or eight could give someone a straight, Hal would want to try to protect those hands with a bet. Therefore, she didn't think the ten gave Hal a full house.
2. That meant that Hal almost definitely had A-K. It was a typical raising hand, plus he would not be afraid to give a free card with that rainbow flop. Furthermore, Hal's quick raise on the turn implied that he had grown a little worried about pro-

tecting his hand. He recognized that the 10♦ was a dangerous card, and he didn't want to fool around any longer.

3. If Diane assumed that Hal had A-K, then her flush draw was live, which meant calling was the correct play.

Thus, Diane decided to call, and then either bet or attempt a check-raise if a diamond came. However, the river was the J♣, for a final board of

Diane could see Hal holding his breath, and she knew why. Assuming he had A-K, that jack was not the river card that he had been hoping to see. Hal was making a concerted effort not to betray any emotion, but it was pretty clear to Diane that he was trying to hide his disgust at the river card.

Diane decided that the pot was big enough to try for a steal, and she fired in $20. In the space of a second, Hal let out an angry growl, slammed down his $20, and started to stand up.

"I missed," Diane shrugged and showed her hand.

Hal tabled his A♣K♥. "Damn, I thought I let you get there." He sat back down and started scooping in the pot, shaking his head dejectedly all the while and mumbling under his breath.

After a few seconds of Hal's mumbling, someone else chimed in, "Hey, you won the pot, cheer up man."

"No, no, it's not that. I'm upset at myself. I should have bet the flop and ended it right away."

In retrospect, Diane wished Hal had done that too.

What Jack and Diane did right in their two bluff attempts:

1. They each identified their opponents' hands perfectly. Diane was able to do it on the turn, while Jack needed the river card to help him out.

2. Once their opponents raised, they correctly called with hands that needed to improve to win. If you include the money they stood to make on the river, they were getting the correct price to try to get lucky.
3. They could tell that their opponents were unhappy with their respective river cards.

What they did wrong: They tried to take advantage of their good reads to somehow win the pot. Sometimes you can read your opponent's hand perfectly, and there's simply no way to take advantage of that information. These were two of those situations. Unfortunately, they didn't recognize that, so they attempted bluffs that were destined to fail.

Why these bluffs *did not* work:
1. It's extremely difficult to get someone to lay down a hand that felt like a monster at some point. Even if, judging by the texture of the board, he no longer has a monster hand on the river, it really doesn't matter. When faced with just a single bet, most opponents cannot get themselves to fold a hand that they had so much confidence in before the river. No-limit is a different story, but in limit poker, you have to expect them to pay you off.
2. With their monster hands, these players helped create sizable pots. It's unrealistic to expect them to fold for one bet, especially when they've already contributed significantly to the pot. Remember this earlier point: From a strictly mathematical point of view, the only thing that should matter to anyone is the size of the pot, not how it got to its current size. But from a psychological perspective, players are more likely to stay in when the pot contains a lot of their own money.
3. Many players have an inherent desire to bemoan their bad luck. Specifically, they like to complain about how the river killed them. All too often, you'll hear someone declare, "That damn river!" or "You know I had you before that last card!"
   Players will often call, even if they think they are beaten, just so they can show that they had the best hand before the

river. Then they'll go on to complain about the bad river card, how unlucky they are, how the poker gods are conspiring against them, and anything else they can whine about. As a bluffer, you have to expect and consider that tendency when deciding whether or not to bluff on the river.

Better opportunities: Even though I said that in limit poker, it's difficult to get a player to lay down a hand that was once considered a monster, it can happen in certain situations. For instance, if someone flops a straight, but watches a fourth heart come on the river, a laydown is much more likely. Sure, he might call, but assuming that neither of you has a heart, I now like your chances of success enough to attempt a bluff.

Similarly, if a player flops a set of tens, but watches the board come J-10-6-Q-K, a bluff is worth trying. It stands a somewhat lesser chance than the one representing a flush, but the reward still justifies the risk.

I don't feel the same can be said about Jack's and Diane's attempted bluffs. If someone has top and bottom pair, and his bottom pair gets counterfeited, he is still going to want to see your hand. If a player flops the nut straight and watches as the bottom two cards pair up, he will call against a lone opponent. I've rarely seen anyone bring himself to fold to a single bet in a heads-up pot in those situations, even if he feels strongly that he is beaten. Your money would be better spent elsewhere.

CHAPTER SEVEN

The Implied Threat

We've touched on this concept in several of the previous bluffs without explicitly referring to it as such. Now let's look more closely at the implied threat, since it's important for you to fully understand it.

General premise: When attempting a bluff before the river, your opponent understands that he must not only consider your current bet, but the possibility of future bets as well. While he might consider calling your current bet, it's the implied threat of future bets that might discourage him from calling.

We said earlier that *tight players look for reasons to fold*. The implied threat is a very legitimate reason. Loose players will often ignore the implied threat, so don't expect them to care whether you plan to bet again. But against tight players, if you bet at them early, and get them thinking about the money they'll have to spend before the hand is over, they'll often talk themselves out of calling.

In limit hold 'em: The implied threat causes certain players to follow a particular Calling Pattern (refer to Chapter 2 to refresh your memory on Calling Patterns). For example, look at CP#2. As soon as they see the flop, CP#2 players decide whether or not they are going to go forward with their hand. It's not so much the small bet they'll have to call on the flop, it's the small bet *plus the two big bets on the turn and river* about which they are concerned. The implied threat of future betting is on their mind every time they make a decision on the flop. So when they call on the flop, you can assume they've already considered the money they'll have to spend later. Therefore, bluffs on the turn and river aren't likely to work against them.

The same is true of CP#3 players; they just delay it by one card. They will call the flop with a wide variety of hands, because it costs them only a small bet. But then, when deciding whether or not to call the turn, they take into account the bet on the river they will have to call as well. If you identify a player as following CP#3, and he calls on the turn, it's usually fruitless to try a bluff on the river, since he's already made up his mind to call.

This demonstrates how the implied threat is a two-way street. It can cause people to lay down the best hand before the river. However, certain players are aware of the implied threat, and if they call on the flop or the turn, they intend to pay off bets through the river. They've already taken all future action into account when calling the earlier bets. You must do your best to recognize that, and to abandon any bluff attempts once they've passed their personal point of no return.

In NLH: Let's say you are attempting a bluff on the river. Your opponent only has three things to consider:

1. The size of your bet.
2. The size of the pot.
3. What he thinks his chances are of having the best hand.

He can put those together, and decide whether or not he thinks a call is correct. In those situations, the size of your bet is important. A large bet might get your opponent to fold, whereas a smaller one he might call.

Before the river, the situation is much different. He not only has to consider the three things I mentioned above, but also a fourth factor, which might be the most important of all:

4. The size of your stacks.

Assuming you have him covered, all his money is potentially at risk on later streets. For that reason, when making a NLH bluff on the flop or turn, *the size of your stacks is more important than the size of your bet.*

It doesn't necessarily take a large bet to move someone off their hand. Let's say your opponent has $2,500. If you bet $200 on the flop, he may or may not call. If that $200 puts you all-in, he's not going to sweat it too much. On the other hand, if you bet $200 *and have another $2,000 in front of you,* it will carry a lot more weight. All other things being equal, he will call the first bet much more often than the second one. For that reason, many top NLH cash game pros keep enough money on the table to cover all of their opponents. They want their bets to always carry an implied threat. Their deep stack sends a message to their opponents: "I can put you all-in at any given time."

The implied threat doesn't work: When your opponent is on a draw. In fact, it actually works in his favor. He has no intention of calling any action on the river if he misses, so the implied threat is practically nonexistent. However, he has a hand that could easily get better, so the prospect of money being spent later in the hand is appealing. He wants his opponent to bet on the river whether he makes his hand or not. He'll either have an easy fold, or he'll get paid for hitting his draw.

That's why, when a player invests money on the flop with a drawing hand, he is often said to be getting "implied odds." He knows he will win whatever is in the pot, but also expects to get paid off by an opponent after it hits. The "implied threat" doesn't threaten the player on a draw.

The implied threat works best: When your opponent has a hand that stands very little chance of improving. A perfect example is a low pocket pair. Even when he doesn't flop a set, he might still have the best hand, but it will cost him several bets to find out. "Keeping you honest" will become expensive. The same can be said when your opponent has a high pocket pair such as kings or queens, but an ace flops. He would love to see if you have the ace you are representing, but the expense of calling you down usually outweighs his curiosity.

Bluff #30. A Simple Example of the Implied Threat

The scenario: $3–$6 hold 'em.

The bluff: A player limps in early position with 6♣6♠. You raise from middle position with A♥K♦. Everyone folds around to the limper, who calls. The flop comes

He checks, you bet, and he folds.

Degree of Difficulty: 1
Rate of Success: High
Frequency: High

The analysis: Obviously, that was not the flop that the player with 6♣6♠ wanted to see. He knows that if you raised pre-flop with any higher pocket pair, or any hand containing a queen, jack, or eight, he is in serious trouble. He also knows that even if you have a hand like A-K, A-10, or K-10, there are still a lot of ways he can lose.

However, if we looked solely at the flop bet, it would seem like he should call. There is $19 in the pot ($4 worth of blinds, $6 from each of you before the flop, and your $3 bet on the flop), and he only has to spend $3 to win $19. The odds are probably better than 6-to-1 that he has the best hand, so from that perspective, a call seems in order.

The reason he folds, and the reason this bluff works, is that it is early in the hand. He knows that he not only has to call the flop bet, but possibly the turn and the river bets as well. The implied threat of those bets discourages the flop call. What starts out as a $3 investment becomes $15 if he is forced to keep you honest to the end, and at that point he is no longer getting a 6-to-1 return on his call.

It would be different if he had only $3 left and calling would put him all-in. In that case, he almost certainly would make the call. You might still get lucky, but your goal is to take the pot without having to produce the best hand. The implied threat of further betting is the primary reason you can do it.

Bluff #31. The Hidden Short Stack

The scenario: Chris was sitting to the right of the dealer in a short-handed $15–$30 hold 'em game. He normally did not prefer that seat, since it was tough to see the opponents to his left, but John in seat one and Lori in seat two were particularly tight, and he enjoyed being able to pick on them. When they were in the blinds, and everyone folded to him, Chris liked to raise with just about anything, putting pressure on and normally getting the better of them.

The bluff: Everyone folded around to Chris on the button, and he looked down to find J♦9♦, certainly a better-than-average hand. He made his usual position raise. John deliberated for a little while, seemingly annoyed by Chris's constant button raises. John hadn't been doing well, and didn't seem thrilled about the prospect of playing his current hand, but he reluctantly threw in the chips to call. Lori folded her BB, so they took the flop heads-up, and it came

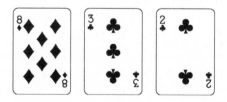

John checked, which Chris was happy to see. He knew that John was a straightforward player, and usually bet whenever he flopped something decent. Checking usually meant that he missed the flop, and Chris could steal the pot. Chris bet, fully expecting John to lay down. John groaned, but then threw his $15 in, which Chris did not expect. Still, he thought it was pretty clear that John didn't have much of a hand, and he figured he could still bluff him out on the turn.

The turn was the 2♠. John checked, and Chris continued his aggression with a $30 bet. John threw in $10 and said, "Okay, I'm all-in, I guess you have me beat," while flipping up the A♣9♠. Chris was taken aback, not realizing that John had started the hand so low on chips. Now Chris was drawing very slim. The river was the 4♥, and John won the hand with his ace-high.

Why this bluff *did not* work: Clearly Chris was correct to be picking on a player like John. Most people would consider A♣9♠ a pretty strong hand in the SB, facing a raise from the button. Instead, John almost threw it away! Obviously Chris's strategy had been working well to that point, which helped to explain why John had only $55 left in front of him when this hand began.

However, because Chris was sitting in seat ten, he couldn't see John's chips, which were on the other side of the dealer. If he had seen how short-stacked John was, he might have changed his approach. I think the pre-flop raise would still have been a good idea. John might have folded and saved his remaining $45.

But once John called the raise, he only had $25 left, and it would have been unrealistic to think he would fold, no matter what he had. Once he came that far, it was pretty likely he would see the hand through. In a typical hand, if he wanted to call Chris down, it would cost him $75 ($15 on the flop, and $30 on the turn and river). Now it would cost him only $25 to keep Chris honest. By being all-in, John removed the implied threat of further betting, which made calling an easier option.

Chris should have made sure he knew everyone's stack size. Then, when he saw John practically all-in, he would have been better off checking the flop and turn. It was highly unlikely that jack-high was the best hand, and it was almost as unlikely that John would fold, once he called the pre-flop raise.

The play that might have worked: If both players checked the flop and turn, and John checked the river, a bet by Chris could win the pot. There's still a good chance John would call, since it would seem unlikely that a board of 8♦3♣2♣2♠4♥ helped Chris's hand. However, once John saw that he had no hope of improving his A♣9♠, he might have thrown his hand away in disgust.

Keep in mind, I'm not saying this play would work the majority of the time. But with $75 in the pot, Chris would be risking $25 to win $75, and I think there's better than a 3-to-1 chance that John would lay down on the river. On the other hand, I don't think there was better than a 3-to-1 chance that John would lay down to a $15 bet on the flop and a $10 all-in on the turn, when there was still a chance he could make a pair with his A♣9♠.

In general, the presence of a short-stacked opponent should make you rethink your bluffing strategies.

Know Your Opponents' Chip Count

You should always know how many chips your opponents have for two reasons:

1. You should know if your opponent is close to going all-in, since that will make it nearly impossible to run a pure bluff on him. Instead, it becomes a good time to make value bets, since you do not have to fear the implied threat of further betting.

   In other words, if a player is going all-in, you'll always make it to showdown without having to invest any additional money. But that is the very reason that bluffing won't work—because you will end up going to showdown. And if you have nothing to show down, then obviously that won't bode well for you (as we saw with Chris's J♦9♦ in the previous example).

2. You should have a general idea of whether your opponents are winning or losing. A losing player is often easier to bluff, because he probably has taken on a defeatist attitude. He may start assuming the worst every time someone bets into him. Also, he is probably not playing his best, and thus he is more likely to make the wrong play. So when you bluff at him, he's

likely to fold when he should call, *as long as he is not close to going all-in.*

On the other hand, a player who is running well usually makes good reads. He is more likely to pick off your bluff, since he is in a frame of mind in which he can do no wrong. Even if, on any other day, he might be just another player, today he is someone you don't want to try to run over, unless the situation is just right.

Bluff #32. Martin Represents an Ace

The scenario: There were three tables left in a limit hold 'em tournament that paid eighteen places. Martin was the table chip leader with about $12,000 and was in good shape to make the final table. On the other hand, Roger was a medium stack with about $5,000. He wasn't in any immediate danger, but certainly had some work to do to get among the leaders.

The bluff: With blinds of $200–$400, Martin raised to $800 from the cutoff position with 4♣4♠. The button folded, and then Roger reraised to $1,200 from the SB. Martin knew Roger to be a tight player who rarely got out of line pre-flop. The BB folded, and Martin called. Before the flop came, Roger grabbed four $100 chips in his right hand, clearly intending to bet no matter what flopped. The flop came

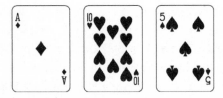

Roger fired his chips into the pot. Martin immediately raised. Roger sighed, looked back at his cards, shook his head, gestured to the flop, and basically did everything to indicate that it pained him to lay his hand down. He showed his Q♦Q♥ to his neighbor before throwing it in, and Martin made a winner out of his pocket fours.

Martin went on to finish third in the tournament, while Roger snuck into the money before being eliminated in seventeenth.

Degree of Difficulty: 6
Rate of Success: Medium
Frequency: Medium/High

Why this bluff worked:

1. Martin knew that Roger's reraise probably indicated a premium hand. But he also knew that Roger, as a tight player, could lay down a big hand if he felt he was beaten. Martin figured that, even if he didn't flop a set, he might be able to outplay Roger after the flop, and he was right.

2. Martin had a solid table image. He had been accumulating chips all day and had rarely showed down a losing hand. His table presence was strong, and it definitely helped him make this play.

3. The flop contained an ace, which is just what Martin needed to bluff successfully. There was a very good chance that Roger had a high pocket pair such as jacks, queens, or kings. It was unlikely that he had A-K or A-Q, because tight players don't usually like to three-bet with those hands. That is especially true when they are out of position, since they know that those hands hit the flop only about one-third of the time.

4. Therefore, Martin assumed that Roger had a high pocket pair, probably jacks or better. Once an ace flopped, pocket aces suddenly became the least likely possibility. Now there were only three ways he could have aces, while there were six ways he could have each of the other pairs.[18] Altogether, that meant there were eighteen ways Roger could have jacks, queens, or kings, versus the three ways he could have aces. The odds were definitely in Martin's favor.

---

18. The A♦ came on the flop, so Roger could have either had A♣A♥, A♣A♠, or A♥A♠. With each of the other pairs, all four suits were still available, so they could be combined into six different two-card combinations.

5. All it took for Martin was one raise on the flop to find out. If Roger had raised him back, then Martin could have safely assumed that Roger either flopped a set or had a hand such as A-K. He could have laid down his pocket fours, and he would have spent only $800 after the flop in his failed bluff attempt, a small portion of his sizable stack. Instead, Roger visibly showed his displeasure at being raised, and Martin knew he had him.

6. Roger had to believe that once Martin raised, he was up against a pair of aces. When you think about it, what else could Roger put him on? He had to imagine that with his queens, he could realistically beat only a bluff. Maybe he would have spent $400 to see Martin's hand, but the implied threat of further betting was a tremendous deterrent. He would have had to spend $400 to call the raise, plus another $800 on both the turn and river, just in the hopes that Martin was bluffing. He didn't want to risk another $2,000, just to see the ace that he was almost sure Martin had.

7. Roger had to consider how close he was to being in the money. If he had called Martin down and lost, he would have become a short stack, and suddenly would have faced the possibility of being out of the money. Martin effectively used not only the size of his own stack, but the size of Roger's as well, when he put him to the test with a raise.

When an Ace Flops After a Pre-flop Reraise

The concepts that Martin employed can be used in many similar situations. Let's say you raise pre-flop, a tight player reraises out of the blinds, and you call. Then the flop comes ace-high, and you don't have an ace. It is mandatory to put pressure on your opponent at least once, just to test him out. If he checks, bet. If he bets, raise. If you have accurately identified him as a tight player, then he is likely to have reraised pre-flop with a big pocket pair rather than just big cards. And he is equally likely to lay it down in the face of aggression once an ace flops.

Even if that player calls your raise on the flop, I would fire one more time on the turn. Many players often call on the flop just to save face, to make it seem like they are not pushovers and aren't going to fold every time someone raises. It's more of a reaction than anything else. Once they face a bigger bet on the turn, they are more likely to stop to think about their situation, and then surrender their hand.

Also, some players call your raise on the flop just to see if you were trying to get a free card. They are hoping that when they check the turn, you'll check behind them, in which case they will definitely stay in for showdown. You can't get timid just because he bet on the flop and then called your raise. You have to give him at least one more chance to throw his hand away.

However, if your opponent does call on the turn, I typically wouldn't bother to bet again. In the situation I described, most players do not spend the money to call a big bet on the turn unless they have already made up their mind to call on the river as well. After all, if they have a big pocket pair such as K-K or Q-Q, they have only two outs to improve. So they are not calling on the turn in the hopes of improving their hand. They're calling because they've decided there is a good enough chance that they have the best hand. For that reason, my general advice would be to save your money on the river rather than try to bluff for a third time.

A word of caution: You must choose your opponent carefully. Not only do you want someone who is tight; you should also choose a player who does not consistently whine about bad beats or look for sympathy from the other players.

You might wonder, what the heck does that have to do with anything? I mention it because there is a certain breed of player that will call you down just so they can see your hand. They figure they are beaten, but they expect you to show ace-rag. Then they can voluntarily show their pocket kings to everyone and whine about what a bad beat they just took. In some cases, they are looking to berate you for playing ace-rag for three bets. They are being silly, and are usually wasting their money, but still it happens. As a bluffer, it's your responsibility to be aware of it, and to avoid that situation whenever possible.

Bluff #33. Bare Ace Play (#2)

The scenario: NLH with $2–$5 blinds. Wayne and Bill were regulars in the game, had logged plenty of hours with each other, and knew each other's tendencies fairly well. At the start of this hand they both had about $600.

The bluff: The UTG player limped, and Wayne called from middle position with A♣J♦. The button called, the SB limped, and Bill checked his option from the BB. Five-handed, the flop came

The SB checked, and Bill came out with a pot-sized bet ($25). The UTG player called, and Wayne called with his nut flush draw and (possibly meaningless) gutshot straight draw. The button and SB folded, so three players remained. The turn was the 8♥, and Bill bet $50. The UTG player folded, and Wayne asked for time. He fiddled with his chips for a bit, then said "$200 straight" (i.e., he raised $150).

Bill looked over at Wayne and asked, "You trying to sucker me in, calling for time?" He smiled, flashed the Q♥ at Wayne, and laid his hand down. Wayne took down the $150 pot with nothing but ace-high and a nice draw.

Degree of Difficulty: 5
Rate of Success: Medium/High
Frequency: Medium

The comparison: There is an obvious difference between the Bare Ace Play in Omaha, which we examined last chapter, and hold 'em. In Omaha, if you don't have the flush with three clubs on board, a fourth one won't help, since you still need two in your hand. You are

ff, and if your opponent has a flush, you

g a better one. On the other hand, in hold

lls your bluff on the turn, you can still get

ting a fourth club to make the nut flush.

u might think this play is better suited for

But in fact the opposite is true. Under the

e Bare Ace Play can be done successfully in

are three reasons for its greater success in

ly, it's much easier to be dealt the A♣ with an-
Omaha than in hold 'em. Most players know
will be much more inclined to believe that you
have ... flush in Omaha. By contrast, it's a lot harder to
convince a hold 'em opponent that you started with the A-x of
clubs and were lucky enough to have three clubs come on
board.

2. Omaha is a game of the nuts, and many opponents are unwill-
ing to give significant action without them. Even with the
second-nut flush, many Omaha players know better than to
commit themselves. On the other hand, hold 'em opponents
are a lot more likely to give you action with the second nuts.
They know there's a chance you have the nut hand, but very
often they will pay to see it.

In our example, if Bill had a king-high flush, there's a decent chance he would have paid Wayne off. However, if the
Q♣10♣4♣ were an Omaha flop, and Bill bet the king-high
flush and got raised, chances are much better that he would
have laid his hand down.

3. Let's say your opponent gets brave and reraises all-in. Somehow he deduced you were bluffing, and now he wants to put
you to the test. In either game, you are obviously not happy
that he played back at you, but at least in Omaha, you have no
qualms about laying your hand down. You are obviously
beaten, and you have no chance of making the best hand. So
you simply give your opponent credit for making a good play,
and you move on.

In hold 'em, you lose a greater amount of equity when your opponent reraises, since you lose your chance to make the best hand. In our example, let's say Bill had pushed all-in for his remaining chips. Wayne couldn't call, because he'd have to put $350 more into a pot that contained about $900, and those are bad odds for him to draw to his flush (assuming he thinks that is the only way he can win, which would be a reasonable assumption). So Wayne would correctly fold, but then he'd not only lose the money he put into the pot, he'd also lose his chance of making the nut flush.

That is one reason why you must choose your bluff victims carefully. You don't want someone who will suddenly get brave on you and reraise without the nuts. *If he is the type of player who is willing to risk his entire stack without the nuts, you shouldn't be bluffing him anyway.* The whole premise of this play is that you know your opponent can't possibly have the nut flush, so you are trying to convince him that *you* have it. Maybe he'll believe you, and maybe he won't, but at the very least, you should be confident that he won't play back at you. If that confidence isn't there, then save this play for another time.

Now let's return to the hand in question. Besides having the A♣, and being able to make the Bare Ace Play, there are two other key reasons why Wayne's raise worked:

1. On the turn, Bill bet only $50 into a $100 pot. Wayne knew that Bill would usually bet more with a strong hand to try to protect it, especially with such a dangerous board. Underbetting the pot was typically a sign that Bill either did not have confidence in his hand, or else he had the nuts and was trying to milk his opponents by betting moderately.

    This is where having the A♣ was valuable information for Wayne. He knew Bill couldn't have the nuts without the A♣, so his $50 bet probably signaled a lack of confidence. Therefore, he correctly decided that a raise could take Bill off of his hand, and in fact it did so with relative ease.

2. Bill knew that it wasn't just a matter of calling the $150 raise. If it was, he might have paid Wayne off. Instead, he was aware that they each had another $400 in their stacks, and if he decided to call the $150, he might have to call another $400 as well. That implied threat made Bill decide he had gone far enough. He had already spent $80 on his pair of queens; he wasn't going to spend another $150, and he certainly had no desire to spend another $400 on top of that, just to see Wayne's hand. This hand illustrates perfectly how the implied threat is a very powerful bluffing tool.

CHAPTER EIGHT

Online Bluffs

Besides giving you some actual examples of online bluffs, this chapter will discuss several online tells, and the adjustments you must make to exploit them. Many players claim that the drawback to online poker is that you can't spot any tells, but they are wrong. The truth is that online play allows you to pick up certain types of information that you couldn't get in a B&M cardroom. Keep in mind, though, that knowledge of these tells by itself won't win you the money. It's your responsibility to observe your opponents and to track their tendencies.

Bluff #34. Call & Push (Early Stages)

The scenario: It was the third limit of an online NLH SNG. Everyone had started with $1,000, but after winning a couple of decent pots, Mark was the chip leader with about $2,200. Meanwhile, Tony, sitting two seats to his right, was slowly closing in on him. Tony had built his stack up to $1,600 with constant aggression. Since no one was standing up to him, he was raising every chance he got. Since Mark figured that Tony was getting out of line fairly often, he was ready to take a stand against him.

The bluff: With blinds of $25–$50, everyone folded to Tony on the button. He raised to $600. The SB folded, and Mark called from the BB. The flop came J♥7♣4♥, and Mark immediately moved all-in. Tony let the clock drip down to the last few seconds, but then let his hand go. Mark extended his chip lead and managed to win the SNG a short time later, while Tony fizzled out in fifth.

Degree of Difficulty: 4
Rate of Success: Medium
Frequency: Low/Medium

The analysis: I am hesitant to tell you Mark's hand, because I don't want to take the focus away from the bluff, but just so you know, he had 9-8 offsuit. Obviously, he was not calling $600 based on the strength of his cards. He was actually running a textbook bluff, and it began with the assumption that Tony did not have a premium hand.

That seemed like a pretty safe conclusion. If he had a big pair, or an A-K or A-Q type of hand, would he really want to put in $600 to try to win $75 worth of blinds? No, he would make a more reasonable raise, and hope to get a call from a worse hand. So right away, Mark suspected that Tony was getting out of line with his oversized raise.

Then it became a matter of how best to take advantage of that knowledge. Mark could have pushed all-in before the flop, but it would not have been his best play. Since Tony had already put $600 in, he could easily have justified putting in his other $1,000, even with a mediocre hand. Then Mark would have needed to make the best hand to win, and that's not what he was looking to do.

The premise behind Mark's bluff: Since Tony did not have a premium hand, he was looking for help on the flop. *But chances were, the flop wouldn't help him.* And once Tony saw an unfavorable flop, he was likely to lay down rather than call all-in.

That's why Mark had planned to go all-in on the flop no matter what came. He knew he stood a better chance of success by letting Tony see the flop and then putting him all-in, playing the percentages that the flop did not help him. He did not want to put Tony to the test pre-flop, because at that point Tony still had hopes of hitting a favorable flop, no matter how bad his hand was.

Consider the wide array of hands with which Tony might have made that $600 raise. He really could have had any two cards![19]

---

19. Which is why it is possible, though unlikely, that Mark was bluffing with the best hand.

However, there are a lot of hands with which he might have called for his other $1,000 pre-flop, even if he thought he was behind, just to try to get lucky. Hands like K-10, K-9, Q-10, A-2 all look pretty meager in the face of an all-in reraise, but he'd still probably call. However, it would be nearly impossible to call all-in with any of those hands after seeing an unfavorable flop.

Mark took a calculated risk, but I think the amount of money up for grabs made it worthwhile. If Tony had raised to $300 (still an oversized raise), there still would have been a good chance that he didn't have a premium hand. But calling his bet and then putting him in for another $1,300 after the flop would not have been the percentage play for Mark. Risking $1,600 to win $300 just would not have been worth it. But to win $600, I think the reward justified Mark's risk.

Other key points:
1. This is one of the few bluffs that doesn't work unless you're out of position. Obviously, if Tony had acted first on the flop, he would have likely moved all-in, killing the possibility of bluffing him out. Typically, this play is made from either the SB or BB.
2. Don't make this play against someone who has put half or more of his stack in pre-flop. Because he is essentially pot-committed, he will probably call even if the flop was no help. On the other hand, you still want him to have bet a large enough portion of his stack to make it worth trying to steal. The perfect victim is someone using about one-third of his stack to make an oversized raise, which is very close to what Tony did.

Bluff #35. Call & Push (Late Stages)

The scenario: You are at the sixth limit of an online NLH SNG. You are short-stacked with $800 and are forced to post the $200 BB.

The bluff: A player raises to $400 from late position. You have a semistrong hand, such as K-Q or K-J. Since you are short-stacked, and you have what you think might be the best hand, you are prepared to go all-in. But, rather than do it pre-flop, you simply call the raise, and *then* push all-in on the flop, no matter what comes.

> **Degree of Difficulty:** 3
> **Rate of Success:** Low/Medium (But that rating refers only to how often your opponent will fold on the flop. The chances of your opponent folding, combined with the chance that you produce the best hand, would be Medium/High.)
> **Frequency:** Very High

The analysis: In this situation the typical player instinctively looks down, sees a playable hand, and decides to push his short stack all-in before the flop. The problem is, his opponent will almost certainly call the extra $400, and now he has to produce the best hand to win. He may or may not end up with the best hand, but with the play I described, he now has an added way of winning. If his opponent misses the flop, he might decide to fold rather than spend another $400.

In similar situations, if you are:

1. short-stacked;
2. out of position;
3. holding a semistrong hand (*not* a premium hand), and are prepared to go the distance with it;

then it makes sense just to call pre-flop and then push in on the flop.

Two key differences between this play and the first Call & Push:
1. In Bluff #34, an argument could be made for reraising before the flop, because you had enough chips to possibly make your opponent fold. In this one, there is no such argument. If you reraise pre-flop, and it costs him only $400 more to call, he isn't going anywhere. That's why waiting until the flop to push all-in is clearly the superior play.

Before the flop he would have to call $400 to win what would be a $1,700 pot, and he will almost definitely do so with any two cards. If instead of a semistrong hand you had a premium hand, then you *would* want to get all the money in pre-flop. You could expect him to call, which is fine by you, since you'd have a hand that would stand an excellent chance of winning a showdown. As such, you'd rather try to get the full $800 out of him, instead of attempting to make him lay down on the flop after spending only $400.

2. In Bluff #34, any two cards will do, since it is less likely that your opponent will call after seeing an unfavorable flop. You are not looking to go to a showdown. However, in this example, you should make the play only with cards that you were prepared to play anyway. Your opponent will call your all-in bet on the flop most of the time. He will fold some-times, though, which is much better than reraising before the flop, when he will almost never fold.

I'm hesitant to call this a bluff because you often have the best hand. But sometimes you get a slightly better hand to fold, and that is when this play pays off big-time. Say you have Q♦J♦ and the flop comes 9♣7♣5♣ and your opponent has K♥3♠. You will probably win with a $400 flop bet, and that is a thing of beauty. He probably would have called an extra $400 pre-flop with K♥3♠, but won't after seeing such an unfavorable flop. The point of this play is to score that occasional coup. Instead of being eliminated by losing to a king-high, you are alive in the SNG with an improved stack.

One might argue that, by causing your opponent to lay down on the flop, you win only $400 off of him instead of $800, and that works against you when you have the best hand. That is true, but tournaments are more about survival. Without a premium hand, you would rather win his $400 without a showdown than try to win $800 by going to showdown. Nothing says that the turn and river cards would be safe. In a cash game, maybe you would take that chance. In a tournament, you should be happy simply to win the pot and survive.

Although I used SNG examples for these two plays, they can certainly be done in multi-table tournaments too, and in B&M tournaments as well as online. But when doing this play in a B&M tournament, make sure that you are not making it obvious. In other words, you don't want your opponent to know that you were planning on moving all-in on the flop no matter what came. Try to sell it. Bet with authority. Make him believe the flop hit you. Remember, the success rate of these plays is not just a factor of the plays themselves. Your execution of them is usually just as important.

Bluff #36. Jerome Bluffs a Multichip Bettor

The scenario: An online NLH game with $2.50–$5 blinds. Both players involved had stacks of nearly $400.

The bluff: Phil raised to $15 pre-flop from middle position. Everyone folded around to Jerome in the BB, who called with J♣10♣. Heads-up, the flop came

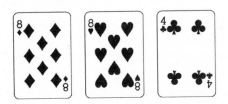

Jerome checked, with the intention of folding. However, when Phil came out with a $48 bet, Jerome changed his mind and check-raised to $120. Phil laid his hand down, and Jerome stole the pot with his jack-high.

Degree of Difficulty: 4
Rate of Success & Frequency: Both dependent on whether or not your opponent is giving off a reliable tell. I will explain below.

The analysis: When playing online NLH, the site usually provides a sliding scale that you drag with your mouse to vary the size of your bet. Typically the scale provides you with round numbers. For example, if you are playing with $5–$10 blinds, the scale might offer you the option to bet in multiples of $10, such that you can bet $10, $20, $30, and so forth. Of course, you can bet any exact amount you wish, but in those cases, the scale won't work. Instead, you need to type in the exact amount you wish to bet. Therefore, when you see a bet that is not a round number, you know that the player had to type in that amount.

Poker players are lazy by nature. If someone went to the trouble to type in the exact amount he wanted to bet, rather than just choose one of the round numbers that the sliding scale provided, then he must have had a reason for it. Therefore, when you see a bet of $9 instead of $10, or $24 instead of $25, you should take notice. Phil's $48 bet was clearly a typed-in number. The question Jerome had to ask himself was, "Why would Phil bother?"

The most common reason for betting in that manner: Intimidation. A $24 bet requires four $5 chips and four $1 chips. On the computer screen it appears as an eight-chip bet, which creates a nice-sized stack, as opposed to the single chip that would appear if someone were betting $25. The player betting $24 is hoping that his opponent will see a large-stack bet and lean toward folding. When players take this concept to the extreme, you'll see $49 bets instead of $50, and $99 rather than $100. Once, I even saw someone go through the trouble of betting $49.75, which put three $.25 chips on top of the pile to make it even bigger!

For the most part, this pattern is a fairly reliable tell. If I'm facing an opponent I've never seen before, and he bets $99, my first instinct is that his hand cannot stand a raise. That was Jerome's logic when he check-raised Phil. He was fairly sure that the $48 bet signaled weakness, because not only was it a typed-in bet, it was an overbet into what was approximately a $33 pot. He didn't think Phil could call a raise, but even if he called, Jerome thought he could win the pot with continued aggression on the turn. Online opponents who bet a big stack generally want you out of the pot, so obviously your job is to disappoint them.

Take caution against the single-chip bet: The flip side of this tell is that players who want a call will often take care to bet in round numbers. Therefore, you should tend to avoid bluffing a player who bets $5 or $25 at you. In a tournament, a $1,000 bet is particularly worrisome. It looks so small, since it is only one chip, but don't be fooled. Typically, your opponent wants a call, and would probably welcome a raise. Save your bluffs for another time.

Keep your own bets normal: You might wonder why I don't suggest betting the big stack for you. After all, it is a form of bluffing, right? The truth is that it works only against your least sophisticated competition. Only novice players look at a big stack and go, "Wow, he's betting a ton!" without looking to see how much the actual bet is. Many players would see through you in a second. So my advice is to not get involved in the silliness of betting $24 or $48, even though it's amazing how many players do.

Take notes: Most online sites make it easy to take notes on your opponents, so take advantage of that feature. Note the players that bet strange amounts, such as $24 or $48, and if you get to see their hand, make a note of whether or not it was strong.

Even though most players bet a big stack when they are weak, some do it when they have a big hand. They want to give off a reverse tell (i.e., appearing strong when they really *are* strong), so you want to try to identify who's who as soon as possible. Whatever pattern a player has, he is likely to stick to it. If you see a player bet $24 with a weak hand, he is likely to do it again, and you should be on the lookout for it. On the other hand, if a player bets an uneven amount and shows down a monster, then you should note that betting a big stack is not an indicator of weakness for him. Then, if he bets the big stack again, you will take caution.

Auto-Betting When Bluffing

Most online sites offer you the option to click on a box or button that lets you select your play before the action reaches you. By checking a given box ahead of time, you can automatically fold, check, call, raise, and so forth once it is your turn to act. The upside is that it speeds up the game. The downside is that, when you fall into the trap of habitually using those boxes, you usually are not considering all the possible plays at your disposal. As a general rule, I advise against using these "in turn" options (more on that to follow). However, in certain, limited instances, using the "bet in turn" button can make sense.

When to "bet in turn": Let's say you're playing some form of limit poker online, either a cash game or tournament. You have already made up your mind that, if everyone in front of you checks, you're going to attempt a bluff. You should consider hitting the "bet in turn" button so that your bet will appear instantaneously once it is your turn to act. It will carry a certain degree of intimidation, since it shows clear decisiveness on your part. Plus, observant opponents will notice that you clicked "bet in turn," and they will fear that you did so because you had a hand you were absolutely sure was worth betting.

A few things to note:
1. If your opponents are not paying attention to the manner in which you bet, then your auto-bet won't matter. It won't help, but it certainly won't hurt. However, it will achieve its desired effect against players who notice it even the slightest bit. Even if they don't identify it as an auto-bet, they register subconsciously that your bet was made quickly, and the typical opponent equates that to a bet made with confidence.
2. This tactic will work only in limit games. For NL or PL, you aren't allowed to "bet in turn," because you have to specify the amount you are betting.
3. Don't worry if someone bets in front of you. Your "bet in turn" box will automatically be unchecked, and you will be allowed to act on your hand as you would normally.

4. However, make sure you do not click the "bet/raise in turn" button. It would be a disaster if there were a bet and raise in front of you, and now you're forced to put in three bets with nothing! Presumably, you want to bluff only if everyone shows weakness. So make sure you click the correct button— "bet in turn"—so that you can simply fold if someone bets in front of you.

5. Keep in mind that your opponents won't know which of those two buttons you clicked. If they are observant, they noticed that your bet appeared instantly, so they know you did something "in turn." But for all they know, you had clicked "bet/raise in turn," meaning that your hand was so strong that you had planned on raising no matter who bet. They might suspect one or the other, but there's no way they can know for sure.

6. You should sometimes, but not always, auto-bet with a strong hand. Otherwise, observant opponents might notice that you are auto-betting only with weak hands, since you are betting in normal fashion with your strong ones. Thus, when they see you auto-bet, they might start calling you down with marginal hands, or they might even play back at you with nothing. If you're going to use the auto-bet button, mix up your use of it a little bit, so that you can maintain a degree of unpredictability.

Bluffing Against Auto-Bettors

Obviously, this section is the flip side of the previous one. Since many players auto-bet, you must know how to respond to it.

First and foremost: You should recognize it. When chips appear in front of a player almost instantly, then he probably pressed the auto-bet button. It's your job to pay attention to the action, and to note when that has happened. Many online players ignore their game until the action reaches them, figuring they can simply look at the screen and see what actions have taken place in front of them. Do not fall into that trap of laziness and lack of observation. Once you start, it's a tough habit to break, and along the way you will miss valuable information.

So I will assume that you are being observant and noticing when your opponents have or have not pressed the "bet in turn" button. Let's say you're involved in a heads-up or three-way pot. As first to act after the flop, you check a weak hand. Now the button auto-bets, and the action is back to you. What should you do? You can't continually fold in that situation, because it's unlikely that he always has a hand, but when should you play back at him?

Some patterns are no help: Certain players auto-bet with any hand they plan to bet, whether it is strong or weak. If you are against such a player, or if this is your first encounter with a particular opponent, then you should ignore the manner in which he bet. In those cases, his auto-bet gives you no information. It's not a tell, and it doesn't carry any special meaning. Simply play your hand based on its strength, and if you think a bluff is possible for other reasons, then that is your decision.

What you are looking for: An opponent who usually bets in a normal fashion, but occasionally shows up with an auto-bet, especially when he is last to act. If he typically auto-bets only from late position, then chances are he does it when he does not want to get called. In short, he follows my suggestion of auto-betting when bluffing, but does not mix up his strategy enough to disguise it.

How to counter him: Against such a player, you should look to make the occasional check-raise bluff. You don't want to overdo it, but you also can't let him keep running you over. Check-raise, and then if he calls, follow up with bets on the turn and river if necessary. If you've spotted a reliable tell, then you should win the pot more than half the time, which makes the play worthwhile. Even when you don't win, you will at least get to see his hand. From that information, you'll be able to determine whether or not you actually picked up a reliable online tell from that opponent, and you'll be better prepared for future confrontations.

The opposite of the auto-bettor: Just as you should note the players who auto-bet, you should also be aware of the players that take a long time to act. If the same player is always taking a long time, then don't read into it. Chances are he simply has a slow Internet connection, or else he is careful to always take the same amount of time to act on each hand. There is no information to be gained there.

However, when an opponent who normally plays fast suddenly takes a long time to act, and then comes out with a bet or a raise, you should beware! It's always possible that he took a long time for a reason completely unrelated to the hand being played, but if he did it on purpose, he's trying to make you think he had a tough decision. He wants to appear weak and indecisive. In fact, he probably has a monster. Don't call unless you have a strong hand, and definitely don't play back at him. Pick a different time to attempt a bluff.

Similarly, if a player consistently plays "in turn," such that his bets or raises always appear instantaneously, it should catch your attention when that same player does not click the "in turn" button in a given hand. It involves the exact same concept as in the previous paragraph, and it is just as reliable a tell. It's just a little tougher to spot. You are looking for the times that his bet takes a couple of seconds to show up, rather than appearing immediately.

A player who constantly auto-bets does so because he wants to continually appear confident. When he doesn't click the auto-bet button, and takes slightly longer to make his action, he wants to somehow make you think that he had a tougher decision this time around. Almost always, it is a ruse. His failure to auto-bet signals a strong hand. You should proceed with caution and again save your bluffs for another time.

Bluffing Against Auto-Folders

By far, the "check/fold in turn" button is the option used most often (for simplicity purposes I will call it the auto-fold button). Before the flop most online players habitually use it, especially those that play in multiple games. They see a hand, immediately decide they're not going to play it, and auto-fold. Some of them give careful thought to their decision. They analyze the situation, looking at all of the factors at work, before concluding that their hand is unplayable.

However, most auto-folders are not that thorough. They simply look at their cards, decide that they don't have a good hand, and click auto-fold without taking into account their position, opponents, stack size, table image, and anything else that should be influencing their decision. Furthermore, they usually pay little or no attention to the hand once they've folded. They only regain interest when the next hand arrives.

What does this mean for you? Those players are tighter than average, and thus are easier to bluff than usual. Don't suddenly become a wild and crazy bluffer just because a player has shown himself to be an auto-folder. But if you have a close decision about whether or not to bluff, it should swing you toward bluffing.

Where do you want them? Having an auto-folder on your right doesn't help you any. Since they fold marginal hands more than the typical player, they are more predictable. Earlier, we discussed why we want predictable players on your left. Whenever it's in your power, get them behind you, where you can best capitalize on their predictability.

How can you take advantage of them? Certain simple plays that we discussed in Chapter 3, such as raising from the button with any two cards, should be done with greater frequency once you have an auto-folder either one or two seats to your left. If both players to your left are auto-folders, then you should stay glued to your current seat for as long as they remain there. You will find plenty of chances to attack them.

You obviously can't know ahead of time whether they have clicked auto-fold. However, if they do it regularly, then you should play the percentages, which suggest that they will deem their cards to be unplayable more than half the time. When they are in the blinds, they will auto-fold often enough to make raising from the button with anything a consistently profitable play. Plus, it is a much safer play than raising against random opponents, who might get tricky and play back at you with subpar starting hands. Most auto-folders don't even consider such possibilities. Their play is based strictly on starting hand value. Thus, if an auto-folder reraises you, you can be pretty confident that his hand merits a reraise, and you can play the remainder of the hand accordingly.

You also now have an automatic raising situation when everyone folds to you in the SB, and the BB is an auto-folder. He has to auto-fold only half the time for your raise to show an immediate profit, and that doesn't even take into account the times that he calls but you win the pot anyway. And since auto-folders typically find more than half of their hands to be unplayable, you'll come out way ahead.

Let's say you're in the cutoff seat. Having an auto-folder to your left doesn't mean you'll automatically raise when everyone folds to you. However, you'll know that there's a better-than-normal chance that you will "buy the button," and you can take that into consideration when deciding whether or not to attack the blinds.

In all of these situations, if you are playing NLH, you don't need to do anything more than double the blinds. If your opponent has clicked auto-fold, any raise will get him out, no matter how small. Therefore, even if your typical pre-flop raise would be greater, you should only double the BB when you are attacking auto-folders. If they've already clicked auto-fold, they won't observe the size of your raise anyway.

Auto-folders are just as prevalent in stud, if not more so. It's amazing how many times the low card starts the action, and in the blink of an eye everyone auto-folds, and the low card wins the antes. At least one of them made a mistake by folding, and it was usually the player to the right of the low card. We've already said that if the low card is to your immediate left, and everyone to your right folds, you should raise with anything (see Bluff #2). Obviously, he wasn't in class that day.

That's fine by you. Be prepared to take advantage of him. Let's say you have an auto-folder to your immediate left. If the low card is two seats to your left, and everyone in front of you folds, then raise with anything. There's a good enough chance that the player to your left clicked auto-fold, and it will just be you against the low card, which we've said is an automatic raising situation.

In summary: Attacking auto-folders has been one of the best-kept secrets in online poker (until now, of course). I've had tremendous success doing so, especially against players who insist on playing three or four games. The vast majority of them can't possibly hope to keep up with the action at every table, and they remain surprisingly oblivious to my constant attacks.

If you use the "find player" or "search for player" option that most sites have in their lobby, you can know for sure whether the players to your left are in multiple games. If they are, and they're auto-folders, then as far as I'm concerned, it's open season on them. Eventually, they might catch on that they aren't getting as many free plays in the BB as they should, or that the same player to the right keeps raising them. But I've found that the typical multigame player takes a while to make that realization. Until he does, you can have a good time taking advantage of his tightness, his lack of observation, and his habitual use of the auto-fold button.

CHAPTER NINE

Unusual Bluffs

These are not plays you see every day. In fact, you might never find an opportunity to duplicate the exact same actions that these bluffers took. But they should at least get you thinking about the creative ways to execute certain bluffs.

Bluff #37. Colin Gives a Tip in Advance

The scenario: A very loose $6–$12 hold 'em game. The players were easygoing and relaxed, and many of them typically followed CP#4: They would call all the way to the river, often with little or no hope of winning. But if they did not make at least a semistrong hand, they would fold. Surprisingly, they made very few loose river calls. Even though they played long-shot draws and made many loose calls on the flop and turn, they didn't necessarily call on the river with any pair. In general, it was a great game for setting up bluffs against players on a draw, and then betting on the river if it seemed as though they missed.

The bluff: Four players called pre-flop. Colin called from the button with 10♣8♣. Both blinds were in, so seven players saw the flop, which came

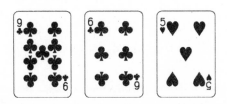

The SB checked, and the BB bet. One player called, then another raised. The action was folded around to Colin, who decided to three-bet

with his straight-flush draw. Every remaining player called the three
bets, so five of them were in for the turn, which was the J♥. Everyone
checked to Colin, and he had a decision to make.

None of his opponents seemed happy with their hand. No one
gave the impression that they had wanted a jack, and nobody seemed
prepared to check-raise. Colin now had an open-ended straight draw
to go along with his flush draw, so he decided to fire again. Only the
SB folded; everyone else called.

The last player to call was the one who had originally raised on
the flop. He implored Johnny, the dealer, to give him the card he
needed. He didn't say what that card was; he just asked for Johnny to
put it out there.

Colin decided to play along. He was friendly with Johnny, so before Johnny had a chance to deal the river card, Colin said, "Hey
Johnny, whatever all these guys need, don't give it to them."

"What would you like?" asked Johnny. "The deuce of spades?"

"That would be great," said Colin.

The river card was the 2♦, for a final board of

"Close enough?" asked Johnny.

Of course, that wasn't the card that Colin had been hoping for,
but he decided to continue the charade as best he could. Before the
first player could even act on his hand, Colin threw three $2 chips to
Johnny!

"Close enough Johnny. Win or lose, those are yours."

"Thanks Colin," said Johnny as he tapped the chips on the edge
of his tray to indicate a tip.

In rapid succession, everyone checked to Colin, and he bet $12.
The next player, the BB, was the only one who hesitated at all. He
looked at Colin, looked back at his cards, nodded, and tossed them
in. The next two players quickly folded, clearly having missed their

straight or flush draws. Colin took down a $180 pot with nothing but a ten-high, a $12 river bet, and a $6 tip for Johnny.

> **Degree of Difficulty:** 7
> **Rate of Success:** Medium (But *highly* dependent on the river card. Medium assumes a random river card. With a favorable river such as the 2♦, the rate is very high, while with a bad one it is very low.)
> **Frequency:** Low

Why this bluff worked:

1. As described earlier, the playing style of Colin's opponents made this play feasible. They weren't just staying in with primary draws (i.e., ace-high flush draws and open-ended straight draws). They were often calling multiple bets with only gutshot straight draws and backdoor flush draws. So with two flush draws and a lot of straight possibilities on the turn, chances were good that his opponents were still drawing. When you also consider that none of them bet or check-raised on the turn, it was clear that nobody had a strong made hand.

2. Having the button was extremely important. Everyone had to act in front of Colin, giving him control over the proceedings. If he had players acting behind him on the flop or turn, he could never have made this bluff with the same degree of confidence.

3. When everyone checked to Colin on the turn, he correctly bet. That created the opportunity to bluff on the river. If he had decided to take the free card on the turn, he could never have successfully bluffed at the end. The BB, who seemed to have a pair of nines or some other weak made hand, would have probably smelled a rat and called.

4. Colin reacted perfectly when the 2♦ came on the river. He acted like it was the perfect card, when in fact it was a total dud. He threw Johnny $6, which was a nice-sized tip, but if you chalk it up as an investment, it's nothing. If $6 helps you, in even the slightest way, to win a $180 pot, you should gladly part with it every time.

5. Out of Colin's three opponents on the river, he knew that the last player did not pose a threat. He's the one that asked Johnny to "give him the card he needed." Since the 2♦ clearly was not that card, Colin knew he wasn't calling.

6. He also knew that the player in the middle was probably not calling. Since that player had never taken an aggressive action, but instead had called bets and raises the entire way, he was probably on a draw too. If so, there was no way the river card helped him either.

7. The BB—the first player to act after Colin's river bet—was the only opponent Colin had to truly worry about. Since he had bet on the flop, he seemed the most likely player to have a pair. The $6 thrown to Johnny was done for the BB's benefit more than anyone else's. Colin knew that if he could get past him, the other two players were not as dangerous.

8. Understandably, Colin's opponents figured he wouldn't throw $6 to the dealer unless he was supremely confident he had a winner. When the BB considered his final action, there's no doubt that Colin's premature tip helped push him toward folding. He lost confidence that he could win with a small pair, plus, subconsciously, he probably wasn't too upset to see Colin take the pot.

9. What do I mean by that? I'm saying that, to some extent, the players probably felt a degree of kindness toward Colin. They saw him as a player who was willing to give the dealer a generous tip, and told him to keep it, "win or lose." On some level, they didn't want to be seen as the "bad guy," the one who beat the player that was so nice to the dealer. Keep in mind that these were not cutthroat opponents. They were playing loosely, enjoying themselves, and did not seem overly concerned about the money involved. The whole time he was playing, Colin acted like he was one of them, which is what you are supposed to do. They fully believed that he was just a generous tipper who happened to have a big hand. Little did they know that in his one quick-thinking act of generosity, Colin was being more of a cutthroat player than they ever would have imagined.

Bluff #38. Tipping with the Nuts

Some background: In one of Tom's first forays into a cardroom, he became amused by a little habit of an opponent named Jake. Whenever Jake bet on the river with the nuts and got called, he would throw the dealer a tip before revealing his cards. Once the dealer acknowledged the tip with a "thank you" or by tapping the chip against his tray, Jake would flip over the nuts.

Tom began to do that himself. Some of his opponents found it amusing, while some were mildly annoyed, but he continued to do it for at least a year. It got to the point where all the regular players in his game knew what it meant when Tom tipped before showing his cards. Some of them would even say, "I hope you're not getting ready to throw in a tip," before they called. Others even returned the favor by doing the same thing when Tom called on the river, and they had the nuts! It became a good-natured back-and-forth jibe, but it was something the other players always associated with Tom.

The scenario: Tom's usual $3–$6 hold 'em game.

The bluff: Joey, one of the regulars, limped in from UTG. Tom then raised from middle position with A♣K♠. Everyone folded around to the blinds. They called, as did Joey. Four-handed, the flop came

Everyone checked to Tom, who bet. The SB folded, while the BB and Joey both called. The turn was the 3♥, and again they checked to Tom. He decided that neither player seemed particularly happy with their hand, so he fired again. This time the BB folded, and only Joey called. The river was the 9♣, for a final board of

Joey checked a third time. Tom didn't think he could win a showdown, so he fired in a bet. Just as Joey reached for his chips, seemingly ready to call, Tom threw a chip to the dealer.

"What was that?" asked Joey.

"Oh, I thought you said call."

"No, I hadn't done anything yet."

"Sorry about that. My mistake." Tom shook his head as if he had just goofed up.

Joey looked Tom over. "I guess you made your flush," he said as he looked back at his cards. He shook his head and said "nice river" as he showed Tom his J♦10♦ and mucked it.

Tom nodded. "Yeah, I finally got there on the end," as he flashed his A♣ and threw his cards in. The dealer thanked Tom for the tip as he shuffled up for the next hand.

Degree of Difficulty: 6
Rate of Success: Medium
Frequency: Low

The analysis: Some of you might consider this an unethical play. Personally, I think as long as no cheating is involved, anything goes. Acting out of turn is clearly unethical, and depending on the situation, it borders on cheating. *Tipping* out of turn, so to speak, can hardly be put in that same category. Besides, if Joey had called, I highly doubt that Tom would have asked for his tip back, so I'm sure the dealer had no problem with it either.

Although it wasn't critical to the success of the play, it didn't hurt that Tom had the A♣ in his hand. He knew that Joey couldn't have it, which was the most important thing, since that would have been disastrous. Tom couldn't exactly throw a premature tip to the dealer, suggesting that he had the nuts, if Joey had a piece of the nut flush in his own hand! Tom knew he could at least pretend to have the nut flush and not be immediately caught in an outright lie.

And then, when Joey folded, Tom was at least able to show the A♣. It might have aroused some suspicion that he didn't show both cards, but not too many players were paying that much attention anyway. They just assumed that it was a typical case of Tom-has-the-nuts-so-he's-tipping-before-showing, and they were ready to move on to the next hand.

Tom hadn't picked up that little habit of his for any particular reason. He just thought it was amusing. But in a split-second decision, he was able to find a practical use for it, and it helped him take down a sizable pot he probably wouldn't have won otherwise.

Bluff #39. Look at This Beauty!

The scenario: $15–$30 hold 'em

The bluff: The UTG player limped in pre-flop, and Kurt limped with J♣10♣ in middle position. The button called, the SB folded, and the BB checked, so there was four-way action. The flop came

It missed Kurt completely. As the BB checked, Kurt's girlfriend, Maria, came up behind him to ask how things were going. "Things are good," said Kurt, "stick around for one second while I play this hand."

"Got anything good?" asked Maria.

Without hesitation, Kurt lifted his cards to show Maria what he had. No one else at the table could see Kurt's cards, but they could all see that he was showing them to Maria. Upon seeing Kurt showing off his hand, the UTG player quickly checked. Kurt fired out a bet, and the button quickly folded. The BB looked at Maria and said, "I'm not liking my hand too much," but he called. The UTG player folded, leaving them heads-up.

The turn card was the 2♥. The BB checked, Kurt bet again, and the BB gave way. Kurt took down the pot with jack-high and turned to flash a smile to Maria, who nodded her head in approval.

Degree of Difficulty: 5
Rate of Success: Medium/High
Frequency: Medium/High

The analysis: This bluff may or may not have worked anyway. But having his girlfriend behind him helped Kurt close the deal. In fact, it's a bluff Kurt might not even have attempted if Maria wasn't there at the opportune moment.

When someone shows his cards to an onlooker, he is usually conveying one of two things: "Check out this great hand I have!" or "I had this great starting hand, but the board wouldn't give me any help!" (See the next bluff for more on that second one.) In this particular hand, Kurt showed his cards as a response to Maria's question "Got anything good?" which was his way of telling the table, "Yes, I have something really good, and I want my girlfriend to see it too." Combined with a bet, it was a really convincing show of having a strong hand.

Kurt took advantage of several favorable factors:

1. The flop came king-high with no obvious draws, which is always a favorable board for bluffing. For example, if the flop instead came nine-high, loose players might have stayed in with hands such as Q-J or J-10, just hoping to spike top pair on the turn. But once the flop brought a king, they no longer had overcards. They knew that if Kurt was betting a king, they could be drawing nearly dead with those hands, so they folded in situations where they might call if the top flop card had been lower.
2. He had position on two of his three opponents.
3. He had Maria show up at the opportune moment.

4. He had the only flop caller admitting out loud that he didn't like his hand. It might have been a ruse, but Kurt didn't think so, and that was confirmed when he folded on the turn.

I have no problem saying that, if I were one of Kurt's opponents, I would have folded anything less than top pair. I'm sure no one else gave the hand a second thought—they were content to let Kurt win with his "strong hand." Only Kurt and Maria knew how good a play it really was.

Verbal Tells

In the previous hand, one has to wonder why the BB chose to say anything. It didn't change the outcome of the hand; Kurt would have bluffed and won anyway. But why would he want to give away information like that?

It's amazing how many dumb things people say at the poker table. Many times, all you have to do is sit back and listen, and you'll know your correct move. Here are a few examples:

1. You flop some sort of draw, and you bet it. The action gets folded around to the player on your right, who says, "All right, I'll call one time." No matter what comes on the turn, I sure hope you plan on betting again.

   As misleading as some poker players try to be, it's been my experience that players who say, "I'll call one time," often mean it. They have some sort of weak draw, such as a gutshot straight draw or naked overcards. They will try one time to hit their draw for a small bet, but they don't plan to spend a big bet unless they significantly improve on the turn. *Chances are, the turn won't help them.* You need to take advantage of that by betting and giving them a second chance to fold.

2. Pre-flop, the action gets folded around to the player in the cut-off seat. He looks like he is leaning toward folding, but then he says, "I'm bored," and throws in the money to call. If you

are on the button, raise with any two cards. If the action gets folded to you in either the SB or the BB, raise with anything, and come out betting on the flop.

If the "bored" player is giving an elaborate act, more power to him. Most times, players who claim to make a call out of boredom are doing just that. They have inferior cards and just want to see a flop, because they haven't had anything decent in a long time. As you know by now, *chances are that the flop won't help them.* Fire into them, and make them pay for deciding to play out of boredom.

3. Three-handed, the flop comes K♣7♦2♠. You decide to bluff from the BB, hoping that the flop didn't hit either of your opponents. The player to your left folds, but you hear the SB softly mutter, "I'm not goin' anywhere," as he calls. On the turn, he checks again.

   In other circumstances, you might try bluffing again. But in this case, you probably shouldn't bother. If he had made the comment loudly, with some bluster, he might have just been trying to scare you into slowing down. But when he says it under his breath, it's probably the truth. With a flop like that, he's not on a draw, so he must have a pair with which he has decided to call you down. Don't be upset that you have to abandon your bluff attempt. Just be glad that he verbalized his thoughts, and that you had your ears open to hear them.

4. You raise from the button with rags, hoping to steal the blinds. It's folded to the BB, who holds the cards up to his girlfriend: "What should I do with these, honey?" "Double down!" she giggles. He laughs along and calls. Now the flop comes A♣Q♠10♦. He checks. Do you bet your rags?

   I sure hope so. If you play blackjack at all, you know that you always double down on a total of eleven. Since she joked about doubling down, it's safe to assume that his cards total eleven, which means that you are up against either 6-5, 7-4, 8-3, or 9-2. No matter which combination he has, the flop didn't come anywhere close to him. A simple bet will win you the pot immediately.

I've repeatedly mentioned the importance of observing your opponents. Watching them should remain your top priority. But listening to them is often helpful too. If they are chatterboxes, who seemingly say things just to confuse you, then you can always ignore them. There's nothing wrong with discounting whatever you hear, and just playing the hand as if they didn't say anything. However, you will often encounter straightforward opponents who are not careful about the information they let slip. You never know what helpful things they might say, as long as you are paying attention.

For that reason, *don't wear headphones*. I have heard all sorts of reasons that people like to wear them: They like to listen to music while they play, they don't want their neighbors bending their ear, and so forth. Hey, I enjoy good music as much as the next guy, and I've had to listen to my share of annoying bad-beat stories. But that's a small price to pay for being able to hear everything my opponents are saying. Winning poker involves gathering information. Once you wear headphones, you deprive yourself of your opponents' verbal tells, and in the long run you'll pay the price.

Bluff #40. Help from an Opponent's Friend

The scenario: $5–$10 hold 'em.

The bluff: Jackie in seat ten limped from early position. Carl called from seat two in middle position. Everyone folded around to Michael in seat seven, who checked his option in the BB with 8♦3♠. Three-handed, the flop came

Everyone checked. The turn was the 4♣. Since no one seemed happy with their hand, Michael decided to take a shot at the small

pot. He threw in a bet. Jackie called, which did not please Michael. As Carl was preparing to act on his hand, his friend came up behind him.

"You almost ready to leave, Carl? I just went busted."

"Yeah, let me just play this hand, okay?"

His friend leaned down next to him. "Whatcha got?"

Carl lifted his cards up with one hand to show his friend, while he called with the other. Michael had not expected to get called, let alone by both opponents! He was prepared to declare his bluff attempt a failure. The river was the A♦, for a final board of

Before Michael had a chance to check, he saw Carl's friend roll his eyes skyward and shake his head sideways ever so slightly. Michael was pretty sure that Jackie, sitting to the right of the dealer, had not been able to see the reaction from Carl's friend. All of a sudden, Michael deviated from his original plan of checking and folding. He bet $10, and looked to see what Jackie would do.

Jackie stared at the board for a second, made a quick glance up at Mike, looked back at her hand, and pushed it in. Carl stood up, flipped up his 8♣6♣, and said, "Yup, I missed, just like I've been doing all day. Good night everyone." He walked away from the table, while he and his friend walked toward the exit sharing their hard-luck stories. Little did the friend know that he helped play a part in Michael's success for that day.

"Was 4-5 any good?" asked Jackie as Michael scooped the pot.

"4-5? What was that, two pair?"

"No, just a pair of fours."

"You're asking me if a pair of fours was any good? Come on, give me a little respect here," chuckled Michael.

"Yeah, I guess you're right," laughed Jackie as they prepared to play the next hand.

Degree of Difficulty: 7
Rate of Success: Medium/High
Frequency: High

The analysis: *Poker is a game of information.* The more information you can get regarding your opponents' hands, the better. In this hand, Michael picked up a valuable bit of information, thanks to Carl's friend. He knew from the reaction to the river card that the A♦ was not what Carl needed, and that he had no plans to call.

Jackie, on the other hand, did not pick up that information. She was not in a position to see the friend's reaction, and therefore had to wonder whether the A♦ might have helped Carl's hand.

Therefore, Michael was able to execute a perfect squeeze bluff, with Jackie caught in the middle. If she were last to act, she might have called with her pair of fours, just to see what Michael was so proud of. She obviously suspected that her hand might be good, as indicated by her question afterward. However, with Carl still left to act behind her, she had to think twice before calling with such a marginal hand. She still had to worry that Carl might overcall or raise, in which case the $10 she spent on the river would have become a complete waste.

Not all seats are created equal: Strictly from an informational standpoint, seat ten is the worst. You have trouble seeing the players to your immediate left, and as a result you miss important visual tells. Here was a perfect example of that. Jackie was generally an observant player and usually did well in that $5–$10 game. However, she couldn't catch the reaction from Carl's friend, and that might have made the difference between successfully picking off a bluff, and folding a winner.

CHAPTER TEN

Bail-Out Bluffs

I would assign all four bluffs in this chapter identical ratings:

Degree of Difficulty: 10
Rate of Success: Very Low
Frequency: Very Low

I call these "bail-out bluffs" because in each case, the bluffer unnecessarily put himself in a bad spot. The victim had a very strong hand, and could not have been expected to lay it down. Strictly speaking, the bluffer's best play was to check and fold. If he had chosen to do that, he could have made his life a lot simpler. But instead, he put himself in danger, and then dug out of that danger by making a magnificent play. He managed to execute a bluff that would almost always fail.

I don't offer the stories of these bluffs as suggestions of what you should do. If anything, I would tell you never to put yourself in similar situations. But while these players made mistakes to be involved so deeply in their respective hands, they deserve recognition for the way they were able to win the money.

When I think of these bluffs, I think of a basketball player attempting a game-winning shot from half-court with three seconds left on the clock. Most of the time he would miss, and the focus would be on why he didn't take a higher percentage shot. He had three seconds to get closer to the basket, but instead he took a wild shot from half-court, and every postgame interview will focus on the bad decision he made.

But on those rare occasions where the shot goes in and he wins the game, nobody remembers what a low percentage shot he took. All that matters is that it went in, and everyone who was at that game will forever remember the spectacular shot that won it. ESPN will call it the play of the week and show the replay dozens of times, and the man who made the shot will be treated like a hero. The only person who might react correctly is the coach. He'll say, "Great shot, thanks for winning us the game. But next time, could you put yourself in a position to take a better shot?" Normally, I am strictly the coach. But right now, you should also think of me as the ESPN commentator telling you about the poker plays of the week.

I'm going to begin with a bluff in which I was the victim. Hey, we've all been bluff victims, probably far more than we realize. Unless you call every bet or raise, you're going to fold the winning hand sometimes, and that's perfectly okay. Since this was a high-quality bluff done by a highly skilled opponent, I have no shame in sharing it with you here.

Bluff #41. Jeff T Spots a Tell

The scenario: PLH with $2–$5 blinds at the Sands in Atlantic City. It was the weekly game in which I got my start as a serious player. Several of us, including Jeff T, were regulars and thus familiar with one another's tendencies. Jeff and I originally bought in for $500 and $400 respectively, but we had both been doing well, so when this hand came up we each had over $1,200.

The bluff: Everyone folded to Jeff, who raised to $15 from middle position. As next to act, I called with A♦10♦. A player behind me called, and the BB called. So four-handed we saw the flop:

The BB checked and Jeff checked. Having flopped top and bottom pair, I did not want to slow-play my good but vulnerable hand.

"I bet the pot," I declared as I put out $62. It was folded around to Jeff, and he called the $62.

Heads-up, the turn card was the 8♥. He checked again. I wasn't crazy about my hand, but I also thought his most likely holding was an A-K or A-J type of hand, and I didn't want to give him a free card. Once again I declared I was betting the pot, and I then proceeded to count out $186. Just as I finished putting my chips in the pot, Jeff check-raised me to $486. I folded, and he showed me 6♣5♣.

The analysis: This play was based on Jeff's knowledge of my tendencies. When he checked on the flop, he intended to give up on the hand. But when I bet $62, and everyone folded to him, he decided he wasn't going to give up so easily. He knew that it was unlikely I cold-called before the flop with A-A, Q-Q, or 10-10. He thought my most likely holding was A-x, and that I was betting the pot to protect a lone pair of aces. It turns out that his read was a little off, but I still did not have a strong enough hand to be willing to risk my entire stack.

He realized that his pattern of raising pre-flop and then check-calling the flop represented considerable strength. I should be specific here. If certain players made that play, it might be considered weak. For instance, there are players who raise pre-flop with K-K and can't release their pair even when an ace flops. Jeff did not fit that description. If he raised pre-flop, and then check-called on the flop, he wasn't doing it with a hand like K-K. It almost always signaled a strong hand. Unfortunately, in the occasional pot like this one, it represented a piece of trash.

For what it's worth, I do not feel that I played the hand well. The call before the flop was questionable, but not bad considering I had position on him. The bet on the flop was fine, but following up with the $186 bet on the turn was not a good decision. I thought there was a good chance he had A-K, but against a player like Jeff, who was capable of check-raising as a bluff, I would have been better off checking and taking the free card. On the one hand, I would have given a hand like A-K a chance to outdraw me. On the other hand, it would have been easy to get away from my A♦10♦ cheaply if a king, queen, or jack came on the river. Furthermore, if a blank came on the river, Jeff would not have been able to bet more than the $186 that was in the pot. At that point I could decide whether or not to call, without my whole stack being exposed.

But what was done, was done. I fired out on the turn, and got it right back in my face. Once Jeff check-raised me, there were really only two possibilities. He either had me beat or was on an outright bluff. I could not see him making a legitimate check-raise in that spot with anything less than A-10. If he had me beat, it would not just cost me another $300 to find out. I had about another $800 in front of me, and with any hand that beat mine, he would probably put me all-in on the river. Reraising was out of the question, since I felt there was a good chance he flopped a set, and it would be tough for him to give me credit for K-J or J-9, the only two hands that could beat him. Basically, I needed a stronger hand than two pair to commit all of my chips. I knew it and he knew it, and he took advantage of it beautifully.

Lesson to be learned: Remember the "How Can I Win This Hand?" game that we discussed in Chapter 3? That game pays off in situations like these. Jeff was always looking for bluffing opportunities, and you should do the same. Even if you choose not to go through with one, at least recognize that you have the *potential* for one.

Very often, I've been in a situation similar to Jeff's. The player to my left bet, everyone folded to me, and my hand was essentially worthless. However, I stopped and asked myself, "Could I steal this pot with a raise? What if I call and then check-raise?" Sometimes I gave it a shot. Sometimes I just folded and played the next hand. Either way, by playing that game in my mind, it helped me see the hand a lot more clearly.

The aftermath: It was only after I had moved to the West Coast that Jeff told me what had made him decide to attempt that bluff. He said that my usual style was to make a bet without declaring the amount. Even if I was betting the pot, I wouldn't announce it. I would mentally calculate the pot, and then either bet the exact amount or something close to it. So this time, when I said, "I bet the pot," it made him stop and think.

He said that prior to that play, in the whole time we had played together, there had been only one other time he had ever heard me verbally declare that I was betting. In that instance, I had a semi-strong hand that I was concerned about protecting. Therefore, he decided that I probably had the same type of hand this time around. And he figured since I was concerned about protecting it, I had to feel there was a good chance it could be beaten, and thus I would respect a check-raise enough to lay my hand down.

Of course, as it turns out, he was absolutely right. He was able to combine his memory skills and his creativity to convincingly bluff me off a fairly strong hand. But while I gave him credit for making a great play, I also remained upset at myself for giving off such a clear tell. Of course, I was happy he told me about it, but I couldn't believe what a mistake I had made.

In the last chapter I talked about verbal tells, and gave some examples of things that you should obviously not say. Here was a much more subtle example. I didn't think I had been giving away any information by simply declaring that I was betting. In fact, prior to that hand, I was proud of myself because I thought one of my strong points was concealing any tells. So much for that! I was overconfident in my abilities, and I got what I deserved. But at least I learned a valuable lesson: No matter the situation, you really can't go wrong by always keeping your mouth shut at the poker table.

Bluff #42. The Bare King Play

The scenario: The first limit of a $220 PLO single-table satellite at the 2000 WSOP. The blinds were only $15–$30, but Shaun and Dennis had each busted an opponent, so they both had about $3,000 while everyone else had roughly $1,500.[20]

---

20. This bluff first appeared in *Poker Digest,* "My 2000 'Bluff of the Year' Award Goes to . . . ," Volume 3, Issue 26, p. 14. Shaun and Dennis are not the players' actual names.

The bluff: When it was folded around to Shaun in middle position, he raised to $100. Dennis then reraised to $300. Everyone folded to Shaun, who called, so they took the flop heads up. It came

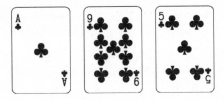

and Shaun immediately came out with a nearly pot-sized bet of $600. Dennis looked as if he was about to raise, but then he paused, reexamined the board, and instead chose to flat-call. The turn was the 4♥. With about $1,800 in the pot, Shaun again bet $600. Dennis immediately called. The river was the 2♠, for a final board of

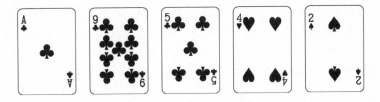

and Shaun pushed all-in for his remaining $1,500. Dennis contemplated for at least thirty seconds. Then he turned up his cards— A♦A♠Q♦10♥—trip aces.

"Are you folding?" asked Shaun casually.[21]

Dennis nodded and mucked his cards, and then Shaun turned up K♣K♦8♦4♦. He didn't have a straight, a flush, or even two pair. He took down the pot with a lone pair of kings. He also went on to win the satellite.

---

21. In 2000 there was no rule that your hand was dead if you exposed it. That rule didn't come into effect until the following year. Therefore, Dennis still had the right to call.

The analysis: Before we examine the intricacies of this bluff, let's take a general look at the hand. My personal preference is never to put in the first raise before the flop in tournament PLO. If someone else raises, and I have aces, I might reraise if I think it will get us heads-up, or if a reraise would put me all-in. The only other time I might raise pre-flop would be if I were the table chip leader. Then it would be primarily an intimidation raise, with opponents knowing that if they call, I might end up putting them all-in before the hand is over.

I would put Shaun's raise in that category. His hand was marginal, but once he decided to play, it made sense to come in for a raise. He was the co–chip leader, and his opponents could easily be intimidated by his stack size. However, his worst-case scenario took place when Dennis, the only player at the table who could bust him, decided to reraise. At least nine times out of ten, a pre-flop reraise in PLO indicates aces, usually with one or both of them being suited. So Shaun, holding kings (one of them suited), could not have been happy with the situation. However, since it only cost 10 percent of his stack, he decided to call Dennis's reraise, and that's when the hand became interesting.

First, Shaun gets credit from me for attempting the bluff at all. Most players in his position would have given up on the hand. After the flop, they would have said to themselves, "I know that my opponent has a set of aces, and I am drawing dead. I have the card (the K♣) that is a piece of the nut flush, but I don't have another club, so it's no good. Even if I try to represent the nut flush, I will most likely get called down and lose a big pot. Better to check and fold, and curb my losses. I'll get him next time." But no, Shaun wanted to get him *this* time. He took the initiative to try to win the pot with a bluff, even though the odds were against him. It took guts not to concede this hand from the outset, and I applaud Shaun for his determination.

Second, Shaun's Betting Pattern helped him pull this bluff off perfectly. He made a pot-sized bet on the flop, a small bet on the turn, and then a large all-in bet on the river. Notice that if he followed *any* other Betting Pattern, his bluff was destined to fail. If he made a pot-sized bet on the flop and then again on the turn, Dennis would probably call, even if he thought he was beaten, to try to make a full house on the river. But then, even if Dennis didn't fill up on the river, Shaun couldn't make a big enough bet to make him fold. Dennis would make a crying call simply because he'd be practically all-in anyway, and he would win the pot with his set of aces.

Similarly, if Shaun check-raised on either the flop or the turn, he would have been faced with the same dilemma. He would not have had a big enough stack to force Dennis out on the river. By making a pot-sized bet on the flop, he properly represented the nut flush. Then, by making a small bet on the turn, he left himself with $1,500 out of his original $3,000. Then, when Dennis didn't fill up on the river, Shaun could make a big enough bet to keep him from calling.

From the beginning, Shaun had to convince Dennis that his set of aces was a *drawing* hand, not a *made* hand. That was the key to this bluff. Remember how Dennis reexamined the flop and then decided to call Shaun's bet rather than raise? That was the exact moment when Dennis shifted his mentality about the hand. He went on the defensive, lost confidence, and ultimately lost the pot.

Isn't that what bluffs are all about? You have to make your opponent lose confidence. Shaun did that perfectly throughout the hand, and then to top it off, his reaction was perfect when Dennis turned his hand faceup on the river. Dennis was clearly looking for some sort of tell, but Shaun didn't oblige him. Instead, he simply asked, "Are you folding?" in a manner that suggested the pot was already his—as if the hand was already a foregone conclusion, and whether Dennis called or not was just a formality. If there was any doubt that Dennis was folding, that simple question helped ensure that Shaun won the pot.

Even though I wasn't a participant in the hand, I was a very interested observer. Truthfully, I began to think that Shaun might be bluffing when he bet only $600 on the turn, rather than making a pot-sized bet of $1,800. But I still would have had a tough time calling his bet on the river. That is one final property of the perfect bluff: You might suspect that your opponent is bluffing, but you still can't bring yourself to call, because if you're wrong, you're out of the game.

Once again, I commend Shaun for making such an excellent play. I think it's creative plays such as his that keep poker so interesting and exciting.

Bluff #43. Jack Straus and the Seven-Deuce

Background: Jack "Treetop" Straus played in some of Vegas's biggest NLH cash games during the 1970s and early 1980s before passing away in 1988. His crowning achievement was capturing the 1982 WSOP championship, but he was equally famous for his many imaginative and innovative bluffs. The play that follows is probably his most famous one. Over twenty years have passed, and it has become part of poker folklore, to the point where I don't think anyone really knows the exact details for sure. But just an overview of it should be enough to make you say, "Wow!"

The bluff: It was a high-stakes NLH cash game, in which everyone had tens of thousands of dollars on the table. Straus had won several pots in a row, so he decided that he was going to play his rush, and raise pre-flop with any two cards. True to his word, he did so, but when he looked down he saw 7-2 offsuit, the worst possible hand. Neil[22] was the only player who called.

The flop came 7-3-3. Straus bet, figuring that was a pretty good flop for 7-2, but then Neil made a large raise. Straus knew that Neil was a pretty tight player, so the raise probably signaled an overpair to the sevens. He was pretty sure he was beaten, but he decided he would try to outplay Neil, possibly by representing trip threes. He called. The turn was a deuce, for a board of 7-3-3-2.

Naturally the deuce didn't help him, but Straus came out with a huge bet anyway, and that sent Neil into deep thought. Straus knew he didn't want a call, otherwise he would need to get very lucky to win. A few minutes passed, and Straus got the impression that Neil was leaning toward calling. So finally, he came up with a proposition. He told Neil that for $25 he could choose either one of Straus's hole cards, and Straus would reveal it.

Neil considered, then threw Straus a $25 chip and pointed toward one of the cards. Straus turned up his deuce, and then Neil went into the think tank again. A lot of time went by, but finally Neil talked himself out of calling. He figured that Straus would make that offer only if both

22. Not his real name.

of his hole cards were the same. So he came to the conclusion that Straus had pocket deuces, had made a full house on the turn, and now had the best hand. Neil laid down his overpair, and Straus raked in the pot.

The analysis: I think this is about as creative and imaginative a bluff as you'll ever see. How many players in the world could think of such a perfect play on the spot? He was able to convince Neil that an overpair was no good when facing a board of 7-3-3-2, not an easy task! Furthermore, he had to risk a small fortune in the process, something that most players would have been too scared to do. This play helps illustrate how poker, when played at the top levels, is truly an art form.

However, while the bluffer in me loves his play, the coldly analytical part of me knows that this was the quintessential bail-out bluff. Straus put himself into a situation he had no reason to be in. Let's look at his various mistakes:

1. He raised pre-flop with 7-2 offsuit. It doesn't get worse than that. Okay, so he was on a rush, and he felt like raising with anything, but I wonder how he would have felt if he had blown back all of his winnings and then some because he decided to fool around with a 7-2. It's one thing to play it as a goof, it's quite another to risk thousands of dollars on it.
2. Betting on the flop wasn't terrible, since he might have had the best hand. But then, when his opponent raised, he knew he was beaten, but he called anyway to try to set up a bluff later. I'm not one to frown upon that creative way of playing, but you'd rather set up a bluff when you know your opponent is weak. When your opponent has an overpair to the board, and enough confidence to raise on the flop, you are really bucking the odds by calling just to try to bluff him out later.
3. His big bluff on the turn could have been a huge mistake. He read his opponent correctly as being strong, tried to muscle him out anyway, and almost paid a tremendous price for it. I'm guessing that he did not have the show-my-opponent-a-card idea when he first made the turn bet. If he had not had that brainstorm, he would have lost a bundle when his opponent summoned up the courage to call.

All told, he could have saved a lot of aggravation by avoiding any of those three mistakes. Each successive one compounded the others. By the time he made his third mistake—betting on the turn—he had buried himself so deep that there was no turning back. So, looking at this hand with an analytical eye, it could be said that Straus did more things wrong than right.

On the other hand, here we are in the twenty-first century, still talking about a play that occurred over twenty years ago! In some ways, I think that supersedes any sort of critical analysis. Sure, from a dollars-and-cents perspective, the risk he took was probably not worth the reward. But can you really put a price tag on becoming part of poker legend? I strongly believe that you must look at not just the few thousand dollars he made on this hand, but also the legacy he left behind. He was one of the forerunners of creative and artistic bluffing, and that's one reason why he is in the Poker Hall of Fame.

Bluff #44. Jason V vs. the Set of Aces

The scenario: A three-handed pot-limit hold 'em cash game at Atlantic City's Borgata. The blinds were $10–$20, and everyone had more than $10,000 in front of them. Two of the players were Jason V, one of the country's top big-bet players, and Charlie K, a somewhat successful tournament player based on the East Coast. They were familiar with each other, having put in many hours playing together. Then this tremendous hand came up.

The bluff: Jason V was on the button with 4♥2♥, and made it $60 to go. The SB folded, but then Charlie K made it $190 to go from the BB. Jason called, and they saw a flop of

Charlie bet out $300, and Jason chose to flat-call with his flush draw. The K♣ came on the turn. Charlie bet $600, and Jason took some time to ponder his next move.

Meanwhile, Charlie decided to start talking. "When you muck," he told Jason, "I'm either going to show you A-A or 7-2." Jason immediately made it $2,100 to go. Now it was Charlie's turn to ponder for a couple of minutes.

"What do you got?" he asked Jason.

"Two cards. What do you got?"

"Two aces."

"Really? Let me see."

Jason was joking around, of course. He didn't expect Charlie to oblige him. But then, unbelievably, Charlie picked up the front of his cards and purposely tilted them toward Jason so that he could see A♣A♠! Then Charlie sat there for another couple of minutes to try to see how Jason reacted to this new information. Eventually Charlie decided to flat-call and see what the river would bring.

At that point there was quite a crowd of people around the table, so Charlie turned his cards faceup for everyone to see! Some of them did not realize that he had already flashed his cards to Jason, so they couldn't believe what they were seeing. Meanwhile there was still another card to come!

The river was the Q♦, for a final board of

Charlie quickly checked. Without hesitation, Jason bet $5,000, and Charlie went deep into the think tank. The whole time, there were at least fifty onlookers, all waiting to see what Charlie would do. Jason decided to needle him a little bit, by engaging him in conversation.

"Three aces is a big hand," he said. "I don't know if I could fold a hand that big." Then Charlie would say something back to him, and

Jason would completely change his tune, "You know, come to think of it, three aces isn't that big a hand. I could lay down three aces."

Their banter continued for at least ten minutes. With everyone watching and waiting, the hand reached its climactic finish: Charlie forcefully mucked his hand, Jason turned up 4♥2♥, the crowd went wild, and Charlie went on megatilt for the rest of the night. Even though it took place several years ago, this remains one of the most memorable hands ever played in Atlantic City.

The analysis: Obviously this was an unusual hand on several levels. The game was shorthanded, the amount of money involved was serious, and for some reason Charlie decided to expose his cards on the turn. Rather than examine the hand myself, I called on Jason V to give me his observations and comments. Here's what he had to say:

The first thing people usually ask me is why I was in there with a hand like 4♥2♥. What they don't understand is that three-handed pot-limit hold'em is a battle of guts, stamina, and insanity. When the money is deep, it hardly matters what cards you have. If I'm going to raise with a hand on the button, I'd better be prepared to call a reraise. Raising pre-flop from the button with a deep stack, and then folding to a reraise, is one of the weakest plays you can make. Your image is shot, all of your future raises get less respect from your opponents, and basically you'll have no chance of winning in a shorthanded game.

Once the flop came, and Charlie bet, I think calling with the flush draw was clearly the play. If I was out of position it might have been different. But since he had to act in front of me every round, I could call and see how he would react on the turn, whether he would keep firing or slow down.

On the turn, I felt his bet could either be an outright bluff or an attempt to protect and/or value-bet a strong hand. So when he started talking about having either A-A or 7-2, it really didn't change anything. That was pretty much what I had figured anyway. But once he started talking like that, I knew he was scared of my hand. Among other things, I was pretty certain he couldn't reraise me if I put in a raise. So I gave it a shot.

I was hoping he would throw his hand away immediately. But when he sat there and thought for a while, I realized he had a real hand. I figured it was either two pair or a set, so now it was a matter of convincing him that I had the goods. He asked me what I had, and, of course, I wasn't going to tell him anything. When I threw the question back at him, I never actually expected him to tell me what he had! And then he showed me his cards! I couldn't believe it! I guess he was trying to get some sort of read out of me, but that was just insane.

Still, I knew I was in big trouble. I had just put a couple of thousand into the pot with four-high. It was time to put on my game face and try to climb out of the hole I had dug for myself. I never talked about my hand; I let him draw his own conclusions based on my betting. Instead, I concentrated on talking about his hand, the set of aces. Not whether they were good or not, but whether I could lay them down if I were in his shoes. I wanted him to think, "He's trying to confuse me. I know a set of aces is a big hand. Whether or not I can fold them isn't the issue. The issue is, do I have the best hand? And why is he so relaxed? If I saw that my opponent had three aces after I raised $1,500, I'd be crapping my pants . . ."

I could see him trying to figure out what I had. He was trying to convince himself that he had the best hand, but he couldn't get away from the possibility that I had Q-J. And I understood his problem, because I would have played Q-J exactly the same way: raise before the flop, call a reraise, call on the flop with an open-ended straight draw, and raise once I hit my straight. When it came time to make the final decision, he decided that I could have Q-J, so he'd call to see if he filled up. In reality, that was the worst of his three options.

Here's why: If he thought I had the straight, then he should have folded. He wasn't getting the correct pot odds to try to fill up, plus he had already shown me his hand, so he obviously wasn't getting any more money out of me if the board paired. If he thought I had anything other than the straight, his correct play was to reraise. That way, he'd shut me out from winning the hand if I had any outs going to the river, or else give me bad pot odds if I decided to draw. The only way flat-calling made sense was if he was 100 percent sure I was either on an outright bluff or drawing dead. That way he could let me bet again on the river, and he'd pick me off. But obviously that wasn't the case, since he couldn't bring himself to make that river call, so I have to believe that he made a big mistake by just calling.

I think the river card really helped my cause. I had already made up my mind that if the river was a queen, jack, or a heart, I would bet without hesitation. So when he checked, I put $5,000 out there pretty quickly, and he nearly jumped out of his seat! I didn't know if the back-and-forth conversation that followed would end up helping or hurting my cause. Truthfully, I was still experimenting with different things, and I thought that the conversation would make him see me as being loose and relaxed. I guess it worked, since I got him to lay down. But little did he know that all he had to do was say "call," and I would've thrown up on the table.

That's one of the few times I bluffed when I knew my opponent had a monster hand. Usually I pick my spots when they are weak or I think they're weak, but this time he seemed so unsure about his hand on the turn that I took a shot on the river. And it paid off.

I don't think there's much to add to Jason's account of the events. I'll just leave you with one reminder: *Your opponents' mistakes become your profit.* Charlie made two huge mistakes, first exposing his cards, and then flat-calling Jason's raise on the turn. Those led to a nice profit for Jason. If you're lucky enough to have an opponent who makes equally big mistakes, you must always be prepared to take full advantage of them.

CHAPTER ELEVEN

WSOP Bluffs and Interviews

We will end this book with some of the greatest bluffs in WSOP history. I believe that they are both educational and inspirational. Sure, we all want to make a steady profit playing poker, but I think that nearly all of us, deep down, want some fame and glory as well. If you get to the final table of a major tournament, and make the same type of plays that these players made, then you'll not only end up with the money, but also with the recognition that you deserved to be there and made a play worthy of a champion. No matter how jaded a poker player you might be, I think that is something most of us aspire to.

When deciding which hands to include in this chapter, I followed these criteria:

1. The bluff was brilliantly executed.
2. It was unquestionably the turning point of the match for both participants.
3. The bluffer went on to win the event.
4. We all got to see the bluffer's hand.

Obviously, that last point says a lot. These are merely the great WSOP bluffs that we know about. One can only wonder how many great bluffs in the past thirty years went unheralded, because we never got to see the bluffer's cards. We can focus only on the hands that the bluffer showed or, in the past few years, the ones captured by lipstick cameras.

For instance, 2004 was the first time ESPN broadcast some preliminary WSOP events, in addition to the main event. Thanks to numerous reruns, I think I caught all of them. They were fun to watch, and I saw some truly interesting plays and confrontations. But after watching hours and hours of footage, I saw only one great bluff.

Only one play merited inclusion into this book. So, with all due respect to the other competitors, I believe that the most perfectly executed televised bluff of 2004 was made by twenty-two-year-old Gavin Griffin, winner of the $3,000 pot-limit hold 'em event.

Bluff #45. 2004 WSOP—
Gavin Griffin vs. Gabriel Thaler

Griffin had come to the final table with the chip lead, and he was clearly the most aggressive player there. For example, early on he got involved in a hand with Ram Vaswani, a member of the famed "Hendon Mob" and a top professional player. Vaswani raised pre-flop with 4♣4♠, and Griffin called with K♠Q♠. On the turn, the board was

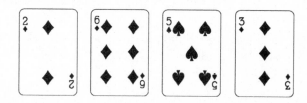

Vaswani bet out $25,000, and Griffin raised to $90,000 on a stone cold bluff! Vaswani reraised all-in, and Griffin had to muck, but that was quite a ballsy play. Even though it didn't work, it made perfect sense. Vaswani had raised pre-flop, and Griffin thought that the low board was unlikely to have hit Vaswani's hand. Still, that one bad read cost him the chip lead.

Many players would have gone into a shell after taking a hit like that. Those players, however, are not the ones who become champions. Gavin Griffin went right back to the aggressive style that got him there. Not only did he regain the chip lead, he eliminated four straight players in the process. His victims included the outspoken Phil Hellmuth, who had some choice words as he departed (no surprise there), and he also exacted revenge on Ram Vaswani. When the smoke cleared, he had only two opponents left.

Griffin clearly had the momentum and the chip lead going into three-handed play, but then he began to cool off. The other two players were creeping up on him, and he needed to do something to regain control of the table. That's when he pulled off the bluff of the tournament.

The scenario: Three-handed, it was Gavin Griffin (seat seven), Gabriel Thaler (seat eight), and Gary Bush (seat ten). Griffin had about $400,000, but Thaler and Bush were within striking range with about $270,000 each. The blinds were $8,000–$16,000.

The bluff: Thaler had the button, and decided to flat-call with A♣6♥. Bush had 6♣5♥ in the SB and limped in. Griffin had 7♦5♣ in the BB and checked his option to raise. The flop came

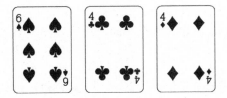

Everyone had a piece of that flop. Bush made two pair, Thaler had two pair with a better kicker, while Griffin had an open-ended straight draw. First to act, Bush bet out $16,000, the minimum bet at that stage. Griffin waited only a moment or two before calling. Thaler then raised $60,000 more.

Bush glanced at Thaler with a bit of an upset expression. He put a chip on his cards, leaned back, and thought for a moment. There really wasn't much to consider. Neither of his opponents seemed scared of his original bet, so top pair with a five kicker was suddenly looking pretty weak. He rocked forward, took the chip off his cards, and folded.

Thaler took on a more confident look once he got past Bush, and under normal circumstances, he had every reason to be confident. As we discussed in "The Weakness of the Cold-Caller" section, the player to fear is typically the first one in the pot. Once you get past him, the difficult part is usually done. Since the player between you and the original bettor showed weakness by flat-calling, he is typically not a threat.

Unfortunately for Thaler, Griffin was not your typical player. After pausing briefly, Griffin announced he was reraising another $135,000. Thaler leaned forward with a wide-eyed stare, like he couldn't believe what he just heard.

"Doyle Brunson's one-word course in poker is 'attack,' and Gavin keeps attacking," admired ESPN commentator Norman Chad. Meanwhile, Thaler was making a clucking noise, stacking his chips together, and talking to himself nonstop.

"You bet right out into me like a champion, huh?" said Thaler. "I mean, you have to have a four, don't you? You just absolutely have to have a four. I mean, you're not gonna raise me with a six; you don't have two sevens or you would've raised before the [flop] . . ." Thaler was talking as much to himself as he was to Griffin. But just in case, Griffin had his left hand covering the side of his face and his head turned to the right so that Thaler couldn't see his face at all.

Finally, Thaler gave a little shrug, looked back at his cards one last time, and tossed them in, without a trace of doubt that he was doing the right thing. The crowd responded with a loud cheer. ESPN commentator Lon McEachern was especially pumped: "And it works! Gabriel Thaler folds, and Gavin Griffin's aggressiveness wins him the hand!"

That hand was truly the clincher. All of a sudden Griffin had $518,000 versus $241,000 for Bush and $191,000 for Thaler. With more than a 2-to-1 chip lead over each opponent, Griffin never looked back. He took out Thaler a few hands later, and then found himself all-in with K♦K♣ against Bush's 7♦7♣. As the board cards started to fall, the crowd sensed the end was near. Griffin was about to claim the title by personally knocking out each of the last six players. On the turn the board was

"Gavin Griffin, one card from becoming the youngest champion in history!" exclaimed McEachern.

"And the way Griffin has played down the stretch here, he would deserve his piece of history," said Chad.

The river was the harmless J♠, and the way Griffin reacted to his victory spoke volumes about his character. He did not jump up and down, did not create a scene or act in an unsportsmanlike manner. He shook Bush's hand, graciously acknowledged the crowd, and essentially acted as though he had been there before. It was his first major win, and a bigger score than most players will ever experience. But between his behavior and his spectacular play, you would have thought he was a seasoned tournament veteran with several titles already.

The analysis: Griffin's bluff was simply perfect. For starters, he avoided the mistake a lot of players would have made. They would have raised the pot when Bush made his flop bet, but that play would have probably backfired. First, it would not have been believable. There is no way his opponents would give him credit for trip fours, since why would he want to make a pot-sized raise with such a monster hand? They would expect him to wait until the turn to raise, if he truly had a four.

Second, it's not likely that a raise would move Thaler off of his A-6. Maybe if Griffin could move all-in, Thaler would talk himself out of calling, but this was pot-limit. A pot-sized raise into a pot that was unraised pre-flop would not be particularly threatening. In all likelihood, it would not be enough to scare out both his opponents. The more likely outcome is that, if Griffin had raised Bush's initial bet, Thaler would have reraised all-in. Then Griffin would have either folded, wasting valuable chips in the process, or made a bad call, hoping to hit his hand. In either case, he would have been on the defensive, which is simply bad poker.

Griffin was too smart to put himself in that predicament. He flat-called the flop, waiting for a better opportunity to raise. Then Thaler raised $60,000, and it was pretty clear that he did not have a monster hand either, for the same reasons I described above. Would he really raise on the flop with a monster hand? Wouldn't he wait until the turn to try to trap his opponents further? His raise signaled a decent hand, but probably not one that could withstand a reraise.

That was Bush's predicament when deciding what to do. He also knew it was unlikely that Thaler had a monster, but his problem was that he still had to worry about Griffin waiting behind him. Bush recognized his vulnerability, and did the smart thing by clearing out.

Now the hand was set up perfectly for Griffin. The pot was big enough that he could make a substantial reraise, and he had properly represented trip fours by just calling the first time around and *then* springing to life when the action came back to him. His raise was big enough that if Thaler called, he would be staking his tournament life on this hand. Griffin didn't believe that Thaler had a hand he was willing to bet his tournament on, and he was right.

Do you need more evidence that it was a great bluff? Hey, he had his opponent talking to himself! Anytime you get your opponent talking, you know you made a great play. It means he's been thrown off his game, and will probably remain that way in future hands. Not only did Thaler offer up an entire soliloquy, but Griffin had him 100 percent convinced that he was doing the right thing by folding! And who can blame him? Not many people would have the guts or the know-how to make Griffin's reraise with no pair. If you can get your opponent to lay down the best hand, and at the same time get him to feel good about his laydown, that is pretty impressive! That hand was unquestionably the turning point of three-handed play, and definitely led to his title.

In the end, everything comes back to mistakes—avoiding mistakes, and inducing others to make them. Thaler made a mistake by limping on the button with A-6. If he had raised, he probably would have won the pot without a fight. Instead, he thought he could outplay his opponents after the flop. He was waiting for them to make mistakes. Unfortunately for him, Griffin did more than just play the hand mistake-free. He had Thaler contribute $60,000 to the pot before getting him to lay down. Thaler's mistakes led to Griffin's profit and, ultimately, his tournament.

Let's put Griffin's achievement into perspective. He defeated a world-class field in pot-limit hold 'em, the game that I believe requires the most skill to master. In doing so, he became the youngest

WSOP champion in history. Not just that, but he personally knocked out each of the last six players. And, somewhere in the middle of all that, he pulled off one of the best bluffs in televised WSOP history. It really doesn't get any better than that.

Bluff #46. 1978 WSOP—
Bobby Baldwin vs. Crandall Addington

If you've only recently become interested in poker, you might be astonished at how much the WSOP has changed over the past thirty years. All you have to do is look at the old WSOP tapes from the 1970s and 1980s to see what I mean. For one thing, almost everyone smoked at the table. It's amazing the television cameras could even see the cards through all that smoke! You'll also appreciate how much the coverage of each hand has improved. Sometimes the camera, which was positioned over the dealer's shoulder, didn't even catch the board cards before the dealer scooped them up.

You've probably seen some of the hundreds of hours of televised tournament coverage currently airing on various stations, most notably ESPN and the Travel Channel. But in 1978, it was CBS and Brent Musburger who covered the four-day WSOP main event. He was a great sportscaster, and I'm sure CBS did its best, but it's safe to say that its coverage did not provide many memorable moments. The running time of the "highlight" video, complete with interviews and analysis? Twenty-one minutes. Suffice it to say, it's a video for serious poker fans only.

But even though the footage was disappointing as a whole, I'm thankful it included the most pivotal hand in deciding who would be crowned 1978 world champion.

The scenario: The final two combatants were Bobby Baldwin and Crandall Addington. Both were top-notch players, even though their appearances were quite different. Baldwin was a twenty-seven-year-old professional poker player wearing a loose-fitting shirt open at the neck. Addington was a middle-aged businessman dressed formally in a suit, tie, and cowboy hat. Baldwin smoked a cigarette; Addington had a long thin cigar. The one thing they had in common was that both of them clearly expected to win, as the confidence on their faces showed.

When heads-up play began at 5:30 P.M. on Day 4 of the main event, Baldwin had a slight lead, $217,000 to $202,000. Over the next hour and a half, Addington relentlessly attacked Baldwin. Through his aggression, he managed to take a 2-to-1 chip lead at the height of his rush. At that point, CBS requested that the players take a break. When they returned, Addington was sitting on a $277,000–$142,000 lead, and Baldwin looked like he might be in danger of going out. But then, suddenly, he came to life.

The bluff: The blinds had just increased to $3,000–$6,000. Someone commented that the heads-up match could go on all night. Before looking at his cards, Baldwin glanced at his watch and proclaimed, "It's 8:15 now. By 9:15 we'll all be home in bed." Not exactly Ruth calling his home run shot, but pretty close.

Addington made it $16,000 to go from the SB/button. Baldwin called. The flop came

Baldwin came right out with a $30,000 bet. Addington called almost immediately. The turn card was the A♦. Baldwin, first to act, pushed all-in. A resigned Addington smiled dejectedly, took one last look at his cards, and flicked them toward the muck. Baldwin brashly announced, "Here's the reason we won't be here that long!" and showed the crowd his 10♥9♥. He won the $92,000 pot with ten-high!

Was Baldwin cocky? Yeah, a little bit. Did he have a right to be? I'd say so. He completely shifted the tide of that match with one bold play. Addington's chip count never made an upward movement again. Baldwin won every important confrontation from that point on, and made good on his promise to the crowd. When his Q-Q beat Adding-ton's 9-9 to make him the 1978 champion, it was only 8:40 P.M.

Fast-forward to today: It's been more than twenty-five years since the hand took place, but Baldwin and Addington remain good friends to this day. Even before talking to them, it made me glad to hear that. Friendship in the poker world usually springs from mutual respect, and since they are two of the most respected players ever, it's easy to see how they would become friends. It reminded me of any two great athletes who can compete hard while playing, but re-main friends once the game is over. Unfortunately, a few of today's poker players are shamefully disrespectful to their opponents. I wish they could learn to emulate greats such as Baldwin and Addington.

The interviews: It was my pleasure to get their perspectives on this famous hand. My first interview was with Crandall Addington. He is currently retired from playing poker, and continues to reside in his home state of Texas.

Matt Lessinger: Even though it's a little off-topic, I feel I must start by complimenting you on how well you were dressed during the 1978 WSOP. It would be nice if some of today's players followed your cue and gave more thought to their appearance. Out of cu-riosity, have you always dressed that way when playing poker?

Crandall Addington: Thank you for the compliment. No, I do not always dress the way that you see me in the WSOP tapes. But never did I dress as some of those players you see today.

At that time, we had a product—the World Series of Poker—that we were selling. Remember that at that time poker playing, particularly professional poker playing and players, had a negative stigma attached to them. Television gave us the oppor-tunity to lift that stigma. I was marketed as the Texas oilman who could compete with the professionals, instead of disclosing to the TV audience that I was a professional as well. People had preconceived notions about what a businessman or oilman should look like, so I marketed to that preconception. The strat-egy worked, as more and more producers showed up at the WSOP and lost enormous sums in the cash games.

Personally, it had the effect of reminding me to remain disciplined, not that I needed much reminding.

ML: I think the image suited you well. Now, let me ask you the most obvious question with regard to Baldwin's bluff: Do you remember what you had in that hand?

CA: I had no hand and no draw. I'm pretty sure it was a 7-8, though I can't say with absolute certainty.

ML: Wow! So you had nothing on the flop? You called simply to try to outplay Bobby on the turn?

CA: Well, I knew what Bobby was capable of doing. He wasn't bluffing at me, even though it might seem like it. Bobby was employing a sublime strategy that he, Doyle [Brunson], and I had mastered. It was the strategy of playing your opponent's hand, not your own. The mark of a master player can be found on those who master this strategy.

You might think that Bobby didn't have a hand, so therefore he was bluffing. But you would be mistaken. Master players are seeking information with their chips. They are willing to sacrifice some of those chips to gain information that may enable them to play their opponent's hand, and Bobby was a master at that.

So, when Bobby bet $30,000 on the flop, he was trying to get information about my hand, but at the same time I received the first bit of information relative to his. I called immediately, which was designed to create the impression of strength. I knew that Bobby had been playing much more aggressively since the break, and he was never a player to let others continually take the lead.

I also knew that Bobby liked to get as much value from a hand as he possibly could. Since he had taken the lead on the flop, I knew that if he had a hand, he would try to get as much value as he could from that hand on the turn. Great players do that. If he had checked, I would have then used that knowledge to attempt to take the pot. If he had made a modest bet, I might have interpreted that as a bet for value. Then again, I might have moved all-in on him, in which case he would have had to be holding a real hand to call me.

Unfortunately, he was smart enough to move all-in. I knew he didn't have a flush or an ace, because he would have bet for value with either of those. I also knew that he didn't have a queen, because the A♦ would have slowed him down. But obviously I couldn't call with eight-high, so he made the only sure play to win the pot.

ML: It's amazing how experts play on a whole different level. Let me ask you about the comment Bobby made just prior to the hand. He told someone in the crowd, "It's 8:15 now. By 9:15 we'll all be home in bed." It almost seems like he was preparing to bluff at a big pot or die trying. Do you remember that comment, and did it mean anything to you at the time?

CA: I remember him saying it, but the comment meant nothing to me.

ML: Tell us about the interruption to the heads-up match. It seems like it couldn't have come at a worse time for you.

CA: As you observed, I had acquired a sizable chip lead, and was playing very aggressively. Then there came a moment when the producer of the TV package, a charming lady whose first name was Suzy, informed us that we would have to take a one-hour break because they had run out of film and needed that time to acquire more from a local affiliate station. My comment was that it would be like stopping a heavyweight title fight when one opponent was on the ropes. She smiled and said that if I didn't agree then she would be unable to get the ending on tape. I looked back at the small bleachers and saw the faces of my friends, the Binions. Well, you know that I consented.

A really interesting analogy had happened to the San Antonio Spurs that same year when they were playing the Washington Bullets in the Eastern Conference semifinal series. The game was in Landover, Maryland, as I recall. The Spurs had a large fourth-quarter lead when suddenly the lights went out in the arena. They stayed out about forty-five minutes, and yes, when the lights came back on, the Spurs had lost their momentum and were beaten.

The funniest part of the story is that the late Jack Straus, who had bet all his money on me, came to where I was sitting waiting for the game to resume, and told me what a huge bet he had lost on the Spurs-Bullets game. He was beside himself when history repeated itself!

The story is just an interesting sidelight to the '78 match. Bobby was a very strong heads-up player, and might have beaten me without the interruption. Bobby played well and deserved the victory.

ML: Spoken like a true gentleman. Before I let you go, are there any words of wisdom you have for my readers?

CA: Let me simply repeat what I said before. Master players do not bluff—they play their opponent's hand. In other words, they won't make a big move unless they have picked up reliable information about their opponent's hand. This is especially crucial in cash games. Less skillful players bluff by recklessly moving their chips in situations in which they have no information.

For what it's worth, I still favor cash games. I think that no-limit hold 'em tournaments have become an aberration of the game. The game was designed to be played after the flop, with a few exceptions.

ML: I agree 110 percent. If it were up to me, the world championship would be played in pot-limit format, so that players would be forced to play after the flop. Maybe one day that will happen. Thank you so much for your time.

CA: You're welcome, and I hope I have given your readers a new perspective relative to bluffing.

♣ ♦ ♥ ♠

I then had the privilege to talk with Bobby Baldwin, who is now president and CEO of Mirage Resorts in Las Vegas. It's not so unusual for someone who succeeded in the corporate world to become a good poker player. But it's a rarity for one of the world's best poker players to then become a success in the corporate world, and Bobby Baldwin is one of those rare people. Then again, we're talking about running a casino, and hardly anyone is more knowledgeable about the casino business.

ML: Let's go straight to your big bluff from 1978. Did Crandall ever tell you what he had in that hand?

Bobby Baldwin: Believe it or not, he never did. We've been friends for the past twenty-five or thirty years, but we've never talked about that hand, and I never found out exactly what he had.

ML: You must have been very confident that his hand was weak, though.

BB: I didn't think the flop made him a big hand. It actually would have made a difference if the flop had come Q♣4♦3♦ instead [with the queen being the nondiamond card]. With that board, he might have flopped a pair of queens with a flush draw, and there would be no way I could have taken him off of that hand. But with the Q♦4♦3♠ flop, I didn't think he had flopped a hand that he would become attached to.

ML: That makes sense. Did your opinion change once he called your $30,000 bet on the flop?

BB: Once he called, it narrowed his possible hands down significantly. In my mind, there were five hands he could have that were the most realistic possibilities. I thought his most likely hand was some sort of gutshot straight draw, like a 5-7 or 6-7. I thought there was a slightly lesser chance he had an open-ended draw with a 6-5. Finally, if he had a made hand, I thought it was probably either K-Q or Q-J, but I thought a straight draw was more likely.

ML: Given that range of possible hands, I guess the A♦ was a good turn card for you.

BB: The A♦ was the *perfect* card. If I could've told the dealer to sort through the deck and find me a card, that was it. Now I knew I had him. I was sure he didn't call on the flop with ace-high, and he didn't call with a flush draw. Given the hands that I gave him credit for, there was no way he could call me.

I would have had a lot tougher decision if a five, six, or seven had come on the turn. Even though I can't say for sure, there's a good chance I would have actually checked and folded, fearing that he either had a straight or a pair with a straight draw. Even if he didn't have a made straight, it would have been tough to take him off of a pair with a draw.

ML: You seemed so sure of your read of him. What gave you such confidence?

BB: It was a combination of two things: playing long hours with Crandall, and having what I call a poker sixth sense. It's not easy to explain it, but there are times when you are absolutely sure that you have made the correct read. I had been watching him for a long time and following his trends, and in my mind, I just knew the A♦ couldn't have helped him.

ML: Let me backtrack to right before the hand. Do you remember making the comment that the tournament would all be over within the next hour? Looking at it now, it almost seems like you had made up your mind to take a stand. He had taken the lead, and now you were preparing to make a big move. Is there something to that, or am I reading too much into it? I said that it was almost, but not quite, the poker equivalent of the Babe calling his home run shot.

BB: I think a more appropriate comparison would be to Muhammad Ali, and the way he used to predict the round in which he would knock out his opponent. I've always admired him, and that was who I had in mind when I said the tournament would be over by 9:15. It was like calling the KO round in advance, the way he used to do when he would rhyme during his pre-fight interviews: "He hits like a flea, so I'll take him in three!" or "He wants to go to heaven, so I'll drop him in seven!" I was ready to make a big move, and that was my way of letting everyone know.

ML: How did you feel about being forced to take an hour-long break right in the middle of the heads-up action? Do you feel it helped you at all?

BB: Actually, it was more like a thirty-minute break. But once I knew we would have that time, I wanted to make the most of it, and I started by changing clothes. Crandall is always a good dresser, so at the start of the day, I wanted to be dressed appropriately. But he was beating me so bad that during the break I ran upstairs, took another shower, and put on a jogging suit that I hardly ever would play poker in. I just wanted to change things up, and give him a new look. Now I was refreshed, and I appeared refreshed, and that definitely gave me a psychological edge for the remainder of the match.

During that time, I was remembering the movie *The Hustler*. Jackie Gleason's character was always getting a clean shave and such, because it gave him a psychological edge over his opposition, and that's what I wanted to do against Crandall.

ML: It just goes to show that great poker players are always thinking, both at the table and away from it. Before we go, do you have any further advice for the readers of this book?

BB: Following the trends at the table is extremely important. Prior to this hand, Crandall had been picking up a lot of big hands for a long time and had been beating me down, and I hadn't been picking up anything. He had whittled away half of my chips. At some point, he knew I was going to make a move, because I couldn't just let him continue to beat me down like that. So this hand was my opportunity to fire back, and he knew I'd be firing back, but he still had to wonder if I had finally caught some good cards, since I had gone so long without any. In a way, it was more believable that I had a good hand, because I had gone so long without one.

ML: That makes sense. Thank you for giving us your time and your thoughts.

BB: You're quite welcome.

♣ ♦ ♥ ♠

Some final thoughts:

1. Some of the most interesting hands you'll ever see are the ones in which neither player has anything. In most cases, the first player to make a move wins. In this case, you had two world-class players, and one move was not enough. It took three to finish the job:

   a. Baldwin bet $30,000 on the flop, which would be enough to win the pot in most cases, but Addington smelled a bluff and countered.

   b. Addington's call on the flop should have allowed him to steal the pot on the turn, but Baldwin sensed weakness and did not back off.

   c. Instead, he followed through on the turn with the all-in bluff that gave him the victory.

   That multitiered level of thinking is something you'll rarely see today. As Addington pointed out, no-limit hold 'em has become a pre-flop game instead of the post-flop game it was meant to be. It's a shame, because as a result, chances are you'll hardly ever see intricate plays such as this one again.

2. Part of the greatness of this play is that Baldwin did not flinch in the face of Addington's quick call on the flop. Most players would have become scared after betting $30,000 and getting called almost instantly. It would cause most players, even some top pros, to shut down their betting, no matter what card came next.

But Baldwin did not panic in the least. He analyzed the hand, made a quick assessment of what he thought Addington had, and made the winning move when the turn card hit. As Addington pointed out, Baldwin made the only play that could unquestionably win him the pot.

3. As with all of the other WSOP bluffs, you have to give extra credit to Baldwin for pulling it off under such a pressure cooker. A large crowd, TV cameras, and a lot of money at stake make it hard for many players to think clearly. Anyone who can thrive under that kind of pressure has what it takes to be a champion, and that intangible should never be ignored. Many of us know the correct play in a given situation. Few of us can execute it repeatedly under the scrutiny of a national viewing audience, with hundreds of thousands of dollars at stake. These men are true champions of the game.

Bluff #47. 1997 WSOP— Stu Ungar vs. Ron Stanley

Stu Ungar had long been considered one of the greatest no-limit hold 'em players ever, especially after winning back-to-back WSOP titles in 1980 and 1981. However, he followed those victories with long years of battling against drug and gambling addictions. He was still considered a great poker talent in 1997, but the general consensus was that his addictions would prevent him from playing at the level he once did. Hardly anyone expected him to make a comeback after a sixteen-year drought in the championship event.

But suddenly, when everyone least expected it, there he was at the 1997 final table with a significant chip lead. He began the final day with $1,066,000 while Ron Stanley, the player considered to be his biggest threat, was a distant second with $694,000.

The two players offered very different appearances. Ungar was at the left end of the table in a loose, drab, button-down shirt with the first few buttons opened. His sunglasses were mirrored, rounded, and perched near the end of his nose. It wouldn't generally be an intimidating look, but his opponents knew that one of the best players in the world was sitting behind those shades, and they could not have felt too comfortable.

Stanley, at the right end of the table, chose to wear a tuxedo, despite the fact that they were playing outdoors in the Vegas heat. He complemented the tux with a white baseball cap, sunglasses, and a full beard and mustache. Neither player allowed his facial expression to vary, so getting a read on either of them was not going to be easy.

Even though Ungar had barely one-third of the total chips in play, he was installed as the 2-to-3 betting favorite to win the event. Most experts predicted that the true battle was for second place. In their minds, nobody was going to overtake him once he had the chip lead.

However, the final table did not begin so smoothly for him. He lost key hands early to Stanley and John Strzemp, and he was suddenly below the million-dollar mark. Spectators felt strongly that he was the best player at the table, but they wondered if the cards would conspire against him. He needed to make a play that would demonstrate his dominance over the competition, and he found the opportunity on hand #36.

The scenario: All six players remained. The blinds were $5,000–$10,000, with $2,000 antes.

The bluff: Everyone folded to Stanley in the SB. He called the extra $5,000, and Ungar checked in the BB. The flop came A♠9♥6♠ and both players checked. The turn was the 8♣, creating a board of

Stanley bet $25,000. Ungar grabbed $25,000 from his stack and began playing with it. Then he reached back, grabbed another $60,000, and raised.

The ESPN commentators that year were actor/poker player Gabe Kaplan and Phil Hellmuth, and they were given a difficult task. They had to describe the action while it was taking place, and without knowing what each player had. As a result, their comments were revealing. While Stanley considered his next move, they were able to speculate on Ungar's possible hands.

"If I had to guess at this point, I would say that Stuey has two pair, nines up," offered Kaplan. "What hand do you put Stuey on, Phil?"

"Well, you know, it's just hard to say. Stuey may have a 9-10 here, I mean, which is a pretty good hand too, nines with a straight draw. It's highly unlikely that he has a straight . . ."

"Sixty thousand dollars was a bet that he would make if he had a straight," countered Kaplan, "trying to get as much money as possible, but not wanting to overload."

Their conversation gave everyone a hint of the dilemma that Stanley was facing. Stanley knew that Stuey would play a big hand, a semistrong hand, or a bluff in roughly the same manner, and that made his decision all the more difficult. He shuffled his chips while pondering his decision, and after about a minute's time, he decided to call.

The river was the K♦, for a final board of

Stanley quickly checked. Ungar reached for his chips, seemingly trying to decide the right amount to bet, and then came forward with $220,000. Stanley leaned back in his chair, looked down at his chips, and fell into deep thought.

"I'll tell you this much. I'm beginning to really love Stu's hand here," said Hellmuth. "It doesn't look like a 9-10 anymore."

"Yeah, and I don't think he's got two pair anymore," added Kaplan. "Having played with Stuey over the years, I would say that Stuey's either got a straight or he was drawing to a straight [and missed]. . . . This is a major, major bet for this time of the tournament."

Stanley was taking his time, and clearly considering a call. But in the end, he decided to slide his cards in. Ungar then immediately flipped his cards faceup to reveal Q♠10♣. He had nothing but a busted straight draw. Even though Stanley mucked his cards face-down, tournament director Jack McClelland had the dealer turn his cards up, so we all got to see that Stanley had folded 9♦7♦.

"What was very interesting about that hand, Phil, was that Stuey played that hand exactly like he would've played it if he'd had a straight or if he'd had nines and eights," said Kaplan. "He raised $60,000 on fourth street and that was not an overwhelming raise, but the kind of raise he would make if he had a big hand, and then he would've followed up with a major bet on the end. . . . So he played it like he had a real big hand, and Ron suspected something, but he couldn't call with the two nines."

"That was a very interesting hand. I mean, had he made that call, who knows how it would've affected Stu?" added Hellmuth.

Instead, Stanley was clearly the one who felt the effects of that play. Through a combination of bad luck and bad timing, Stanley found himself on the short end of every major confrontation for the rest of the day, and finished a disappointing fourth. Ungar, on the other hand, made history by winning his third WSOP title, and his remains one of the greatest comeback stories in WSOP history.

The interviews: My first interview was with Ron Stanley. He still lives in Las Vegas and continues his career as a successful professional poker player.

ML: First of all, I thought it was an extremely classy thing for you to be dressed in a tuxedo. What made you decide to do that?

Ron Stanley: That was something I had thought about for a long time. I had been telling my wife and other people that I would wear one if I ever made it to the final table of the World Series. I wanted to be the first one to do that, and I was. I guess, at the very least, I'll be remembered for that [chuckles].

After all, it's the biggest poker tournament in the world, and it's televised, so it should be a classy event. I see no reason why everyone shouldn't wear one. Back in the day, you used to see televised pro billiards events where everyone was wearing tuxes. And they actually had to play pool in them! We're not doing any physical activity, so I think we should make a better effort to dress nicely, especially for televised events. I think it would look good for poker.

ML: I agree completely, and I applaud your show of class. But it must have been tough to wear a tuxedo outdoors in the Vegas heat! Was that a disadvantage for you?

RS: I hadn't known ahead of time that the final table would be outside. I still would have worn my tux, but that made the playing conditions really difficult. Getting to the final table is hard enough as it is. We had been playing late hours every night, and I wasn't getting my regular meals in or getting good amounts of sleep, especially the night before the final table. Now there was the hundred-degree heat to deal with too.

They had tiny air vents blowing up at us from the floor, but if anything, they only made things worse. I had cold air blowing up to my face while the rest of me was sweating like a pig. I had been feeling a little sick leading up to that day, and those conditions definitely did not help. All in all, it was a rough day.

ML: Speaking of rough, the seat draw seemed like a really bad break for you. How tough was it to sit to Ungar's right for the entire final table?

RS: That was another bummer for me, but it didn't really change my strategy too much. I went into the final table figuring I would play a little more conservatively than normal. But once the play started, and I got a feel for how everyone was playing, I was ready to loosen up and try to make plays on everyone, including Stuey. Unfortunately, I didn't have too much chance to do that [laughs softly].

It's a shame, because I felt I was playing really good poker in the days leading up to the final table, and I had made several key bluffs along the way. I feel like, if I could've gotten heads-up with Stuey, I could've given him a good run for his money. Unfortunately, I made a couple of mistakes, and I lost the key hand to Strzemp, so I never got the chance.[23]

ML: Let's talk about the hand against Stuey. Do you remember your thought processes as that hand was taking place? On the turn, when you bet and Stuey raised, did you call presuming that you needed to improve in order to win?

RS: When I checked the flop and he checked behind me, I liked my hand. As aggressive as he was, I was pretty sure that he would've raised before the flop with ace-anything, so I didn't think he had one. I also felt he would've bet the flop with middle pair or any decent draw. I figured, if he flopped anything, it was at best bottom pair or a bad gutshot draw, so I felt pretty good with middle pair.

Then the eight came on the turn, and I made a small bet. Stuey raised me $60,000, and it was the size of his raise that bothered me a little. It was a decent-sized raise, but not so big that he was trying to muscle me out. It led me to believe that he wanted a call. At that point, I decided that his most likely hand was 8-6 for bottom two pair. I thought it was possible that he had 7-5 for the low straight, but I definitely saw 8-6 as the more likely possibility.

So when I called his raise, I did think I needed to improve to win, but I wasn't just looking to make a straight. I also thought that I could win with a nine or a seven, so if my hand improved in any way, I was looking to take a nice bite out of his stack.

ML: When Stuey bet $220,000 on the river, you took a long time before folding, so you obviously thought he might be bluffing. It

23. In an all-in confrontation, Stanley had K-K while John Strzemp, the eventual runner-up, had 10-10. A ten came on the turn to save Strzemp and leave Stanley short-stacked. Mel Judah also claimed to have folded a ten pre-flop, making the bad beat that much worse.

seemed like you were seriously considering calling. Do you remember what went through your mind?

RS: Truthfully, I had made up my mind pretty quickly that I would fold. I sat there for a while because I wanted to make him sweat a little bit, but I didn't really consider calling. I had already put him on either two pair or a straight, and when the river card was no help, I stuck with my original read.

Looking back now, I wish I had thought about the hand a little longer, especially after he made such a large bet on the river. That should have caused me to adjust my thinking. I should have said, "This is Stuey, he could be putting a move on me." I should have realized that he bet too much to expect to get called, and I should have spent more time considering a call. I had plenty of chips, and it would not have crippled me to make the call and lose.

Plus, I was there to win. I wasn't even thinking about the jumps in money between second and third, or third and fourth. So it's not like I was looking to fold in order to save chips and move up a spot. If I had thought my hand was good, my money would have been in the pot. Instead, I made up my mind too quickly that I was beat, and I threw it away, and now it makes me look bad.

ML: I think it was made worse when your hand got turned faceup, and I was surprised they did that. You mucked your hand without showing, but then Jack McClelland asked for your cards to be shown. I still don't understand why that happened. Was it ever explained to you?

RS: Nobody ever gave me a specific reason, but it was pretty clear why he did that. There were a bunch of reporters and TV cameras around, plus this was the first year that they were attempting to write a play-by-play of the entire final table, so they were trying to get as much information as they could. Before that hand, they had just been showing called hands and all-in hands, but for some reason he decided it was okay this time to show a mucked hand too.

No one wants to show their cards unless they have to, and I certainly didn't like it. Once Stuey voluntarily showed his bluff, Jack knew it would look good to show the hand that got bluffed out. Still, he should have asked me, "Ronnie, do you mind turning your cards up?" instead of doing it without asking. I honestly wasn't bothered when Stuey showed me his bluff. He was showing off, and that was his style. But I was really taken aback when they showed my cards too, even though I didn't visibly react.

ML: It's unfortunate that they chose to do that, but you kept your cool, and I think everyone who watched the 1997 final table can appreciate that. Thank you so much for taking the time to talk with me. Before I let you go, do you have any general advice for my readers?

RS: I would just impress on them how important bluffing is in tournaments. You can't possibly expect to win any major tournament without bluffing. I guess, if it's a one-day tournament, you might get a tremendous rush of cards and win that way. But there's no way you can win a multiday tournament just on good cards alone. You have to not only hope that your good cards hold up, but you have to play your opponents too, and pick up some additional pots that way.

If you have any aspirations of winning a major event like the World Series, you had better learn to bluff well. Especially now, with the seven-day format or however long the main event is, bluffing is simply a must. You cannot win, or even hope to make the final table, without it.

It would have been nice to also get Ungar's perspective on this famous hand. Unfortunately, he passed away less than two years after his 1997 world championship, at the age of forty-five, of a heart attack brought on by his years of drug abuse.

So instead, I turned to Nolan Dalla. Besides being the current media director for the WSOP, and a successful gambler and writer, Nolan was handpicked by Ungar to co-write his autobiography, titled *One of a Kind: The Rise and Fall of Stuey "The Kid" Ungar, The World's Greatest Poker Player*. As a result, Nolan arguably knows more about Ungar than any man alive.

ML: Nolan, give us a little bit of history leading up to the 1997 WSOP. Ungar had won back-to-back titles in 1980 and 1981, but then fell off the map for a while. What helped spur on his spectacular 1997 comeback?

Nolan Dalla: His comeback might have appeared glamorous when all was said and done, but believe me, it didn't start out spectacular at all. He was in bad shape, both physically and financially. The 1997 WSOP main event started on a Monday, and that Sunday night, he was a complete wreck. He was still trying to win an entry through single-table satellites, and he didn't even have the $1,000 to enter one—he needed to be staked.

Late in the night, he got down to heads-up in one satellite, and at one point he had his opponent all-in and completely dominated. He had Q-Q versus two undercards, but somehow he lost. His opponent went on to win the satellite, and that was Stuey's last shot at getting in. He was completely demoralized. He went out and got high, and no one expected to see him back for the main event.

The next morning he enters the Binion's coffee shop having clearly been awake the entire night before. He sits down with a fellow named Doc Earle, and explains how he lost the night before, and how his confidence was completely shot. Between the lack of sleep and whatever drugs he had taken that night, he was totally out of it. Probably no one in the world would have backed him, looking the way he was.

ML: Wow. So, how did he even get into the tournament?

ND: Out of desperation, he called Billy Baxter, a professional player who had backed him in the past, and asked Billy to stake him. Baxter was completely distracted by a combination of sports bets and trying to get to Binion's in time for the main event, so without really thinking about it, he agreed to back Stuey. If he had known the bad shape Stuey was in, he never would have staked him. Stuey was tired, high, and had no confidence. As it turns out, Baxter was lucky that he didn't see him in person, otherwise he would've never staked him and never won his share of the million.

Here's an amazing story that not too many people know about: Back in 1990, Stuey was one of the chip leaders going into Day 3 of the main event, but he never showed up! If he had been there, he would have probably been the favorite to win the whole thing, but instead he got blinded down and eliminated in ninth place. Baxter had a piece of him for that one as well, and he swore he would never stake Stuey again after he disappeared like that. For some reason Baxter changed his mind in 1997. He never really explained why he said yes to backing Stuey. He had a lot of stuff on his mind, and he later said if he had thought it through, he probably would've said no. It's lucky for both of them he said yes.

ML: So Ungar had to get lucky just to get into the tournament, but it must have taken even more luck for him to make it to the final table, given the condition he was in.

ND: It was practically a miracle that he lasted as long as he did. By all accounts, he played terribly for the first few hours, and came very close to elimination. He kind of gave up in a sense, but in a way, that made him dangerous because he decided he had nothing to lose. He played with abandon, managed to stay alive, and by the end of the day he had made a decent comeback.

It seemed like he took on a new attitude that night, once he made it through the first day. Stu showed up in the Binion's coffee shop on Tuesday morning, and once again he ran into Doc Earle. This time Doc saw a completely different man. Stu was cleaned up, shaven, had on new clothes, and he looked ten years younger. He clearly had gotten a good night's sleep, had not taken any drugs, and he sat down to a huge breakfast. He clearly was in much better physical shape going into Day 2, and he spent the day accumulating chips and making progress toward the final table.

By Wednesday, he was completely back in top form. He was totally focused, and back to his A game. I think, once he realized that first prize was within reach, it became a big motivating factor. After all, one million dollars was much more than he won in either 1980 or 1981. Also, he knew that Billy Baxter had trusted in him, and he wanted to live up to that trust.

Wednesday night, once Stuey had played his way to the final table, Baxter called him up to his hotel room to try to motivate him. He said, "Stuey, I've gotta tell you something. You know it's over, don't you? The tournament, it's over. They're all gonna be playing for second prize down there."

Stuey knew at that point he couldn't let his backer down. "If I would've come in second that tournament, I would've killed myself," he said later. He was half-joking, but it's the half-serious part of it that was a little scary, and more than a little foreboding.

ML: Do you know of any general comments that Ungar made prior to the final table, strategic intentions, anything like that?

ND: Not only did he never say anything to me, I'd be stunned if he ever said anything to anyone about that sort of thing. Internally, he thought plenty about strategy, but he would never discuss it with others. That would've been completely out of character. It was not his nature to discuss his strategy with anyone at all, even people he trusted.

Besides, I don't think he ever really had preconceived strategies. Other players go into the final table thinking, "I'm going to start out tight, and then loosen up," or "I'm going to steal the first few pots." Stuey didn't think like that. If he saw an opportunity, he would attack, simple as that. If he felt like he could make a person lay his hand down, he would go with his gut. He adjusted to his opposition as well as anyone, and did whatever it took to win.

Keep in mind that over the course of his life, he entered thirty major tournaments [ones with a $5,000 buy-in or higher], and won ten of them! He was there to win and nothing else.

ML: Did he ever say anything about the specific hand against Ron Stanley?

ND: The only comment he ever made to me was that he knew he could make Stanley fold. He was just supremely confident that Stanley would lay down his hand, and obviously he was right-on. I felt like Stuey almost had a narcissistic view of the situation. It was as if he thought, "How dare someone call me after I bet $220,000!" Perhaps anyone else would've been considered overconfident, but given how often he was correct in those situations, it's hard to say that Stuey wasn't simply telling the truth.

ML: Is there anything else he said in post-WSOP interviews that might provide some insight for my readers?

ND: It's kind of sad, but nobody ever got a good interview with him after the final table. In fact, he was a horrible interview subject. It was not a reflection of his intelligence; if anything, he talked above everyone. That is, when he was clearheaded. And then, when he fell back into his drug habit soon after the 1997 WSOP, his interview answers were simply lacking. He was constantly in assorted states of disorientation, and it was impossible to get more than a yes-or-no answer out of him. In terms of getting insight into his thinking at the final table, I don't think anyone ever made much progress in that area.

At the very least, I can tell you this much: Going into the final day, he had no doubt he was going to win. He never once thought about moving up in prize money [which is pretty obvious, given his comment that he would commit suicide if he came in second]. Even though Strzemp could have been a threat near the end, anyone would have had to get very lucky to beat him, playing the way he was. They simply couldn't read Stuey as well as he could read them. He could effortlessly put himself in his opponents' shoes, whereas no one else shared that talent to the same degree. Of course, I can't say that's a fact, but I think it's the opinion of most of the people who watched him play.

There's no question that he was one of the all-time greats, but I wonder if he would have been equally successful in today's poker world. Truthfully, I'm not sure. The true question is whether Ungar was great because he was intuitively gifted or simply because his poker thinking was ahead of his time. During his era, no one used the size of their stack or their aggressiveness as well as he could. Nowadays, a lot of people have developed those skills. It would have been interesting to see how he would have performed in the twenty-first century, but of course we'll never know.

Since I know this is for *The Book of Bluffs,* I'll end with a story that your readers might appreciate. For a long time, the Super Bowl of Poker was the second biggest poker event behind the WSOP, and Ungar won the main event of both of them three times. One year, I think it was 1990, Ungar came to the final table of the SBOP with a medium stack of about $125,000. In two hours, he doubled his chips and took the chip lead, without showing down a single hand. At the ensuing break, a friend said to him, "You must have had a good run of cards." Ungar replied, "I had no cards whatsoever. I had nothing."

Given the fact that he picked up no hands, just keeping his stack size at $125,000 would have been a good accomplishment by anyone's standards. To double his chips without showing down a hand was just incredible. And keep in mind, this was an all-star final table. That performance showed what a true master of the game he was. Anyone can win with good cards. It takes a true player to also win with garbage.

♣ ♦ ♥ ♠

Some final thoughts: When I relayed the story of this bluff to a young friend, he replied, "Maybe I'm missing something, but I don't see why it's such a big deal that Ungar was able to push his opponent off of third pair with a large bet on the river. In the grand scheme of things, was it really that big of a deal?"

I think, without realizing it, my friend answered his own question. It's only when you consider his bluff in the grand scheme of things that it becomes a big deal. By itself, the play was not extraordinary. For example, if Ungar's bluff were made in a $1–$2 blind NLH game, it would be considered a solid bluff, but not much more.

But in this case, it was the turning point of the 1997 WSOP. Had Stanley made that call, it might have given him the necessary confidence to take down Ungar in a heads-up duel—something that only one player had done in Ungar's entire tournament history. Instead, it just gave Ungar's opponents one more reason to fear him, and his lead was never threatened again.

The intangible effect of Stuey's play was not just felt by his opponents. Many spectators chose to sit through the hundred-degree heat just so they could see one of the all-time greats in action. They knew that Ungar was something special, and they were waiting for him to make a special play. He gave them one. They could go home satisfied, knowing that they had witnessed one of the greatest NLH players in the world at his best.

In short, Ungar's bluff put an exclamation point on his legacy as a NLH champion. Despite the negatives associated with his life, no one can take that legacy away from him.

Bluff #48. 2003 WSOP—
Chris Moneymaker vs. Chuc Hoang

A lot of people talk about how lucky the recent WSOP champions have been. Let me let you in on a little secret: *Every* WSOP champion needed a lot of luck on his road to victory. Doyle Brunson is one of the greatest champions ever, but it was not his extraordinary skill that allowed him to win with 10-2. Stu Ungar took an A-4 against an A-8 in his final hand, and made a straight to win the 1997 title. Nobody wins without luck. Even if you somehow manage to always get your money in with the best hand, it takes luck to have it hold up time and time again, for several days in a row.

But, just as every WSOP champion needed some luck, they needed some serious poker talent too. That goes, not just for the Doyle Brunsons and Stu Ungars of the world, but for the Chris Moneymakers and Greg Raymers as well. Unfortunately, most observers tend to focus on the times that those players got lucky, rather than giving them credit for the hands that demonstrated their excellent skills.[24]

This was the first year that ESPN covered some hands from each day of the main event, not just the final day. As a result, we got to see many of the hands that Chris Moneymaker played on his road to the championship. Somehow this play never made it onto TV, even though it might have been his best hand of the entire tournament.

The scenario: Day 4 of the 2003 WSOP main event. There were thirty players left, and Moneymaker was one of the chip leaders with about $700,000. Chuc Hoang, a solid, professional player sitting to the right of Moneymaker, had about $350,000.

---

24. Several of the figures, such as the size of the blinds and the pre-flop raise, are educated guesses. However, even if they are not exact, they are close enough that it makes little difference. Rest assured, all the subsequent actions described are accurate. Moneymaker gives his personal account of this bluff in his book, *Moneymaker*, pp. 157–61.

The bluff: The blinds were $4,000–$8,000. Hoang raised to $30,000 pre-flop. Moneymaker flat-called, and everyone else folded. Heads-up, the flop came 8-9-10 rainbow. Both players checked. The turn was a six, for a board of 8-9-10-6.

Hoang came out betting $15,000, a small bet into what was approximately a $75,000 pot. Moneymaker smelled weakness and raised $15,000, just to see if Hoang had anything. Hoang, a very deliberate player, waited a few seconds, and then reraised another $15,000. So far this was an unusual Betting Pattern for a no-limit hand. At that point Moneymaker decided enough was enough. He came back with a $100,000 reraise, and then the action was back on Hoang.

He sat back and thought for a *long* time. Onlookers said it was the longest they had ever seen someone take to make a poker decision. After what seemed like an eternity, he said softly to Moneymaker, "I'm going to pay you off," while tossing in the $100,000 to call.

The river was a jack, making a straight even more likely. Hoang checked. Moneymaker thought briefly and then pushed all-in, covering Hoang for his remaining $180,000 or so. Again Hoang took his time before deciding what to do. He stared down at the 8-9-10-6-J board for a while. Then he looked up at Moneymaker and said, "I guess you have the queen," while waiting to see how he would react. Moneymaker made no response whatsoever. Hoang tried to wait him out, but it was clear that Moneymaker had no plans other than sitting like a statue. Finally, Hoang looked him over one last time and tossed his cards in.

At that point, Moneymaker said, "No sir, no queen," and with a quick snap of his wrist he flipped his cards faceup to reveal the A♥3♥! He didn't even have a pair or a draw of any kind! The gasp from the other players at the table could be heard throughout the room. Hoang later admitted that he had folded a seven (presumably pocket sevens), which would have been the winning straight. Moneymaker became the chip leader with almost $900,000, and at the dinner break that followed soon afterward, his bluff was all that everyone was talking about.

The analysis: Wow! I wish that ESPN had shown this hand, so the world could have seen it. What a play! Still, it took two to tango, so let's take a closer look at this hand, keeping both players in mind.

1. Moneymaker's call pre-flop is debatable, but can certainly be justified. He had position, a deep stack of chips, plus he knew Hoang to be a notoriously tight player. The opportunity to steal the pot could easily present itself, and that was something Moneymaker had been doing often. So just looking at the A♥3♥ makes a call seem questionable. But when you combine it with all those other factors, it makes more sense.

2. Up to and including the turn, Hoang outplayed Moneymaker. That's not an opinion, just a simple fact. When Hoang made his straight, he came out with a really small bet. It was designed to look weak, and that's exactly how Moneymaker saw it. He came back with a minimum raise, and then Hoang continued to milk his hand by reraising the minimum. At that point, Moneymaker decided to make a $100,000 raise with no outs, drastically misreading the strength of Hoang's hand.

   Hoang then took a long time to decide on his course of action. The only hand he had to fear realistically was Q-J, but that fear was legitimate, since that's all it would take to knock him out of the tournament. To his credit, Hoang came up with the perfect set of actions. He felt there was a chance Moneymaker could be bluffing, but he didn't want to stake his tournament life on that chance, so when he called the raise, he said out loud, "I'm going to pay you off."

   That was a masterful ploy, wasn't it? Think about it. If you were in Moneymaker's shoes, pulling an outright bluff, how would you feel if your opponent said, "I'm going to pay you off"? It would make you think twice about bluffing on the river, wouldn't it? Hoang was hoping that he wouldn't be forced to go all-in. He thought that his combined words and actions would cause Moneymaker to abandon any bluff attempt and give him a free showdown.

3. That is why Moneymaker's all-in bet on the river was so fantastic. He knew that Hoang had to have a legitimate hand to call his $100,000 raise. Furthermore, he had every reason to believe that Hoang would call if he went all-in. But the hell with all that. He knew that he had to follow through one more time, if he was really going to take control of his table and, ul-

timately, the tournament. He was able to fire the last barrel
when almost every other player would have quit firing. He deserves a tremendous amount of credit.

Admittedly, he didn't do it alone. A favorable river card
helped his cause significantly. When the jack hit, the final
board was 8-9-10-6-J. It was extremely unlikely that Hoang
had a queen. If he had Q-J he definitely would have pushed
all-in once Moneymaker raised $100,000. The only other
hand he could have with a queen would be Q-Q, but that too
was unlikely. He probably wouldn't have checked on the flop,
and then chances are he wouldn't have been willing to call
such a large raise on the turn. Any other hand with a queen
would have been unplayable. Therefore, Moneymaker could
be fairly certain that Hoang did not have one.

However, Hoang could not be as certain about Moneymaker's hand. Moneymaker was representing Q-J with his
raises on the turn, and, if that was his hand, the jack on the
river didn't change anything. So he decided to continue representing Q-J, as if the river card was meaningless. When the
moment of truth came, and with his tournament life on the
line, Hoang couldn't pull the trigger to call. From that point
on, he was simply a defeated man, while the rest of Moneymaker's ascent to world champion is history.

Hoang outplayed Moneymaker before the river. But in the end,
that made no difference. Moneymaker outplayed Hoang on the river,
and that was all that mattered.

Bluff #49. 2003 WSOP— Chris Moneymaker vs. Sammy Farha

Now we come full circle, as the same bluff that started this book will
end it. Even though Moneymaker came to the final table as the chip
leader, no one considered him the favorite to win. He was against a
slew of professional players, with Sammy Farha possibly the toughest of the bunch. Nevertheless, he refused to be intimidated. He man-

aged to string together a series of knockouts against Tomer Benvenisti (as described in Bluff #22), Jason Lester, and former WSOP
champion Dan Harrington. Just like that, he was heads-up with the
chip lead against Farha, and that led to what was arguably the most
famous confrontation in WSOP history.

As with many of the other pairings in this chapter, the two combatants offered very different appearances. Moneymaker, who had
won his WSOP seat online on PokerStars, had a tan hat and a black
polo shirt both prominently advertising the site. Given the stigma
that was attached to online qualifiers, everyone's immediate assessment of him was that he was merely an online player, and thus at a
distinct disadvantage.

That's not to say that he looked like a pushover. His thin mustache and rounded goatee gave him a fierce look, especially when he
stared an opponent down. Plus, he had an intimidating pair of mirrored Oakley sunglasses that stayed glued to his face unless he had
someone all-in. Combined with the stoic facial expression that he
constantly maintained, the sunglasses made it extremely tough for
anyone to get a read on him.

Farha gave a much more professional appearance. He was clean-
shaven, often with an unlit cigarette in his mouth. He also had a
sleek pair of shades, but chose not to wear them heads-up against
Moneymaker, instead leaving them folded up in front of him. He
wore his dark suit unbuttoned, with the sleeves rolled up slightly. His
light blue button-down shirt was wide open at the neck to reveal a
tasteful gold chain. He looked formal, yet extremely relaxed. It was
as if he had just finished an important business meeting, and now
this card game for millions of dollars was his way of letting off
steam. Just by looking at the two of them, it was hard not to give the
edge to Farha.

The stage was set. Farha was on the left end of the table, Moneymaker was on the right, and $2.5 million in cash was sitting squarely
in the middle, there for the taking. It was just a question of who was
going to claim it.

The scenario: They had started the final table at 2:00 P.M., but by
the time the action got heads-up, it was almost 1:30 A.M. Money-

maker had the lead with \$4.62 million to Farha's \$3.77 million. The blinds were \$20,000–\$40,000 with a \$5,000 ante.

The bluff: On the SB/button, Moneymaker looked down at K♠7♥ and reached for his chips. "Don't do it!" joked Farha, but Moneymaker was not dissuaded from making a small raise to \$100,000. Without hesitation, Farha called from the BB with Q♠9♥. The flop came 9♠2♦6♠. Farha checked his top pair, and Moneymaker quickly checked behind him.

The turn was the 8♠, creating a board of

and that's when things became interesting. Farha bet \$300,000 with his top pair and flush draw. Moneymaker waited only a second before quietly declaring, "I raise." He pushed twelve chips forward and said, "There's the three hundred."

"Chris calls," said tournament director Matt Savage over the PA system, having not heard Moneymaker.

"No, I *raise*," he said emphatically, making sure there was no misunderstanding. "Five more," as he pushed \$800,000 total toward the pot.

Farha counted out a stack of \$25,000 chips, grabbed them, and confidently placed them into the pot, all within a matter of seconds. "We said it's going to be over soon," he said with a smile, trying to get a reaction out of his opponent, but Moneymaker remained expressionless.

The river was the 3♥, for a final board of

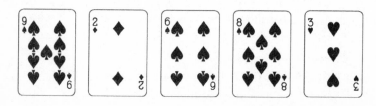

Farha studied the board, tilted his head inquisitively, and checked. Moneymaker glanced at his chips, clasped his hands together, and announced, "I'm all in."

"Chris Moneymaker going all-in, with nothing!" declared ESPN announcer Lon McEachern excitedly.

"A stunning play from Moneymaker," said ESPN's Norman Chad, "who missed his draws, has nothing, and now has put Sam Farha all-in. . . . Moneymaker bluffed at this once and Farha came, he's now bluffing at it again. . . . This would be a tough, tough call for Sammy."

At first, Farha maintained his confident expression. "You must have missed your flush, eh?" he asked with a smile. In fact, that was exactly what happened. For the second time in the hand, he was looking for a reaction out of Moneymaker, who again refused to move a muscle.

As the seconds ticked by and Moneymaker continued to remain motionless, Farha's confidence waned. He leaned back and adjusted his jacket, suddenly looking uncomfortable. Then he stuck his hands in his pockets, beginning to appear pained by the decision he faced.

Still not ready to concede, he decided to take one last shot at getting some kind of tell on Moneymaker. "I could make a crazy call on you. It could be the best hand," he said as he stared at the felt. Then he quickly shifted his glance to see if Moneymaker had shown any reaction. Still nothing.

Farha continued to ponder his decision for a little longer. But finally he picked up his cards, and with a quick snap of the wrist he threw them in. The crowd, which had been waiting for something to cheer, went wild.

"Considering the situation—and I know we're early in the century—but that's the bluff of the century!" exclaimed Chad. "What a play from Chris Moneymaker!"

Farha never recovered. Less than an hour later he was eliminated, and Moneymaker took home the title.

The interviews: Farha politely declined to be interviewed, citing that he will be putting out a book soon and that he wanted to save any material about the 2003 WSOP for his own book. But it's no secret that he viewed this hand differently from most of the poker-playing world. While most people (myself included) gave Moneymaker credit for making a fantastic bluff, Farha did not. Consider these comments from an interview during the 2004 WSOP on ESPN:

> *As a poker player, I read people really good. At that moment, it was fifty-fifty in my eyes. I said [to myself] "I can beat this guy . . . let me lay it down." What bothers me is people talking about it as the best bluff of the year. The play was horrible, but I made the mistake, and I made the play look good. That's the difference.*

As further evidence, consider these words from an interview with *Bluff* magazine:

> *We went heads-up and I felt so tired. I wasn't myself and, eventually, I made an error of judgment. I laid down that big hand—the hand that everybody talks about. It took me about fifteen minutes, but I laid it down. I could write a whole book about that hand. People talk about it as though it was the biggest bluff of the year, but it was a bad play. Any average poker player can spot a bluff and an amateur would have called his all-in bet.*
>
> *He raised on the button and checked the flop. Now, a good player in position will normally bet the flop, in an attempt to represent a hand, but he just checked. I checked as well with my top pair, preparing to trap him. On fourth street, he picked up something. I knew that. I bet and he raised, which was a horrible play on his part. I called. People ask me why I didn't go all-in on fourth street and I say: "This guy had luck on his side. I didn't want to be beaten by luck." So I called his bet in an attempt to set him up. I thought to myself, "I know he's going all-in at the end if he misses."*
>
> *And that's exactly what happened. I checked and he went all-in. But I don't know what happened to me; I was so tired, I wasn't myself. A good poker player would have called him,*

because it was common sense that he was drawing and that he missed his draw. I told him that when I laid the hand down. I said: "I guess you missed your draw."

After that, I thought, "That's it, I've achieved my goal, I'm bored and this guy has luck on his side." I just gave up, I guess, and I played a bad hand. I went all-in just to finish the whole thing."[25]

Farha was clearly upset with himself, which is understandable, but I think he was unduly harsh toward both his own play and Moneymaker's. Maybe he doesn't think that Moneymaker's play should have been considered the "bluff of the century." But if he had made that call with the Q♠9♥, I think we'd just as easily be calling that the play of the century.

It's one thing to suspect a bluff. It's quite another to stake your tournament life, and $1.2 million in real money (the difference between second and first), on that suspicion. It would have taken a player with tremendous courage to make that all-in call with only a pair of nines, and I don't think it reflects poorly on Farha that he couldn't bring himself to do it. He has gone through a lot of aggravation from the media and the poker world for his laydown, which is unfortunate, as I think it is largely undeserved.

On the other hand, I think Moneymaker clearly deserves more credit for his play than Farha is willing to give. Similar to Bluff #42, a great bluff makes your opponent think twice about calling, even if he strongly suspects that you're making a move, because you are putting him to the test for all his chips. Farha suspected that Moneymaker might have been bluffing, but he couldn't bring himself to call, knowing that if he was wrong, he was done. I think that simply reinforces the excellence of Moneymaker's play.

Moneymaker agreed to be interviewed despite the fact that his book, *Moneymaker,* is now in stores. It's an enjoyable read, and it does a great job of describing his road to victory. The only drawback is that it doesn't spend too much time talking about this famous

25. *Bluff* magazine, June–July 2005, p. 51.

hand. And of course, since I had the chance to talk with him, I wanted to know more about it.

ML: Let's go straight to the big hand. Once Sammy bet the turn, that's when things began to get interesting. What was running through your mind at that time?

Chris Moneymaker: When he bet the turn, I couldn't put him on a hand. But I liked the way the board put me on two draws, so I made the $500,000 raise. In my mind, that committed me to the pot. When Sam called, I put him on something like the ace of spades with a small pair, maybe second pair. At that point, my mind was made up that no matter what card came on the river, if it wasn't a spade, I was moving all-in. I wasn't sure of his exact hand, but I really didn't think he could call. I truly, truly thought he would lay it down.

ML: So then you moved all-in and put Sammy to the test. What was going through your mind at that point? Was it tough to sit there completely still?

CM: The first thing that crossed my mind was the earlier hand between Amir [Vahedi] and Sammy. Amir was bluffing, but he started talking also, and that provoked Sammy to call. I just told myself not to make a sound or a move. Then I thought that in my worst-case scenario, he would call, and I'd still have chips. And then, even if I lost, I'd still win $1.3 million, which was still unbelievable. Then I just tried to think of all the things I'd have to do the next day, such as catch a flight, and make arrangements to get to the airport. Pretty much, I just tried to think of anything other than the fact that Sammy was sitting there staring at me.

But it wasn't tough for me to just sit there. Once I put all that money in the pot, there really wasn't anything else to do. Besides, that was something I had done for five days straight. Anytime all my money went in, I just tried to control my breathing and get my heart rate under control. It was like that John McEnroe game show, where if your heart rate got too high you would be eliminated. I just tried to pretend like I was on that show, and needed to keep my heart rate low in order to stay in the game. Basically, I tried to come as close to falling asleep as I could without actually falling asleep, although in the hand against Farha, my eyes were actually closed after I moved in.

ML: Wow. Those glasses worked, because I don't think anyone could tell that your eyes were closed. It was late, and everyone must have been pretty tired at that point. How tired were you? In your book, you said that one of your strengths is your stamina, that you can play for thirty-six hours straight without a problem, so that must have been an advantage for you. On the other hand, you had been playing poker for five long days, and it was 1:30 in the morning, so I'm sure you were feeling it.

CM: All in all, the stamina factor worked in my favor. When I talk about playing thirty-six hours straight, understand that I'm talking about playing limit poker, and when I do that, I'm usually not paying full attention. I'll be watching TV, or doing something else while I'm playing, and that's part of the reason I can go for so long. Here, I was paying full attention to every hand for five days straight, and that was a lot tougher than what I was used to. I spent every hand trying to put players on what they had, and that was rough.

But I also felt that once I reached the final table, I had a lot more adrenaline than the other players. I felt like being there was a much bigger deal for me than it was for them. They all looked kind of run-down and tired, and through a combination of adrenaline and Red Bull, I was still pretty energetic. It helped me bully the table a little bit more, especially when we got shorthanded. They all just looked worn out, and that gave me more incentive to stay fresh.

ML: Let me backtrack to your hand against Chuc Hoang. So few people saw it, and yet it might have been an even better bluff than the one against Farha. Was that a confidence boost, or was your confidence already pretty high?

CM: That hand was the best hand I played during the entire WSOP. That took just as much, if not more, guts than the one against Farha. Whether I made a great move, or just got lucky that he didn't call, it really gave me momentum.

My confidence was already pretty high after putting out [Johnny] Chan and Humberto [Brenes], but this was a different situation, since this time I was on a complete steal. My biggest fear all tournament was that players would start picking up reads on me, but once Hoang folded, it helped ease my mind that no one was getting any information off of me. I think that added confidence—that no one was picking up reads on me—helped as the tournament went along.

ML: It's pretty amazing that in such a short time, you made two great bluffs like that. Is bluffing a big part of your overall game?

CM: [Laughs briefly] Not as much as it used to be! Bluffing has gotten a *lot* tougher for me since the WSOP. Now everyone thinks I'm bluffing! It's tougher to win a lot of hands, but for the ones I win, the pots are a lot bigger than they used to be. I recently bet $500 into a $10 pot, got called, and won. So obviously, I'm getting a lot of action now, but I've also had to tone down my bluffing a lot.

Bluffing is pretty situational. I always preferred being in a position where I didn't have to bluff. But once I put someone on a hand, and I think I can bluff him out, I'm gonna do whatever I can. That's how it goes. First, I put them on a hand. Then I decide whether I think I can get them off it. And then, if I feel that I can, I go after them.

But at the same time, the bluffs have to make sense. I've found that when scare cards come on the turn, those are the bluffs that have worked best for me. Scare cards came on the turn against both Hoang and Farha, and they would have needed very strong hands to call either time. I put them to the test, and thankfully they backed down. Of course, if they had chosen to put me to the test, I obviously could not have called either time.

ML: It's been great talking with you. Before I let you go, do you have any general advice related to bluffing that you could share with the readers?

CM: Well, like I said, bluffs make the most sense when a scare card comes. It doesn't really matter how good the situation is otherwise. If your bluff isn't believable, it won't work.

I've had a lot of bluffing situations come up when I've bet on the flop and an opponent flat-called. You have to ask yourself, what does he have that he would just call with? They usually either flopped a draw or a monster. Or, in some cases, they are calling with a marginal hand like second pair, just waiting to see what you'll do.

People don't flop monster hands that often, so you can't continually play in fear of that. If you thought the situation was right to fire the first bullet [on the flop], then go ahead and fire the second one as well. Don't be the guy that bets once and then backs off. If it's good enough to bet once, bet it twice. A guy that flat-calls should not give you any reason to slow down. If he's got either a marginal hand or a draw, you'd be giving him a big break by checking the turn, so don't do it.

ML: Great advice, Chris. Thank you so much.

♣ ♦ ♥ ♠

Some final thoughts: Against both Farha and Hoang, the greatness of Moneymaker's bluffs stemmed from his fearlessness on the river. It was his brave, all-in river bets that made brilliant plays out of busted bluff attempts. In both cases, his opponent didn't budge on the turn. Most players in Moneymaker's shoes would have backed off and given up. They couldn't bring themselves to risk their tournament lives by going all-in on the river on a total bluff. They check the river, they lose the pot, and they usually forfeit their hopes of winning the tournament. Moneymaker was a cut above. He may have been "just" an online qualifier, but he played with the heart and strength of a world champion, and he consequently reaped the rewards.

Many years from now, people will still be talking about the spectacular confrontation between Moneymaker and Farha. As poker players, we owe them a debt of gratitude. They played a large part in transforming poker into the worldwide, televised phenomenon it is today. They marked the beginning of a new era of poker, as witnessed by the thousands of new players who are attempting to become the next Chris Moneymaker.

And hey, if that is your goal, there's no reason it can't be you. Just keep in mind that a solid knowledge of poker fundamentals, by itself, won't be enough to get the job done. Just like Gavin Griffin, Bobby Baldwin, Stuey Ungar, and Chris Moneymaker, you'll need to mix in some well-timed, well-executed bluffs if you hope to become a champion.

About the Author

Matt Lessinger was born and raised in the Bronx, New York, and attended Haverford College outside of Philadelphia. Upon graduation, he moved to Atlantic City, where he worked as a casino floor supervisor by day and played endless hours of poker by night. After honing his skills against many of the East Coast's top players, he moved to Las Vegas to play poker full-time and enjoyed immediate success. After winning the 2000 Carnivale of Poker pot-limit hold 'em championship, he was highlighted in a *Poker Digest* article and began his writing career as a columnist for the magazine.

He lives in the San Francisco Bay Area, where he continues his career as a professional poker player and writer. He writes for both *Card Player* magazine and the *Online Poker News*. He also gives private poker lessons to a select handful of students, who have enjoyed tremendous success.

The Book of Bluffs is his first full-length book.